THE FRENCH FACE OF EDGAR POE

THE FRENCH FACE

OF

EDGAR POE

Patrick F. Quinn

Carbondale

SOUTHERN ILLINOIS UNIVERSITY PRESS

1957

ACKNOWLEDGMENT

OF COURSE almost every book is in some sense a collective enterprise, and this one is no exception. For their encouragement, advice, and criticism I have many people to thank, Mr. Ralph L. Rusk and M. Jean Hytier especially. I am grateful also to Mr. Richard Chase, Mr. Lewis Leary, Mr. Mark Van Doren, Mr. Wilbur Frohock, and to my colleague Miss Ruth Michael, for the careful readings they gave the manuscript when there were many more weaknesses in it than I hope there are now. In talking about Poe with Mr. Joseph Slater, Mr. Stephen Stepanchev, Mr. Edwin Honig, Mrs. Sophie Ehrlich, Mrs. Mary Doyle Curran, and Mlle Marie-Hélène Pauly, I learned much about my subject; and for suggestions on how to treat it I am glad to recall at this time some conversations in Paris with Mr. Wallace Fowlie, M. Henri Peyre, and M. Gaston Bachelard.

For permission to use in this book material that was originally printed in *Yale French Studies No. 6* and *The Hudson Review* (Winter, 1952), I am obliged to the editors of those publications. I wish also to thank the Yaddo Corporation for enabling me to bring the manuscript to completion during several months residence at Yaddo, in Saratoga Springs, New York.

P. F. Q.

Wellesley College
May, 1956

CONTENTS

INTRODUCTION   3

1   THE FRENCH RESPONSE TO POE   9

2   BUT WHAT DO THEY SEE IN HIM?   28

3   SINGULAR EXCITEMENT, INCREDIBLE SYMPATHY   66

4   THE POET AS TRANSLATOR   109

5   "MON SEMBLABLE, MON FRÈRE!"   135

6   POE'S IMAGINARY VOYAGE   169

7   "THAT SPECTRE IN MY PATH"   216

8   THE POOL AND THE PORTRAIT   257

NOTES   279

SELECTIVE BIBLIOGRAPHY   295

INDEX   303

THE FRENCH FACE OF EDGAR POE

INTRODUCTION

IN 1862, at the age of twenty, the French poet
Stéphane Mallarmé went to London and began
work on his translations of the poems of Poe. He had
learned English before going to England, learned the
language, he said later, for one simple reason: "the
better to read Poe." [1] If it was Mallarmé's hope that in
England he would come to a better understanding of
Poe than was possible in his own country, his excursion
was, at best, unnecessary. If in the same hope he had
come to America, the trip would have been a failure.
Residence in either country would surely have improved his knowledge of English, but for an understanding of Poe he would have been better off had he
remained in France. For it was in France, as Jean
Richepin said some years ago in a series of lectures on
American literature, "It was in France that Poe was
soonest and most fully understood." [2]

This opinion, with which I now agree, would once
have seemed to me fantastic. For I was aware of the
high regard which the French have for Poe and I
thought it misplaced. I knew, for instance, that in "La
Bibliothèque de la Pléiade," a superb set of books devoted almost exclusively to the classic French writers,
there were editions of Plato, Shakespeare, Tolstoy—

and Edgar Poe! I could not believe that Poe belonged
in this company. Nor can I now. When I came upon
Mallarmé's description of Poe as "one of the most
marvelous minds the world has ever known," [3] I did
not subscribe to it, nor do I now. The extravagant esteem in which Poe is held in France, and in Europe
generally, will remain something of a mystery to me;
and I feel sure that Perry Miller was speaking for
most of us when he described his astonishment at wit-
nessing the lengths to which an enthusiasm for Poe
can be carried in even so sensible a country as Holland.
In the autumn of 1949 he was invited to Leeuwarden, a
city in the province of Friesland, there to attend a
public ceremony commemorating the hundredth anniversary of the death of Edgar Poe. For this occasion,
Mr. Miller writes, "solid citizens—bankers, lawyers,
the Queen's commissioner, and the provincial government—suspended their affairs for an afternoon and
gravely devoted four hours (with an intermission for
tea) to hearing orations on Poe and readings of his
poems. . . . During the intermission came the inevitable question: 'What are they doing in America on October 7?' " [4] What, indeed? Mr. Miller admits that he
had no satisfactory answer to give the solid citizens of
Leeuwarden, and he concludes that the Poe they were
honoring and the Poe they expected him to praise was
only a mythical construction of the French imagination.

It was with this same assumption and others like it,
and with also, I might add, an entirely lukewarm appreciation of Poe's writings, that I began my investigation into Poe's immense reputation in France. I
thought that my inquiry would take me back to the
origins and up through the history of a great misun-

derstanding, or even a great hoax. Frankly, I had it in mind to write a kind of exposé, and I suspected that the villain of the piece would be Baudelaire, the man who, on the subject of Poe, had led France and most of Europe up the garden. Only get to the bottom of the matter, I told myself, and it should not be too difficult to explain how and why Poe came to be so mistakenly overrated in France. Such were my thoughts at the outset of this inquiry, and I went to France with the expectation of developing them. But now, some years later, I have rather different proposals to make.

For a while I was able to retain the viewpoint I had brought with me. But the more I became aware of how securely and widely established Poe's fame was, the less certainty I had that my prejudgment was correct. In time it occurred to me that there might, somehow, really be a good French case for Poe. Evidence of this possibility began to accumulate, and to such a degree that at length I put aside my original convictions; and with more of an open mind I became interested in the French response to Poe, not primarily to refute it but to see what it was. I turned, then, to a reading of the Baudelaire translations of Poe, compared them with the English originals, and in this dual reading sought the literary experience which the French seemed to find in the stories of Poe and which I, together with most other Americans, had apparently never known. In my judgment, the experiment succeeded. And hence the major purpose of this book is to show that by participating in the French response to Poe it becomes possible to bring a new and enlarged understanding to one of our own writers.

By this definition of purpose I may have adequately clarified what the subject of the book is. But it may be well to put the matter negatively and say at once that "Poe and France" is not the subject. "Poe and France" —so much is encompassed in that sweeping phrase that it should be reserved as the heading for not one but a whole series of books. For the phrase involves, first of all, the question of Poe's knowledge of French and of French literature; and secondly, there is the reverse question, that of Poe's influence on, or his relationship with, French writers from Baudelaire to the present. There have been a number of studies of both questions—the second especially, in volumes by Seylaz and Lemonnier—and work of this sort, already well advanced, will no doubt continue. But to date virtually nothing has been done about a third question, which is fully as relevant as the other two, and for us in America much more so: What is the significance of the French response to Poe so far as our understanding of him is concerned? May we not have something to learn in this area? I think we do. For in taking Poe up in the way I am suggesting we will, in effect, be reading him anew under the guidance of what amounts to the testimony of almost an entire people during the space of a hundred years.

The Poe with whom I am concerned in the way I have described is the Poe of the great stories. This is the writer whom Baudelaire gave to France and to the world; and in my opinion it is the stories of Poe, rather than his poems or critical writings, that are his major accomplishment. Only incidentally, therefore, will this study allude to Poe as poet, the Poe of Mallarmé. As for the writer who meant so much to Valéry—Poe the critic, the aesthetician, the philosopher of literature— this, the third Poe, also has a diminished role to play in the pages that follow. It may well be that for some purposes another kind of emphasis would be called for; and had it been my objective to determine the total impact of Poe on modern French literature this book would be rather different from what it now is. The last three chapters would be largely irrelevant, and much more would need to be said about the significance Poe had for the Symbolists in general, and for Mallarmé and Valéry in particular. But I consider myself an interested visitor in, rather than a custodian of, this province of French literary history. My attention has been focused on Poe within the context of his reputation and influence abroad. It happened that Mallarmé and his successors did not reveal Poe's poetry to me in the way Baudelaire and French critics after him revealed Poe's tales. Nor did I find in Valéry's remarks on Poe's aesthetic a sustained reappraisal that I could make my own. I hardly expected to. For most of what Valéry had to say on this subject was said in the form of unpublished lectures at the Collège de France in the 1930's. Only within recent months of the current year (1956) has his material become available. One would like, some day, to examine it. Meantime, an attempt to do justice to the Poe of Valéry would have to be a very tentative and truncated affair. But this is no reason to postpone a consideration of the Poe of Baudelaire.

In more ways than one Baudelaire is the central figure in this book, and I have accordingly given the central chapters to three related topics: an account of Baudelaire's discovery of Poe, an examination of the translations which he was thereby led to make, and a discussion of the "affinity" which the French poet at once felt he had with a then almost unknown American writer. The first two chapters provide the pre-

liminary context, first in a general way and then in
some detail, of how France has reacted to Poe since
the time Baudelaire made him famous there. In the
last three chapters the focus narrows, and the objective is to see how what we have learned of the French
response to Poe may illuminate our understanding of
his work when we return to it in English. Guided in
part by Baudelaire and in part by some other French
critics, I offer these chapters as a demonstration that
we can do more than inventory, or even admire, the
ways in which Poe has been read in France. We can
put this information to use. The last section of the
book is therefore concerned with a re-examination of
a number of Poe's major tales.

In an essay entitled "From Poe to Valéry," T. S.
Eliot remarked: "Now, we all of us like to believe that
we understand our own poets better than any foreigner
can do; but I think we should be prepared to entertain
the possibility that these Frenchmen have seen something in Poe that English-speaking readers have
missed." [5] In an earlier version of the same essay,
printed in French, he suggested that critics in France,
England, and America undertake an "examen collec-
tif" of the differing opinions of Poe that prevail in
those three countries. In this study of the French face
of Edgar Poe I have attempted to read some features
there that have not been clearly seen by critics who
have written in Poe's own language. To some extent,
then, the book may serve as a contribution to the collective enterprise Eliot recommends.

1

THE FRENCH RESPONSE TO POE

EDGAR POE, who isn't much in America, *must* become a great man in France—at least that is what I want." [1] When Baudelaire wrote those words to Sainte-Beuve in 1856, he had already given nine years to a task that was to preoccupy him for seven years more. It was only when a paralytic stroke shattered him in 1866 that Baudelaire abandoned, along with all lesser interests, this one which had dominated most of his mature life. One of the results of this remarkable devotion is that of the twelve volumes of Baudelaire's works in the definitive Crépet edition, five are translations from the work of Poe. This simple arithmetic involves a fact of major significance. For in Baudelaire there was a great creative genius, a writer who had, and knew he had, one of the rarest of all gifts: the power to alter and revivify his own country's literature. And yet this man, for nearly twenty years, gave himself with an almost ascetic energy and ardor to the wearisome and specifically uncreative work of sedulous translating. Certainly this was no pastime for him, nor was it simply the means of obtaining an income, although it did serve that end, too. One is almost tempted to go so far as to say that Baudelaire's life work, his great achievement, was not so much *Les Fleurs du*

mal as it was his Poe translations. However this may
be, the five Poe volumes fulfilled and surpassed all that
Baudelaire had hoped for them. Not only did Poe become a great man in France; he has become, thanks to
Baudelaire, a world figure, and this despite the fact
that his reputation as a major writer in America has
hardly been better than precarious. Let us examine
this astonishing paradox.

Although it is a commonplace that in American literature there are few writers of really major rank, it
is perilous to offer an opinion as to just who these writers are. Whatever the list, the objection will be made
that the prizes were not fairly awarded. But it seems
fairly certain that if the list is a brief one Poe's claims
for inclusion in it are by no means considered self-
evident in this country, and have seldom been convincingly sponsored. The general reading public, which
might be expected to show a warm interest in Poe, or
at least a dutiful respect for him, has shown neither.
Some forty years after his death, when a poll was
taken to discover which ten books were generally considered the best to be written in America, Emerson's
Essays and Hawthorne's *Scarlet Letter* reached the top
of the list. Nothing by Poe was voted to rank among
the first ten, or the first thirty! [2] No doubt Poe would
fare better today if a similar competition were arranged, but it seems true nonetheless that his status as
a classic American author exists, in the mind of the
general public, rather by default than acclaim.

If apathy will serve to characterize the attitude of
the common reader towards Poe, something more like
hostility has been the usual response of American writers from Poe's time to our own. Emerson, for example, employed his considerable talents as a phrasemaker

to dispose of him in three words, "the jingle man." [3]
Whitman's feelings were mixed: although he finally
came round to admitting Poe's genius, it was its narrow range and unhealthy, lurid quality that most impressed him. But Whitman did manage to attend the
Poe Memorial ceremony in Baltimore in 1875, and
although he declined to speak publicly there, he at
least had the charity to lend his distinguished presence
to that pathetic occasion.[4] This was more than the
other leading American poets of the day could bring
themselves to do. From Bryant, Whittier, Longfellow,
and Holmes came brief and "appropriate" tributes,
none of which approached the intensity of feeling and
conviction expressed in the letter Swinburne sent from
England. And to compare the perfunctory doggerel offered by Bryant as a tombstone inscription with the
incandescent sonnet Mallarmé had submitted is to realize, quite apart from the abyss that separates verse
from poetry, in which hemisphere Poe's work had been
really welcomed. Only recently, in some essays by T.
S. Eliot and Allen Tate, has American criticism begun
to treat Poe in a way that suggests an awareness of the
implications of that sonnet.[5] From Henry James ("An
enthusiasm for Poe is the mark of a decidedly primitive stage of reflection") through Paul Elmer More
("Poe is the poet of unripe boys and unsound men")
to Yvor Winters ("Poe . . . whose literary merit appears to the present writer a very frail delusion"),[6]
our critics, far from pushing Poe onto the stage of
world literature, have rather insisted that his name be
retained exclusively as a minor one even in the cast of
American letters.

How different a chart must be plotted to show the
history of Poe's reputation in France! His American

contemporaries were reluctant to pay him merely conventional homage; for his French admirers the problem was to find a language of praise sufficiently sublime. Baudelaire, of course, carried away by his missionary zeal, was not one to hesitate on this subject. In *L'Art romantique* he calls Poe simply "the most powerful writer of the age." [7] Make what allowances we will for this as a statement intended for public consumption, the sincerity underlying it may be inferred from the allusion, in *Journaux intimes*, to his morning prayers to God and to Edgar Poe as his intercessor in heaven.[8] For Mallarmé also, Poe was a writer altogether unique, *the* poet, as we know from "Le Tombeau d'Edgar Poe." For him as for Baudelaire the stature of Poe was evidently that of a literary deity. Thus when Mallarmé sent to his friend Cazalis a copy of his sonnet "L'Azur," the first in which he had completely succeeded in the style that was to be distinctively his own, he remarked in his letter: "The more I continue in this direction the more faithful shall I be to those severe ideas which I owe to my great master Edgar Poe." [9] And for Valéry in the next generation Poe was also to be a great master: "Poe is the only impeccable writer. He was never mistaken." [10] In the first letter he wrote to Mallarmé, in 1890, Valéry was careful to underline their common admiration of Poe; and fifty years later he was to specify Poe, along with Leonardo Da Vinci, as the major influences in his literary and philosophical career.[11]

That an enthusiasm for Poe should have been shared by the three most influential poets in modern French literature, that this American writer should have become the pivot on which for the past century French literature has turned, this by itself is sufficiently extraordinary. But even this statement of the case does no more than suggest the force of Poe's impact. There is scarcely one French writer from the time of Baudelaire to the present who has not in one way or another paid his respects to Poe. Villiers de l'Isle Adam, Verlaine and Rimbaud, Huysmans, Claudel, Gide, Edmond Jaloux—these are names at random, but they will serve to indicate the scope of the interest Poe has had for France. Indeed the only *short* list of French writers that would be relevant to this subject would consist of those men, like Barbey d'Aurevilly and Sainte-Beuve, who did not join the pilgrimage to the Poe shrine. For this interest became something very like a religious cult. If Baudelaire was unique in actually praying to Edgar Poe, some of Baudelaire's successors were not far behind him in their fervent devotion. For the adherents to this cult Poe becomes immense, transcendent, to be associated, as he is by Jules Lemaître, only with the very greatest figures, Plato and Shakespeare.[12] The Poe text, accordingly, is conned with the fanatic zeal appropriate to sacred books. Thus Jean Moréas, in an article in *Le Symboliste*, could assume that the readers of that journal would appreciate a reference to one of Poe's least known stories, "The Devil in the Belfry."[13] And what if not religious awe is this, registered by Albert Samain in his *Carnets intimes:* "Have read Edgar Poe, *Eureka*. Overwhelming sensation, especially towards the end. The grandeur of the hypotheses, the limitless nature of the concept, terrify me. I wanted to read it through in one night, and this dizzy flight through the incommensurable makes me collapse on my bed, my body aching, my head splitting."[14]

No matter how the chart is read, therefore, whether

we attend to such men as Baudelaire and Mallarmé or to writers of secondary and tertiary importance, the results are identical: Baudelaire made Poe a great figure in France, and not for his own time only but for the next hundred years. This apotheosis is probably unmatched in literature. Precisely because it is such an extraordinary thing, involving a great mass of subtleties and complications, it will perhaps never be definitively explained. But, to cut through the mass of detail for the moment, we can discern one unmistakable fact: the values France has attached to Poe are not those his own nation has seen in him. May it not be possible now to recapture Poe, as it were, for America, with at least some of those values still intact? It seems assured, to repeat a basic point, that if Poe is ever to be seriously appreciated in this country it will not be owing to traditional American criticism. It is rather to France that we must look; and in this chapter, in order to get a general impression of the central French thesis regarding Poe, we shall here survey three related instances of the French response to him, and then, in the next chapter, examine the whole phenomenon in greater detail.

— I —

IN AUGUST, 1845, a translation of "The Purloined Letter" appeared in a Paris journal, but neither Poe's name nor that of the translator was given. Later in that year a version of "The Gold Bug" was printed, this time with Poe named as the author. These were the beginnings of Poe's career in France.

Baudelaire did not become aware of this new writer immediately. He dated his discovery of him to some time in 1846, or 1847. But the strange commotion which he experienced in first reading Poe was a subject he never tired of alluding to. From the few French translations that were available he went on to what he could find in English. He wrote to London for a copy of Poe's works in book form; he collected a file of the *Southern Literary Messenger* during the period of Poe's editorship. And the more he investigated the matter the more his original feeling about Poe was confirmed. This American was his *alter ego*, his brother. "The first time I opened one of his books I saw, to my amazement and delight, not simply certain subjects which I had dreamed of, but *sentences* which I had thought out, written by him twenty years before." [15] This experience of the shock of recognition as Baudelaire describes it here is unparalleled in literature.

There is no reason to doubt that the experience was genuine. For one thing, Baudelaire recurs to it, in his letters and elsewhere, again and again, and always in the same terms and in the same tone. Any effort to dodge the implications of such evidence derives not from an expert understanding of Baudelaire but rather from a tacit assumption regarding Poe: that he is not really so impressive as Baudelaire thought he was. To examine Baudelaire's reaction to Poe with the premise in mind that he was not speaking in earnest is inevitably to befog the entire question. No such reservations are called for. The language Baudelaire uses to describe the effect Poe had on him is quite devoid of ambiguity.

There are other grounds also for not questioning the sincerity of his enthusiasm on this subject. Precisely because the experience was so profound, so unusual, Baudelaire was never able to examine Poe with any degree of critical detachment. Thus it is that after we have taken note of the extraordinary expression which Baudelaire gave to his interest in Poe and turn to the three long essays which he wrote on this subject, we feel, inevitably, rather let down. Nowhere in them does Baudelaire sustain his discussion on the level which his brief remarks elsewhere have led us to think is the level on which Poe should be treated. These essays, as examples of criticism, are therefore disappointing. What Poe meant to Baudelaire as a kind of literary hero comes through clearly enough. But what is said about the work of Poe seems rather superficial. It is as if Baudelaire, no matter how intense his emotional response to this work, could not readily communicate the secret of his feelings about it. He could only make some suggestions; he could not coolly stand apart and analyze. That so gifted a critic should have become tongue-tied on the subject of his greatest enthusiasm is an indication of how deeply implicated in Poe's work Baudelaire felt himself to be. To probe into it, to discourse on its significance and the nature of its life, would be, so it seems, to explore himself. This Baudelaire was unwilling or unable to do. Hence his repeated requests to Sainte-Beuve to write some critical articles on the subject of Poe. "You, who so love profundities, why not investigate the profundities of Edgar Poe?" [16] But Sainte-Beuve never fulfilled this request, or any other which Baudelaire made regarding Poe. And so those "profundities" which Baudelaire was sure existed in Poe's work, but which he himself did not explore and could only point to, remained unsounded for many years, until in our own time Baudelaire's invitation to Sainte-Beuve was accepted by other writers.

There is some irony in the fact that the very feature which makes Baudelaire's essays on Poe disappointing is their similarity to the kind of essays Sainte-Beuve himself wrote.[17] From our contemporary point of view, the attention given to the man and the milieu is excessive. We would rather have, if we had the choice, much less of that, and, instead, a much more detailed inquiry into what Poe wrote. But despite their biographical emphasis, Baudelaire's essays are not simply portraits of an artist who was exhausted and crushed in a materialistic, "counting-house" world. Naturally this interpretation of Poe's career would be favored, for Baudelaire saw in it all the more reason for his initial and intuitive feeling of kinship with Poe. Thus one clear purpose of the essays was to inscribe Poe's name in the roll of literary martyrs, along with the classic cases of Chatterton and Nerval. However, Baudelaire was not content with a merely sentimental view of the matter, one which would amount to saying that Poe's greatness was nothing more than an index of his weakness. Poe as a lame giant, then—this is what the portrait comes to. But a giant nonetheless, and this because of the complex interest which Poe's work contains. Baudelaire did not stop short with the presentation of a curious personality whose sad career furnished a lesson for the times. He called attention to a writer who should be taken seriously, and he indicated the channels down which this interest should move.

As Poe's translator, Baudelaire gave his attention almost entirely to the stories. But in his essays he had something suggestive to say of every aspect of Poe's work. "His poetry, profound and plaintive, is nevertheless wrought and pure, correct and brilliant as a

crystal jewel." [18] Inspired? That too; but in addition
the work of a man of will, master of himself, who realized that in art there can be no minutiae. Mallarmé
was fascinated by hints such as these and took up a
task which Baudelaire had thought impossible, the
translating of Poe's poems. Poe's aesthetic, exacting
and disciplined, calling for a union of inspiration and
method [19]—this was to be the focus of Valéry's interest. Of Poe's *Eureka* Baudelaire had said that it would
require an essay all to itself; in "A Propos d'Eureka"
Valéry wrote that essay.

Baudelaire's successors thus found in the articles on
Poe a number of hints which they acted on according
to their own interests and predilections. For Baudelaire himself it was Poe's work in fiction that chiefly
mattered, and it is not surprising that his most illuminating remarks are those he made on this subject.
In general, he indicated that the stories were not to
be read as mechanical melodramas, as contrived exercises in the horror genre. The "new literature" which
Poe had created would be devoid of all novelty if they
were merely that. Consequently, Baudelaire took care
to underscore the psychological content of these stories
as their distinguishing feature. Much as he admired
Poe's talent for ratiocination, and the "impeccable"
quality of his style, the real Poe, for him, was "the
writer of the nerves," who in exploring mental and
moral disease had opened up for literature an order of
experience that seemed to have been effectively sealed
off. In his preface to *Tales of the Grotesque and
Arabesque* (1840), Poe hinted that the terror he was
writing about was "not of Germany but of the soul."
In substance, this is what Baudelaire had to say about
the spirit in which Poe's stories should be read.

Here again we find no more than a direction given.
It was something, however, to make this point clearly,
to define Poe's characteristic subject matter as belong-
ing to the psychological order, and, if only by implication, to warn against the superficiality of seeing his
work as the imitative productions of a sensational journalist who had some skill at writing weird tales. Baudelaire succeeded in setting up a strong barrier against
such a misconception. It is chiefly as a result of this
that subsequent French commentary on Poe has been
so fecund. In this country, on the other hand, the pre-
vailing view has been at best an uneasy one, unsure
whether Poe's tales should not be dismissed as so much
claptrap. In American criticism, ancient or modern,
the treatment Poe has received has as a rule been
either lean with censure or fat with platitude, and thus
has generally failed to give a satisfactory account of
his undeniable permanence and power.

— II —

BAUDELAIRE pointed in a general way to the psychological interest of Poe's work, and this interest, as we
shall see in more detail later, has been to the fore in
France ever since. But the most striking demonstration
of it is the two-volume study by Marie Bonaparte,
Edgar Poe, published in Paris in 1933. It is one of the
many ironies in the history of Poe's reputation that
this, the most exhaustive scrutiny of his work, should
have been written in French; that it should remain at
this date so little known in this country (unmentioned,
for example, in the bibliographical volume of *Literary
History of the United States*); and that the recent
(1949) translation should have been published in

England, but not here until 1954. In his review of this book Edmond Jaloux called it the most important critical study of Poe ever written in France.[20] And he added the interesting qualification that this holds true quite apart from the veracity of the particular psychological theory which Mme Bonaparte employs.

Thus he forestalled a common objection; for the theory employed is psychoanalysis, and when that word comes up in a literary context it is usually considered good form to knit one's brow and show signs of impatience. Often enough, perhaps, this stock response proves to be the right one. But in the realm of what is called literary psychoanalysis *Edgar Poe* is, I think, unique. No other study based on similar assumptions presents so elaborately detailed an examination of a writer and his work.[21] This is far from being the production of an amateur who, after leafing through a number of Freudian manuals, set out to develop a thesis on a likely author. Nor does it in any way resemble the rather cut and dried "depth" studies which some professional psychiatrists with a bookish turn have contributed to *The American Imago*. Once a friend and disciple of Freud, and today his most active and best known exponent in France, Marie Bonaparte does bring a rare professional competence to her task. But she brings also two other qualifications that are not often encountered in works of this kind, a wide erudition and a high degree of literary sensitivity. Thoroughly acquainted with English, she works with the standard "Virginia" edition of Poe, and, for the biographical section of her study, she follows the Hervey Allen volumes, the most authentic life of Poe that was available to her. Thus, whatever reservation is finally taken to the premises she starts from, no drastic demur

may be raised against the scholarly foundations on
which her work rests.

Her central thesis may be stated in this way: Poe's
life and writings are fully intelligible only if it is assumed that they both derive their character from an
infantile oedipal experience of great intensity. Love
for his sickly, dying, and finally dead mother became
a kind of protean matrix which shaped the pattern of
his life, and the recurrent themes of his tales, poems,
and even *Eureka*. Poe was, in her description, "sado-
necrophile." Such was his illness, and from that rank
source arose the strange growths of his literary creation.

Yet to reduce *Edgar Poe* to an abstract statement of
its theme is to distort it rather crudely. Nothing less
will suffice for an understanding of the full complexities of the case than a careful reading of the entire
work. Not that such a reading will dissipate all the difficulties that a study of this nature entails. It may be
objected, for example, that psychoanalysis is, properly,
nothing more than a therapy for living human beings;
and therefore to read Poe's stories and poems, as Mme
Bonaparte does, as if they essentially were transcripts
of dreams, is to do violence to psychoanalysis as well
as to Poe. Or one may suspect that the particular *kind*
of Freudian explication used in this book is unduly
primitive—too hard and fast, labored, Ptolemaic. And
one needs no wide acquaintance with Freudian speculation to notice the technique which this writer employs whereby the distinction between fact and hypothesis is conveniently blurred so that the latter may
be put to work as if it had all the strength of the former. Nevertheless, in spite of such objections as these,
the impression that remains after reading her book is
a formidable one. Once a few inherently unprovable

assumptions are granted, *Edgar Poe* goes on to cast a powerful light on its subject. Poe himself, who so loved ingenious and astonishing solutions to complex puzzles, would have applauded this remarkable reading of his career and writings.

For although Marie Bonaparte is a psychoanalyst first of all, she is also a highly gifted reader. It is possible that her main intention was to "prove" psychoanalysis by a demonstration of its exegetical power. However, she could not have gone very far in that direction unless she had possessed the essential art in literary criticism, the art of reading well. Responding to Poe's work with a highly sensitive intelligence, she calls our attention to many details that are inescapably present in it, but which, prior to her study, have generally gone unnoticed. No other critic, for example, has said such illuminating things about "Loss of Breath," "The Man That Was Used Up," and the other baffling items of this kind which even Poe specialists prefer to leave alone. Or, to name a story that is universally famous, "The Murders in the Rue Morgue," how are the introductory and the main episodes of the story related? Why is the corpse of the murdered daughter discovered in the chimney head down? Why does the detective Dupin fail to explain that detail, or to inquire why the two murdered women should have been looking through a packet of letters at three in the morning? And how is this story related to "The Purloined Letter," where again a fireplace and a letter are important factors in the plot? Questions of this kind, which lead us directly to the author's text and on into a theory of what the text communicates, are raised and answered throughout her book. It is surprising enough that specific questions like these have not been raised before, but it is even more so to find how plausibly they may be answered in the light of Mme Bonaparte's guiding hypothesis. For that hypothesis, lurid as some of its results are, enables her to show an amazing homogeneity throughout the entirety of Poe's work. On any showing this is an impressive achievement.

— III —

LIKE almost all the discussions of Poe that have been written in France since the appearance of the Bonaparte volumes, those of Gaston Bachelard are indebted to her analysis. Bachelard's readings of Poe cannot be treated, however, as if they were merely an extension of her theories. They must be seen in the light of the rather special work he has been concerned with during the past twenty years, and on this intricate subject I shall attempt a word of explanation here.

For some years prior to his recent retirement at the age of seventy, Bachelard was professor of philosophy and head of the Institute of the History of Science and Techniques at the University of Paris. Encyclopedic in his interests, at home in physics, chemistry, and mathematics, and apparently as widely read in literature as any man in France, this extraordinary figure is above all a philosopher, creative, seminal, original. Original, and therefore iconoclastic. It was this bent that led him, in the course of his research into the work of the alchemists and pre-scientific "scientists" of the seventeenth and eighteenth centuries, to go beyond merely descriptive cataloging. Granted, he seems to have said, that these men were not really scientists and so gave us nothing that we recognize as scientific knowledge; yet neither were they merely stupid men. What, then, is the lesson their pre-scientific experience contains? In his analysis of this problem Bachelard developed the thesis that a psychology could be worked out for subjective knowledge, for intuition and reverie, the realm midway between dream and conscious thought. This is, precisely, the realm of the imagination. It was accordingly to the evidence of imaginative literature that he turned for the detailed demonstration of this theory. Resurrecting the ancient intuition that correspondences exist between the four elements and the human temperaments, Bachelard has presented in five volumes—from *La Psychanalyse du feu* (1938) to *La Terre et les rêveries du repos* (1948)—his amazing studies in the psychology of the imagination.

The rich suggestiveness of these books may be gauged from the fact that although relatively few pages deal with Poe those pages present some of the most illuminating commentary Poe has ever received. For Bachelard, Poe is, in general terms, a poet of water. That is the element towards which he was orientated and which polarized, so to speak, his imagination. This insight makes possible, among other things, a clear-cut demarcation between Poe and a writer with whom he is often associated, E. T. A. Hoffmann. A study of their imagery of water and fire shows how different they are: Hoffmann fascinated by flame, Poe recoiling compulsively from it, so that, as in "Ulalume," a volcano image is given in the form of "scoriac rivers," even though this fluvial effect weakens the figure Poe must have intended.[22] More specifically, Poe is the poet of darkened water, water which is stagnant, heavy, and dead. It absorbs life, drains it away. In a word, the water which fascinated Poe and which,

in "Ulalume," "The City in the Sea," "Usher," and
so on, is a dominant image, is no longer the "real"
water which is drunk, but *that which drinks*. In an essay of thirty pages in *L'Eau et les rêves*, Bachelard examines the stories and poems of Poe, bringing into
relief the great attraction the symbol of the dank tarn
and the sullen, melancholy pool had for the imagination of this writer.

Another valuable reading of Poe which we owe to
Gaston Bachelard is contained in the preface which
he wrote in 1944 for a new French edition of *Arthur
Gordon Pym*. This book, he tells us, is much more than
what it is usually taken to be. It is, of course, a realistic narrative of adventures at sea; but at the same time
it involves more than a merely social, human, conflict.
It presents a drama of cosmic forces, a drama in which
man is struggling against not simply human adver-
saries but the elements themselves. If the reader is to
become aware of this drama he must bring to the book
a special sympathy which grows out of the recognition
that in Poe's best work there is both a manifest and a
latent content. Beneath the surface account of more
or less credible incident there is a subcurrent which
flows from the world of dreams. Bachelard defines
Poe's special quality in these terms. He admires Poe as
one of the few writers who have been able to work
along the frontier between the real and the dream
worlds, a shadowy frontier where the writer's experience is strangely blended of elements drawn from both
those realms.

Thus, in his comments on Poe, Bachelard accom-
plishes two important things. For one, he directs attention to the particular element-symbol in terms of
which the Poe imagination was frequently aligned;

and in addition he indicates and illustrates the technique of the double-reading, through which alone, in his opinion, we can become aware of the kind of life that sustains Poe's melodramas. It is true, then, that although Bachelard treats Poe incidentally, as simply one exemplification of a recondite hypothesis, his discussion refines the exhaustive critique of Marie Bonaparte. Making a subtler use of some of the assumptions of psychoanalysis, less dogmatic and systematic in method, he nonetheless retains the essence of her theory (it was Baudelaire's as well) : that Poe's singular gift was to probe into the caverns of the psyche and to bring up to the level of imaginative literature the dark scrolls—of fear, guilt, and obsession—that those caverns contain.

However true it is that the final and defining task in literary criticism is the task of evaluation, it is certainly true also that the initial work that must be done is to determine as exactly as possible *what is there*. With a writer like Poe this first step is indispensable, for it is a hallmark of Poe's work that it cannot easily be accounted for under any of the conventional headings. Baudelaire was aware of this when, with no success, he urged Sainte-Beuve to investigate the profundities of Edgar Poe. If now we have some conception of the extent of those profundities, some definable sense, in other words, of what lies latent in Poe's work, it is in part because through their development of this suggestion of Baudelaire the analyses of Marie Bonaparte and Gaston Bachelard have given it to us, and indicated at the same time what particular power it is that has insured Poe's permanence among the great writers of the world.

But these are only some preliminary instances of the French response to Poe. With Baudelaire in one century and Bachelard in another, we have two widely separate points; it remains now to draw the line that connects them.

2

BUT WHAT DO THEY SEE IN HIM?

IN DECEMBER, 1861, only four years after the
French government had taken legal action against
Les Fleurs du mal as a scandalous and impious book,
Baudelaire announced that he was a candidate for election to the French Academy. It was a surprising move
in any case, but especially so when he compounded his
original breach of decorum by asserting that he aspired to the chair of the revered Dominican Lacordaire.
He had a reason ready: "Lacordaire is a *romantic*
priest, and I love him." [1] But on the advice of his
friends, and guided also by his own estimate of what
the probabilities were, he withdrew his candidacy before the election took place. He could not possibly have
been successful, and even his admirers took the view
that this was only one more specimen of his extravagant and eccentric humor. Very likely there was some
spirit of irony behind it; but Baudelaire's gesture, as
we look back on it now, strikes us as a legitimate one,
and in its superb defiance a noble one. At least *he*
knew what his stature was, if his contemporaries did
not. How appropriate, then, that he was willing to
make this dramatic affirmation of it, to state his credentials and list his claims for recognition. Among
those claims, as he described them in a formal letter

to the secretary of the Academy, was his work on Poe:
"a translation that has popularized in France a great
unknown poet." [2]

Baudelaire no doubt was using the word *poet* here
in its most extended sense, for it was not precisely the
poetry of Poe that he had brought to attention in
France. But the fact remains that he did succeed in
giving to an obscure American author a posthumous
career that has endured with few interruptions from
1857 to the present. One reverts constantly to the astonishing quality of the thing. It is as if we in America
considered such a writer as Gérard de Nerval among
the literary glories of the world, as if we named streets
in his honor, formed a Nerval Society, and incessantly
published translations of his work. The French would
have as much reason to marvel at this transformation
as we do at their high regard for Poe. There may be
other writers in our literature more deserving of foreign recognition, but what we find so puzzling is less
the fact that France welcomed this particular one
than the warmth of that welcome and the extraordinary scale of his popularity there. What *do* they see
in him?

The essential clue to this, according to Laura Riding, is that Poe always preserved a very respectful attitude towards French culture, and the French have
been gracious enough to return the compliment. [3] The
two Poe heroes who are pre-eminently perspicacious
and logical men, Dupin and Legrand, are endowed by
Poe with French ancestry so that their intellectual
clarity may seem the more plausible. Poe had, or seems
to have had, a wide acquaintance with and a warm
appreciation of French literature and philosophy. And
by using, for the most part correctly, a good many

French words and phrases, he offered the best credentials the French could wish to see—a good knowledge
of their language. All this is implied and apparently
seriously meant in Miss Riding's hypothesis, which
indeed is the only one she could formulate that would
be in keeping with her own estimate of Poe: "a
gloomy and sentimental hack," [4] and "a mediocre but
vulgar talent, placed in the less immediate foreground
of public attention, seeking to distinguish itself
through affected refinements." [5] This is the view of
one American poet who is not at all eager to find her
cousin in Mr. Poe.

But if she is right, how could serious readers and
still more serious critics have been so much in error as
to take Poe seriously? "The only solution to be advanced," she says, "is that the readers are serious and
the critics still more serious, but they cannot have read
Poe." [6] This is one way out, certainly; but it may prove
too hasty an exit. Miss Riding's notion of Poe's great
respect for the French calls for sharp revision if, in
reading Poe, we read his story "Why the Little
Frenchman Wears his Hand in a Sling." This is in
fact hackwork, thoroughly mediocre, vulgar in quality. But in it there is no evidence of respect for the
French. Contempt and derision are what we find instead; and so, unless Miss Riding is to have it both
ways, her solution to the problem of Poe's adoption by
France is simply too contradictory to be of any help.
Let us look elsewhere.

— I —

ONE must be wary of attempts to generalize about an
entire people, to state in a phrase the essence of a na-

tional character. And yet there does seem to be a measure of truth in emphasizing the logical quality of the French mind. *Ce qui n'est pas clair n'est pas français*—the motto has been enunciated often enough to take on the status of an axiom; although what is meant by *clair* stands itself in need of some clarification if much French poetry from Mallarmé to the present is not to be regarded as antithetical to the national genius. But even the "disordering of all the senses" which was cultivated by Rimbaud was supposed to be "long, immense, et raisonné." [7] The final word is unexpected in this context, but its presence is a sign of how pervasive is the respect for logic in France, or how deep-rooted is at least the tendency to be logical. This is a cast of mind the French especially revere. Could it be, therefore, that they have taken to Poe primarily because this cast of mind was his?

This suggestion was made a good many years ago by the American critic Curtis Hidden Page. "Poe appeals to the French mind," he wrote, "because the essence of his work is logic—logic entirely divorced from reality, and seeming to arise superior to reality." [8] This would appear to be logic in a very pure state indeed. Page has overstated the matter, but there is some point to what he says. Apart from the detective tales and such analytical demonstrations as "The Philosophy of Composition" and "Maelzel's Chess Player," Poe's work does not impress us as the output of an especially rational mind, not if the distinction between reason and imagination is a meaningful one. On the other hand, it must be admitted that his extraordinary fantasies are far from aimless and uncontrolled effusions. They have a shape and an individuality that they would not possess unless there were a firmly controlling intelligence behind them. And to become aware of that control, as it operates on material that seems by its very nature intractable and anarchic, is to realize on at least one level of literary experience what Poe's capacities were.

In his study of the influence of French literature on Poe, Régis Messac explores with a sensitivity rare in source studies of this kind how it is that Poe succeeds in treating his macabre subject matter in a way that is not at all the way of a man who is fumbling to express his incoherent nightmares. There is no groping, very little confusion. He is able rather to clarify and order almost everything he touches. "Indeed his mind is one of the most remarkably lucid in all literature." [9]

This is the conclusion which Messac reaches after examining the relationship between *The Narrative of Arthur Gordon Pym* and a book that could have inspired it but which is in any case a precursor of it in the literature of the "imaginary voyage": *Relation d'un voyage du pôle arctique au pôle antarctique par le centre du monde*. An anonymous work, first published in 1723, the *Relation* has a number of features which call to mind not only *Arthur Gordon Pym* but Poe's Maelstrom story and "MS. Found in a Bottle." Messac does not try to enforce his suspicion that Poe must have been familiar with this book; he does something much better: he analyzes the similarities and differences between it and the analogous work of Poe.[10] The author of the *Relation*, intent on emphasizing the exotic and strange, overplays his hand. He accumulates such a mass of bizarre detail that the reader's imagination is quickly surfeited, and what was at first extraordinary becomes dull and even commonplace when met with at every turn. Poe does not make this mistake.

In *Arthur Gordon Pym* we encounter only one unknown bird, one strange animal, one river of extraordinary water. In the *Relation* an odd meteorological
phenomenon is described as lasting for only forty-five
minutes. The same kind of phenomenon in Poe's story
continues intermittently for several days, and thus
what was merely a passing curiosity in the one case
becomes something inexorably and fatally menacing
in the other. The French author, too, describes all his
strange phenomena very vaguely. In Poe's hands,
similar sights and visions take on a marble-like solidity,
although their strangeness is not one whit diminished
thereby. This effect he obtains, in part, by his restrained understatement, by the avoidance of a direct
account when suggestion and implication will serve
the purpose better. Poe is frequently thought of as a
writer whose technique consists principally of piling up
horrible and astonishing details so that the reader will
somehow be moved, by main force if necessary. But
Messac proposes a quite opposite opinion: "Instead of
setting forth under full sail on the ocean of fantasy
and imagination, he constantly maintains course along
the limits of the real world. He is careful to keep it in
sight, and he leaves it behind only at the moment when
our attention is distracted. The sureness of touch with
which he manages this is never lacking." [11] And in
this sureness of touch, Messac concludes, in Poe's ability to choose and govern his effects, he is very French.
This is the reason for his nearly limitless success in
France, although when they read Poe not all French
readers are necessarily aware of the way in which he
brings a classical sense of control to his handling of
romantic material.[12]

It is Messac's basic contention that even if Poe did

not derive his ideas and his literary strategies from eighteenth-century French authors, he had in common with them a strong spirit of reasoned inquiry; and hence such comparisons as those which Messac makes are highly illuminating, even though the problem of influence is not finally solved.[13] The Poe of "The Philosophy of Composition," for example, says a number of things that echo the Boileau who wrote "L'Art poétique," although at first glance scarcely any two other writers would appear less compatible. And the Poe of "Morella" and "Ligeia," on the other hand, is reminiscent of the Balzac who wrote *Louis Lambert* and *Séraphita*. Baudelaire was cognizant of this kinship, and alluded to it, but he did not go so far as to draw the inference which Messac finds in order: "Of the two men [Poe and Balzac] it is Poe, a writer whom so many people are pleased to consider as some kind of mad visionary, who is the more rational. It is in his work that one finds the greater regard for order, clarity, and coherence. In a word, it is he who is the more French." [14]

This, we should notice, is the opinion of a Frenchman, and as such it deserves to be taken more seriously than if it were forthcoming from some other source. Nor is Messac the only French critic who has lingered over this peculiarly "French" quality of Poe. Rémy de Gourmont saw in him not a "sickly dreamer" but a lucid intelligence of the order of Pascal's.[15] Another of the literary critics associated with the Symbolist movement, André Fontainas, minimized Poe's relationship to English and German romanticism in order to underline his French sympathies, particularly with the French culture of the seventeenth and eighteenth centuries.[16]

But both these men were admirers of Poe, a fact that may have something to do with their efforts to naturalize him. He was not, however, one of the major enthusiasms of Charles du Bos, and yet du Bos too believed that there was a French cast to the mind of Poe.[17]

In just which sphere of its activities, one may ask, is the mind of Poe most clearly demonstrated? Is he French in his criticism to a greater degree than he is in his poetry or in his fiction? But it was through his reading of the tales that Baudelaire recognized a kindred spirit in Poe, and it was this Poe that he gave to France with the result that the *Histoires extraordinaires* are to be found in bookshops everywhere in that country today. Translations of Poe's poetry and criticism are of interest chiefly to French poets and critics, to a more restricted audience made up of professional writers rather than common readers. But if a good case is to be made for the French quality of Poe's work, it seems that his criticism provides the most appropriate basis for it.

In a brilliant article which emphasizes this division of Poe's writing, Marcel Françon is able to show that it was most appropriate, and in fact inevitable, that the American writer should have been warmly received in France.[18] Baudelaire, he argues, found nothing new in Poe. He only thought he did; actually he was recognizing ideas that were authentically French in origin. He was therefore receptive to them. A factor that helped in this was the similarity that then existed in the mental climates of France and America. On both sides of the Atlantic there was a strong interest among intellectuals in what may be called, generally, Transcendental philosophy; and, specifically, Emerson's re-

mark that his was a Swedenborgian age was as true
for France in the 1840's as it was for the United States
in the same period. But Poe's literary theory, Françon
explains, derived chiefly from the thought of Coleridge
and in this way may be tied up to antecedent ideas in
Germany, those of A. W. von Schlegel especially. But
behind Schlegel, in turn, there is eighteenth-century
French thought. A minor French critic of that era,
Houdart de la Motte, emphasized the "unity of interest" principle, which is found in both Schlegel and
Poe; and Hédelin, another eighteenth-century French
writer, seems to be the man remotely responsible for
the theory that a long poem is a contradiction in terms.
This also is an idea dear to Schlegel and Poe. Such
ideas were born in France, offspring of the French
mind, but were brought to maturity elsewhere. And
so Françon's conclusion [19] is that when Baudelaire encountered them in the writings of Poe he made the
mistake of considering as new and original what was
really quite old and originally French.*

But that it is a sound partial answer is unquestion-
able. However determined were Baudelaire and his
contemporaries to break their ties with the French literary past, they could not have been completely successful in their attempt. Two centuries of a solid and

---

* It is a curious thing, by the way—to embark on a half-frivolous
digression—how readily Poe may be given a position in a closed circuit
of one sort or another. For example: Assuming the influence of the
French Symbolist poets on men like Eliot and Wallace Stevens, and
accepting the professions of the Symbolists that they were guided in
their practice by the precepts and example of Poe, then we may deduce
that Poe's poetry, after a long detour abroad, has at last had some effect
on his distant American successors. As for his stories, they have what
Baudelaire called mental illnesses as their subject matter, and several of
these stories deal with the phenomenon of hypnotism. Now, it was under
the influence of Charcot, a French pioneer in psychiatry, that Freud
began his career; and for Charcot hypnotism was a subject of major
clinical interest. *Therefore*, it is not surprising that Marie Bonaparte's

coherent literary heritage is too much to be disowned all at once. And so it well may be that those elements in Poe's aesthetic doctrine which bear some resemblance to the criteria which held sway for so long a time in France did call forth a cordial response in the minds of those writers who, consciously, were intent on making all things new.

— II —

IN READING Poe, however, could they not also have found something that *was* new? In their literary interests the French are far from xenophobic: Ossian had a considerable vogue in France, as did Hoffmann, Shelley, Oscar Wilde. More recently, William Faulkner was given readier and warmer recognition in that country than he was in his own. Surely it is not a specifically French quality in all these writers that made possible their success in France. By that test alone, the vogue of Poe should be explainable in terms wider than those proposed by Messac and Françon.

And in fact Charles du Bos, although he too takes notice of some French character in Poe's genius, does attempt to account for his success on the grounds of the foreign interest that Poe presented. As a poet and

---

psychoanalytic study of Poe should be the impressive book it is. For she was a student of Freud's, who had been in his time a student of her countryman Charcot; and she applied her teacher's theories to a writer whose tales of psychological unrest had been extremely popular in the country where her teacher had received his introduction to psychology. *Q.E.D.* There is hardly less logic in this fanciful theory than in that proposed by Françon to account for the *déjà vu* response of Baudelaire. In Françon's article the devious filiations among the critical ideas of Poe, Coleridge, Schlegel, and several obscure French writers are traced with a great deal of skill; but one cannot put down the reaction that the neat circular pattern which this tracing reveals is too aesthetically satisfying to be altogether correct.

as a theoretician in poetics, he had something of moment to say to poets in France. He preached, for one thing, the gospel of originality, and of course in his own writing he assiduously cultivated this quality as Keats, Shelley, and Coleridge never did. According to du Bos, this captured the attention of French poets because to be great in France it is necessary to be original. The "relative scarcity" of the French vocabulary is an important reason for this. It results in giving to even the best French poems an air of having been too carefully, and even fastidiously, elaborated. And since French words are sharply outlined and rigorously defined, the French poet finds it difficult to avoid being commonplace and conventional. Furthermore, eloquence and poetry were for a long while so intimately allied in France that Verlaine's famous line, "Take eloquence and wring its neck!" had the force of a battle cry. However, a very large body of French poetry was written before the neck of eloquence was wrung, and in that poetry an enormous number of poetical themes had been used. By the time poets appeared who could have given superlative treatment to these themes, many of them had become stale. And so, therefore, "more and more as the poetical themes go on exhausting themselves, will the great French poet be condemned to originality; and to the dicta of an Edgar Poe, from which a Keats would have turned quietly away, he gives and in a sense is bound to give an attentive hearing." [20]

Some of the assumptions here are not immediately intelligible. One would like to know, for instance, which themes are intrinsically poetical, and how themes may be worn out by use. This du Bos does not explain, but what he says about the French vocabulary seems true enough, and at least in a general way he explains why Poe was held in so high regard by Baudelaire, Mallarmé, and Valéry. Evidently they found in both the theory and practice of Poe a guidance that no other English or American writer could have so explicitly given them. It cannot be an accident that so much of Poe's criticism has been translated into French when there is as yet no translation of what we would consider the magistral source for this part of his work, Coleridge's *Biographia Literaria*.

We have some reasons, then, to explain why French writers took to Poe as critic and to Poe as poet. But a more searching question, and one more germane to our inquiry, is why the Poe of "Usher," *Arthur Gordon Pym*, and the other great stories became a classic not only for writers but for the whole literate reading public of France.

The most convenient explanation is that Poe "improves" in translation. When Baudelaire turned the stories into French, so this theory goes, he removed most of their flaws. He brought to his task more than a sympathetic understanding of what Poe had attempted. He brought also a much surer hand and a more delicate taste, and so, in effect, he as much rewrote the stories as translated them. The French, therefore, in appreciating Poe, are appreciating something that Poe himself did not have and that Baudelaire gave him.

This is certainly a plausible theory, for a translation is by definition a different thing from its original, and it is possible that the differences between the text of Poe and the text of Baudelaire are all to the advantage of the latter. How well this theory holds up we will determine in Chapter Four. But we may retain it,

for the moment anyway, as a likely suggestion. And
it recommends itself the more because it does not assume either that the French response to Poe is the exclusive result of the French character of his mind and
his work; or, quite oppositely, that it was the daring
originality of his work that evoked enthusiasm in an
audience jaded with the results of too codified a literary tradition. To adopt either one of these two possibilities is to fall back on too simple an explanation. Poe
does echo Boileau, and some of his stories are like some
of Balzac's. These connections may have served to give
Poe an entry into France; but if this was the sort of
thing he had to offer the French, they would have had
no reason not to go on as usual with Boileau and Balzac. On the other hand, if his work was altogether exotic, it is unlikely that a *rapprochement* could have
been made. His work was neither too French to be ignored as superfluous, nor too exotic to be unintelligible. It had, rather, the right proportion of both qualities, and for this reason it became popular in France
at the middle of the last century.

What those right proportions are or should be cannot be stated in a formula, but their combined presence in the work of Poe was the paramount factor in
its success abroad. Over half a century ago Charles
Morice all but defined the reasons for this success, and
did so in terms that are not narrower but wider than
those favored by such later students of the matter as
Messac and Françon. In *La Littérature de tout à l'heure*
(1889), Morice wrote:

What we admire most is not so much the expert construction
of his tales, or the perfect mastery with which he builds up
our interest, step by step, to a final explosion. Rather it is the

deep sense he has of an aspect of nature and man hitherto
unnoticed: the grotesque and the horrible. V. Hugo saw this
only from the outside. Quasimodo is merely a vulgar monster,
his one claim to our interest the hump on his back. It is
within the soul, the heart, and above all within the mind of
man that Poe sees the grotesque; and it is to our souls, and
not our eyes, that he appeals.[21]

Less, in other words, for the presumably French character of his craftsmanship than for the new thing
which he brought to literature and which could not be
found in even so great a romantic writer as Victor
Hugo. I quote and paraphrase Morice's opinion; I do
not defend it. For surely what Hugo saw, whether
from the outside or from within, was not written down
once and for all in one novel. Morice and his generation had not discovered the really great work of Hugo
in his late visionary poems, "Bouche d'ombre," "Dieu,"
"La Fin de Satan." And so in the starkly invidious
comparison Morice makes we find Poe praised at
Hugo's expense. Hardly fair; but the juxtaposing of
the two names in this way is a revealing one. The implication is that in the great literary changes of the
nineteenth century the role of Victor Hugo in France
was that of the lost leader.

One finds a similar attitude towards Hugo implied
in the account of French romanticism with which Guy
Michaud, in 1947, began his immense study of the
Symbolist movement. The romantic revolt in France
was given a noisy start with *Hernani* in 1830, and
Hugo later claimed that he had set a red bonnet on
the French dictionary. Was that gesture so very daring? Michaud thinks not. In his opinion, the French
romantic writers of the 1830's were rebels in only a
superficial way, "révolutionnaires de salon." Hence

they chose to take issue with the old guard on the subject of the theatre. It was for the stage that they demanded a return to truth—and the truth they had in mind pertained to costumes, diction, "local color." Michaud dismisses the quarrel as merely academic in interest, and exclaims: "In all this, how far removed we are from the lonely explorations of a Shelley or a Hölderlin, from that journey to the end of the night which had been undertaken by other writers in other lands!" [22]

In other lands, but especially in Germany—the Germany to which Irving was sent by Sir Walter Scott, which drew other American visitors like Ticknor and Longfellow, and which for Emerson and Margaret Fuller was the spiritual homeland described by Gérard de Nerval: "Ancient Germany, mother of us all, land of Goethe and of Schiller, country of Hoffmann." [23] It was also the country of Tieck and Novalis, of Herder and Kant, and its importance for the thought and literature of nineteenth-century France, England, and America can hardly be overstressed. We lose sight of Poe at this point, but only that he may reappear a page or so later in a context that will help explain how he came to be all but assimilated into the literature of France.

When he chose to invoke Germany as "the mother of us all," Nerval may have been remembering how differently a similar phrase was used in a famous passage of French Revolutionary eloquence, Marie-Joseph Chénier's exhortation to the Convention in 1793: "On the ruins of dethroned superstitions can be founded the one natural religion, having neither sects nor mysteries. Her preachers are our legislators, her priests our executive officers of the state. In the temple of this re-

ligion humanity will offer incense only on the altar of
our country, the mother of us all, and our divinity." [24]
Nerval never abandoned his French citizenship, but
allegiance to the intellectual heritage of eighteenth-
century France he did renounce. The Revolution's
goddess of Reason, in whose name Chénier spoke, had
no sanction that Nerval acknowledged. In turning to
Germany he was embracing a different faith, one that
had Imagination and Mystery, Intuition and Dream
as its divinities. He could say, therefore, ". . . I believe
that the imagination of man has invented nothing
which is not true, either in this or in other worlds; I
cannot be doubtful about what I have so distinctly
seen." There is scarcely a difference between this and
the aphorism of Novalis: "Poetry is the absolute reality. The more poetic something is the more true it is." [25]

These two quotations, chosen from hundreds like
them in Albert Béguin's *L'Ame romantique et le rêve*,
are affirmations evoked by the great spiritual revolt
that was German romanticism. The complex nature of
that phenomenon and its bearings on the history of
modern French poetry are amply treated in Béguin's
book. These matters do not concern us here. But following Béguin, and not, I hope, unduly simplifying
his argument, I think the point to be made is that the
German romantics, both in literature and philosophy,
had developed what may be called a *poetic* vision of
the world. Or, if not a vision, precisely, then modes of
attaining one. Dreams were such a mode. In the realm
of dreams, as Nerval's statement suggests, a new spiritual adventure seemed possible. Its goals: an exploration of the interior life, non-social and non-rational;
and along with this a new and felt understanding of
the relation between the subjective self and objective

reality. New values, new "events" were to be discovered; but in this search the systematic lucidities of the intellect could unearth only misleading clues and had therefore best be avoided.

While these new winds of doctrine were rising to the east, most French writers remained, if not becalmed, at least on course at cruising speed. It is a commonplace, in other words, that the literary activity of France during the first part of the nineteenth century was relatively restrained in quality. Compared to what was going on elsewhere, the romantic movement in France was largely a matter of surface attitudes and theatrical gestures. It did not innovate. It was not radical. Perhaps the superficiality of early French romanticism was owing to the longevity of the Cartesian outlook and the priority it set on clear and distinct ideas. And to this legacy of Descartes was added that of the eighteenth-century *philosophes*. In France the ideals of reason, science, order, and system remained firmly entrenched. It seems that a bomb was needed, imported from abroad, to displace them. At home neither Nerval nor even Hugo, for all his genius, could bring off the great upheaval. Much less could Hoffmann in French translation. His stories were found intriguing for a while, but their popularity went into immediate decline once Baudelaire's translation of Poe appeared.[26] It was the discovery of Poe by Baudelaire that finally brought France into the mainstream of modern literature. For here was a writer who combined what the French could see and appreciate, a sense of form and a respect for the intellect, with the very thing that Nerval, for one, had gone to Germany to find, the ability to move as in dreams through the depths of the mind and to illuminate the kind of

verities the reason knows not of. It was the second of
these qualities that Charles Morice emphasized when
he cut down Hugo in order to exalt Poe. But Morice
did see that the two qualities are present in Poe's work.
Their combined presence apparently impressed Baudelaire as evidence that a new kind of literature was
possible. It became his mission, therefore, to chart a
new course for French writers; and the Symbolist line
that derived from Baudelaire gave France once again
at the end of the nineteenth century the literary pri-
macy of Europe that she had lost to Germany at the
end of the eighteenth. Thus at the right time, in this
instance the exactly *indecisive* moment, Poe's work
made its appearance in France. If only by its action on
the mind of Baudelaire it served to give a new direction to French literature.

— III —

IN A country other than his own a prophet is custom-
arily accorded the honor which is his due. But it does
not follow that such recognition is always unanimously
bestowed or given always with equal fervor. There
were perhaps two men, friends of his, with whom
Baudelaire was particularly eager to share his enthusiasm for Poe. He was able to sway a great many
others, both in his own time and later, but with Sainte-
Beuve and Barbey d'Aurevilly he was not successful.

How is it that among all the multitudinous critical
essays of Sainte-Beuve there is none on Poe? Not, certainly, because Sainte-Beuve reserved his *Lundis* for
considerations of more famous or more firmly established writers, or of French writers only. One could
easily compile from the many volumes of his essays a

roster of mediocre names, of various nationalities, which seem now consigned to oblivion beyond any hope of recall. In preparing this list one would notice that if there is no essay on Poe neither is there one on Baudelaire.

The record of the relationship between Sainte-Beuve and Baudelaire begins as a story of master and disciple and ends, as such stories often do, with the disciple in the ascendancy and the master disgruntled and embittered. But with a difference: the disciple, in this case, despite all the evidence warranting a change of heart, never abandoned the warm feeling of loyalty which he had for his distinguished predecessor. In 1856, after the appearance of *Histoires extraordinaires*, Baudelaire requested a review article from Sainte-Beuve, and the critic agreed to write one. He failed to do so, however, and when the second volume of Poe translations appeared in the following year, Baudelaire renewed his original request. This too was ignored, and in the same year, when Baudelaire needed all the support he could get in contesting the lawsuit occasioned by *Les Fleurs du mal*, the conduct of Sainte-Beuve was most politic and circumspect. And then, in 1858, Baudelaire made his last appeal to Sainte-Beuve to do something about the work of Poe. Silence once more, and although it may be that the lack of full biographical and historical information regarding Poe was what deterred the master from attempting an essay, it seems more likely that he took no action because it would have been in Baudelaire's interest for him to have done so. His silence on the subject of Poe is simply a special case of his silence on the subject of Baudelaire. Sainte-Beuve had been blind to the great merit of the younger poet, and when the latter had demonstrated his massive superiority, the envy of a minor talent for a much greater one effectively sealed his lips.[27]

Barbey d'Aurevilly, on the other hand, was of immediate assistance when Baudelaire, having trouble in arranging for the publication of his translations, asked for his support. It was due to d'Aurevilly's intervention that the editors of *Le Pays* decided to give space to Poe in the columns of their paper. He took this course not only out of his warm regard for Baudelaire but also because of his interest in the newly discovered American writer. He, too, had been impressed by the samples of Poe's work that had begun appearing in France, and he was eager to see more of it in the French of Baudelaire. But when the *Histoires extraordinaires* came out in book form he professed some disappointment. Reviewing the book for *Le Pays*, d'Aurevilly had nothing but praise for Baudelaire's gifts as a translator, but on almost all other counts his enthusiasm was decidedly temperate. He doubted that Baudelaire had made a wise selection of the stories, for those published showed that Poe was a dupe of all the contemporary vulgarities: pantheism, materialism, fascination with hoaxes and bizarre sensations. Not a good start, nor a good omen for the second volume.[28] D'Aurevilly passed that one by in silence, but after the appearance of *Les Aventures d'Arthur Gordon Pym* he wrote a review which almost ended his friendship with Baudelaire.[29] For Poe, in his judgment, should be considered as no more than "king of the Bohemians," a writer of extraordinary talent, but one altogether lacking in an awareness of the essential concerns of humanity: God, society, the family. The instincts of curiosity and fear are the only ones that are of interest to him. Perhaps Poe could have been a poet; but he let his virtuosity as a *jongleur* dominate all his work. No; the most that may be said for Edgar Poe is that he is "the most beautiful corpse in literary Bohemia," and in that respect only is he worth any consideration.[30]

Four days after this review was published, d'Aurevilly wrote to the outraged translator and sponsor of Poe and attempted to make some amends for the severity of his article. He explained that he wrote as a critic just as he believed and acted as a man, on the basis of deep moral convictions. Looked at from that point of view, Poe's work must be found deficient. D'Aurevilly refused to reverse himself on that judgment. But what he had said was by no means entirely derogatory. He had called Poe a Bohemian: "A Bohemian—and so he is! . . . and of all the writers worthy of that name Poe has the most strength, is the most poetical, and is the greatest, in his way; which is why, in my view, he is their king." [31] But the damage was done, and a private letter of this sort would not avail to undo it. In his investigation of the reaction of French criticism to Poe, Léon Lemonnier suggests that as a result of the d'Aurevilly review in 1858 Poe's reputation went into a decline that lasted until, around 1875, he became as great a literary hero for Mallarmé as he had been for Baudelaire.[32]

We need not stop to inquire here whether it is possible to fix a date and an article as the pivotal facts in so unsystematic a phenomenon as the vogue of a writer. Perhaps in order to lend some dramatic interest to a study which could very easily bog down in a morass of dates and quotations, Lemonnier was moved to find a pattern of rise and fall and rise again in the history of Poe's reputation in France. The pattern he presents seems remarkably symmetrical and tidy—perhaps some other complicating evidence has been overlooked.[33] But it is of importance to notice that not everyone in France with an opinion worth hearing was in absolute and favorable accord on the subject of Poe. Some of the reviews which the Baudelaire translations received were trenchantly hostile, and from 1857 to the present there have been a number of writers and critics who have declined to share in their compatriots' general enthusiasm for Poe and who have spoken their minds accordingly.

— IV —

IN HIS essays on Poe, Baudelaire stressed the point that there was a grave conflict between the man and his environment—in his eyes the usual thing when an important artist attempts to follow his own genius rather than the taste of the bourgeois society in which he finds himself. But this thesis was not universally accepted. Some critics insisted on seeing Poe as all too typically American, a true heir of Franklin, despite some superficial indications to the contrary. Their view was that the American grain in him made poetry impossible. He could not accept the marvelous—everything had to have a scientific or a rational explanation. He was American—indeed more than that, a Yankee —in that he attempted to let mathematical reasoning supplant human emotions; one needs to be a mathematician to enjoy reading Poe, and to call his work literature is to confuse literature with highly contrived ingenuity. Nor was he in any sense an idealist, for all his talk about "ideality." He is American in the consistency of his materialistic outlook, which is especially evident in his positivistic and mechanistic aesthetic and philosophy. By eliminating passion and truth from poetry he reduced it to nervous excitation, produced by mechanical means. There is in fact no human soul in any of his work. Sickness, crime, and death define his province, and even here the crime does not grow out of passion or anger, but is simply the reaction of a deformed brain or a depraved moral sense. His heroes are only monsters, his horrors meaningless and monotonous. The sources of his inspiration are also eccentric and unhealthy. Nightmares rather than dreams provided him with material, and the nightmares were those induced by drink. Thus he could not fuse poetry and science, as his admirers allege he did, but only reason and madness, and he perniciously gave madness the appearance of reason. His stories are as abnormal and unhealthy as the man who wrote them, for all the morbid states of mind which Poe described he had experienced in himself. This makes his stories moving, gives them considerable power, but there is neither originality nor beauty in them. They are the productions of a kind of madman and should have more interest for students of medicine than for readers of literature.

In brief, this was the way in which Poe was attacked by some French critics from 1855 until about twenty years later.[34] This side of the French response to Poe has considerable intrinsic interest, for it comprises the most detailed negative criticism that his work has received. There is nothing in English to match it. But it is also an index of the kind of attention which France has been unique in according Poe. So much ammunition is not wasted on a negligible target. Even when French writers have seen fit to deplore the work of Poe they have shown by the care and acumen they brought to this task their implicit acknowledgment of its importance.

When Mallarmé's first translations of the poems began to appear in 1873, the partial eclipse of Poe in France, as Lemonnier describes it, was almost ended. He became *the* name to reckon with so far as the Symbolist writers were concerned; and for the past seventy-five years Poe's French reputation has had all the appearance of solidity and permanence. There have been, of course, a number of demurs. Recently, Jacques Vallette registered some doubts about the enduring worth of the poems and tales: "Only so much stage scenery; the abortive effect of too conscious an art, exclusively concerned with form." [35] But the criticism of Poe, he says, retains an inexhaustible interest. Vallette's article is too brief to have any lasting interest. It is an indication, however, that Poe remains a live topic for literary discussion in France, which is not at all the case in this country. The book which occasioned Vallette's article has had no discoverable reviews in the United States.

One of the four or five best discussions ever written on Poe is also an example of something other than the adulatory response which is presumed to be universal in France. In "La Méthode intellectuelle de Poe," Denis Marion scrutinizes with great acuity the claims that are made on Poe's behalf in favor of his reputedly rare analytical powers.[36] Poe's rationality is really no more than intuition. The detective Dupin, for example, does not reason and analyze his way through the Rue Morgue case. He has hunches which happen to prove correct. He disposes plausibly of certain possibilities regarding the murders, but other possibilities

could also have been operative, and these he never
stops to consider. The case of the purloined letter is
similarly solved by intuitive means, and *vraisemblance*,
for all the fuss made about it, is the weakest feature
of "The Gold Bug." The intuition on which Dupin
relies for entry into the minds of the human agents
whose actions he afterwards reconstructs is also Poe's
means of inquiry in *Eureka*, where the problem is to
enter into the mind of God. For Poe's subject in *Eureka* is creation. But what he says of the divine creation is hardly more than an analogous description of
artistic creation, and that of a kind which he himself
tried to practice. As Marion shows, the cosmology of
Poe is a cosmic aesthetic:

Identifying himself with God, Poe sees beauty as the only
path to truth, for he began by projecting his own personality
into the divine consciousness. "This Heart Divine," he writes,
"what is it? *It is our own.*" Thus he is not surprised to find a
God in his own image, a God who is a poet, and whose creation, the universe, is "the most sublime of poems"; and a God
who is a story-teller, with the dénouement of the divine story
"springing out of the bosom of the thesis—out of the heart of
the ruling idea." [87]

The precise intellectual method with which Marion
examines the intellectual method of Poe would suffice,
if the essay were better known, to dispel the widespread opinion that there was a peculiarly French cast
to the mind of Poe. For if, as is assumed, that cast of
mind is characterized by its clarity, precision, and
analytic edge, then it is Denis Marion who is genuinely so endowed and not at all the subject of his
essay.

— V —

ALTHOUGH it is incontestable that the French response
to Poe is and has been markedly affirmative in character, it is fortunate that there exists also a body of resolute minority opinion which is not. Unless some kind
of dialectic were at work, we would hear from France
nothing but encomiums and witness nothing but the
lavish pouring of libations, a kind of thing which
while impressive in its way seldom proves especially
illuminating. Rhapsodic appreciation of the sort evidenced by André Faurès: "[Poe] was always noble,
pure, and fine . . . in his era there were few souls more
beautiful than his"; or by Mme Suzanne Jackowska:
"Poe was the most unusual, the most original, and the
most marvelous writer who ever enriched English literature with gems of purest ray, and in addition one
of the most remarkable savants," and so forth, gets us
nowhere.[38] No matter how sincere, a laudatory note
sustained too long at such a pitch is bound to become
taxing, and we are relieved to hear occasionally the
contributions of a Vallette and a Marion in a dissonant
register. But by and large, from the first stirrings of
the Symbolist movement in France, Poe has been the
theme for a chorus of praise. That chorus is much too
large to permit us to single out each individual voice
for careful appraisal of its timbre and volume. But a
sufficiently accurate notion of what the French have
seen in Poe may be derived from listening to only a
restricted number of solo parts.

For the Symbolists, it was the poetry and the critical ideas of Poe that were of major interest, and in
these areas they freely acknowledged him as their an-

cestor. How sizable his status was in their eyes may be
easily determined: the evidence is direct and plenti-
ful.[39] And when indirect it is just as impressive and
maybe a little more so. For example, when one of the
more active proponents of the Symbolist doctrine, Jean
Moréas, felt called on to answer an attack made against
him and his colleagues as obscure and extremist *Deca-
dent* writers, his strategy consisted for the most part
in unruffled paraphrase and quotation from the literary theory of Poe.[40] The authority of *that* name, he
seems to have assumed, would be adequate to quell all
doubts. But since to enter fully into these matters
would be to deviate too sharply from the subject of this
study, it will suffice to say that in the poetic revolution
that was the Symbolist movement Poe, even more than
Baudelaire, was looked to as the source of inspiration
and guidance.[41] With the triumph of Symbolism he
regained the stature that Baudelaire had given him:
that of a great classic.

Though concerned primarily with Poe's criticism
and poetry, the Symbolist critics had nonetheless some
acute observations to make about the stories. The remarks of Gustave Kahn on the subject of "The Fall
of the House of Usher" and the function that "The
Haunted Palace" has in that story are of the first interest in this regard: "We take 'The House of Usher'
as the dramatization of a psychological fact which Poe
experienced in his own being." [42] A sombre and sul-
furous sadness pervades the atmosphere of the story.
The house, with its great crevice down the front, is
like a soul engulfed in mourning. And in this house
the visitor meets a friend whom he now can scarcely
recognize, and yet whose strange mental life he can

describe as if the man were a double of himself. To
bring out as fully as possible the character of the lost
soul that is Usher and the lost soul that the visitor too
may become, Poe introduces the stanzas of "The
Haunted Palace." Kahn writes:

The function "The Haunted Palace" has at this point is twofold, to make Poe's leading idea more concrete and at the same
time to refine it. It is made more concrete by being presented
in a simpler symbolism, one more easily understood, for the
introduction of this poem is a call, a warning to the soul of
the reader, who knows that traditionally a lyric poem is the
translation of essential truths. It is refined in so far as the
truth at stake in the story, the truth of the allegory and of the
complex symbol which is invested with all the appearances of
a fact of life, is presented here in a short poem lacking all the
manifold details with which this truth was presented in its
first appearance.[43]

Kahn was interested in discussing the symbolical nature
of Poe's poems, but in doing so he stated, not always
with maximum clarity, what has remained a consistent French thesis regarding the stories: psychological
dramas which were staged first in the person of their
author, but an author who was unique in his ability
to give formal literary realization to what must have
been originally a tumult and chaos of abnormal emotional experience. This was Baudelaire's line on Poe,
and if it has been most fully developed in our own time
by Mme Bonaparte and Gaston Bachelard, it did not
lie dormant until they, with their rather specialized
psychological interests, came to their study of Poe.
Kahn's remarks are dated 1888, and they are not the
only instance of how the viewpoint of Baudelaire has
prevailed in France. The same point was made by
Jean Dornis:

If the Anglo-Saxons have wished to see Poe as above all the inventor of the detective story, his Latin admirers have been stirred by something very different: the electric shock of his intense and morbid psychology, his fascinating and surprising analyses of all the feelings, the depravities, the scars that are brought about by mental illness. His audacity in examining his own intentions, in searching the most secret corners of his brain, probing himself, hearing his own heartbeat, cross-examining his will—all this makes Poe their "master of induction." [44]

And this, too, is the thesis, or at least the point of departure for the ambitious critical study of Camille Mauclair, *Le Génie d'Edgar Poe.*

And yet in writing this book Mauclair intended to present a refutation of the too narrowly psychological thesis that had been advanced some years before by Émile Lauvrière. If it should still be necessary to emphasize the point that Poe has been much more seriously studied in France than in America, the best way of doing it is simply to indicate the nature of these two works. Lauvrière's *Edgar Poe: sa vie et son œuvre,* published as early as 1904, was the first attempt ever made at an exhaustive treatment of Poe. Detailed and voluminous, it is matched only by Hervey Allen's *Israfel,* which appeared in this country twenty years later. Both books are considerably dated now, but it is instructive to see that the first full-length study of Poe's life and work was written in France. Mauclair's book, published in 1925, remains without a rival in English, for it is concerned almost exclusively with an analysis of Poe's mind and art. No English or American critic has yet attempted a book-length study of that subject. But if the attempt were made, a knowledge of Mauclair's volume would be indispensable.

The same cannot be said for the 1904 work of Lauvrière or his three later adaptations of it.[45] A pioneer in the effort to bring the findings of medicine and psychology to bear on the character and the work of a literary artist, Lauvrière fell victim to the dangers inherent in such an enterprise. His scientific equipment became very quickly outmoded, and his insights into the literature he was dealing with were never better than commonplace. Poe, according to him, was a "dégénéré," the product of tuberculous and alcoholic heredity, who became, somehow, an "artiste fou." The theory is not too unlikely, but it would be a valuable one only if Lauvrière had been able to show more than an external resemblance between the alleged sickness of Poe and the work Poe produced, and show also how the work of a madman may still be art. Lauvrière lacked both the psychological and literary perceptions competent to deal with these problems.

This weakness in his case—and a grave one it is—provided Camille Mauclair with reason and incentive to write his own analysis of Poe. Committed wholeheartedly to the aesthetic of Symbolism and hence to its faith in the possibility of a rigorously controlled and conscious art, Mauclair perforce had to deplore the incursion of a heavy-handed psychiatry into the domain of literature. And that Poe, of all writers, should become the subject of an alienist's inquiries seemed to him especially objectionable. For merely to read Poe, says Mauclair, is to see that his creations are "constructed objectively by a will absolutely in command of itself," and to know anything at all about genius is to know that *authentic genius is always sane.*"[46] If Mauclair had no more to offer than a set of affirmations such as these, his book would be of

slight intrinsic interest at present, although twenty-
five years ago it might have achieved its purpose in
casting some doubt on the opposite contentions of
Lauvrière. But despite a certain lack of measure at
times, *Le Génie d'Edgar Poe* is perhaps the most suggestive, as it is the most ambitious, of all critical studies of Poe's work.

Ambitious, because Mauclair tries to see all of Poe's
work as a whole, or rather as the effort to achieve one;
and as key to this partial accomplishment Mauclair
offers *Eureka*. This, he says, is the book in which Poe
expressed himself most fully, although it is not a perfect performance; indeed it is hardly more than a
sketch. But had Poe lived longer and under less excruciating circumstances than those that had marked
most of his mature life, he would have gone on to the
great metaphysical work of which he was capable.
And how negligible then would his poems and stories
have seemed to him! [47] The Poe of Camille Mauclair is
primarily a philosopher, an *idéologue*, and something
of a mystic, whose purpose it was to unlock the secret
of the world. One cannot but be impressed by the devotion and skill with which this thesis is developed;
and although a number of partial truths are brought
to light by Mauclair's argument, it is doubtful that
many readers will be willing to accept his view of Poe
as final. Mauclair contends that the Poe of Baudelaire
was a "mere" writer, a story-teller.[48] This is not quite
true, but if it were, Mauclair would not be free from
the same kind of error. For his own oversimplification
consists in describing as the very essence of Poe's work
what exists in it only as a tendency.

But in the course of developing his theory Mauclair

makes a great many incidental observations that cut
to the heart of the matter. His purpose is to get at the
"interior current," to present "the implicit meaning
in the work of Poe; hitherto only its explicit side has
been praised." [49] He would charge Baudelaire with
this kind of limitation; but in his desire to compensate
for too restricted a view Mauclair goes far in the opposite direction and finds in Poe's writings "a rich
content of ideology." En route to this opinion, however, he discovers for himself something which Baudelaire had been the first to suggest. Mauclair writes:
"The imagination was Poe's means of exploring the
deeper levels [of the mind]. Thus it is no paradox to
say that he neither was nor wished to be merely a
writer of fantastic fiction. Everything in his work is
psychological allegory." [50]

Everything? Not really, and by saying this Mauclair gives the shrill ring of hyperbole to a view that
would stand up much better if more accurately phrased.
For though he can make out an ingenious brief for
such failures as "Lionizing" and "Four Beasts in One,"
Mauclair cannot read these tales as psychological allegories. But for the most part he is equal to the task
of elucidating the subsurface life that many of Poe's
best stories have. A good instance of this is what he has
to say of "A Descent into the Maelstrom." The Norwegian fisherman who lived through this unprece-
dented experience describes how he was at first overcome by fear as his descent began. But when he
acknowledged to himself that death was inevitable, a
new emotion took hold of him, the emotion of which
Baudelaire speaks in his line,

Les charmes de l'horreur n'enivrent que les forts.

And once this kind of drunken fascination with the mechanics of the maelstrom begins to dominate the man, he loses his fear and at that moment becomes an image of Poe. "The fisherman, like the author, is freed from his fear by an almost serene contemplation of the impassive Law which brought the fear about. To understand this Law is to be consoled for falling victim to it." [51] The meaning of the story, as Mauclair reads it, parallels what Pascal expressed in more explicit terms in his image of man as a thinking reed.

Following the author's own lead in the matter, Mauclair insists that the element of terror in Poe's stories is not an end in itself, but only a theme, a pretext. Fear acts as a great mainspring of the psychological life, and only for this reason was Poe fascinated by it.[52] He was neither catering to a popular taste for horror stories nor working out derivative variations on examples borrowed from the German romantics. Mauclair insists similarly that the true subject and therefore the real interest of such stories as "The Gold Bug" and "The Purloined Letter" is not the kind of subject and interest that is met with in conventional detective fiction. The final solution of the problem is only a pretext again; *how* the problem is faced and solved is what really counts.[53] Hence the importance of method throughout Poe's work, and not merely in the stories that have some explicit intellectual and analytical interest to them. Poe's method consists in making his readers unconsciously collaborate with him. He does this by leading them gradually and by imperceptible degrees from the real to the extraordinary, and thus introduces them into a psychological order very different from the one in which they are normally at home. Mauclair does not set great store by

Arthur Gordon Pym, although he grants that there are some wonderful details in it. But here also he finds the characteristic Poe method at work: "The real world is kept very much in evidence, and yet a fantastic element appears that eventually takes charge of the whole drama and gives it a very different color. By nice gradations the credibility accorded to Pym dissolves in the unreal light of the enchanted Polar landscape to which he brings us, where everything is at once nightmare and apotheosis." [54] How true this is we may defer for consideration in a later chapter. But in general, and in many specific cases, Mauclair is able to discuss the stories of Poe in a way that answers to our felt experience of them, even if the strictures of a fastidious contemporary aesthetic would urge us to dismiss them as pretty poor stuff. He is able to do so not because in seeing Poe as a philosopher he caught sight of the essential Poe, but rather because he set out from the assumption that prior to the ideology there is a psychological concern basic in these stories. In this assumption and in his ability to make use of it Mauclair belongs with those French critics from Baudelaire to Bachelard who have demonstrated the efficacy, and indeed the necessity, of our bringing to Poe an awareness that the kind of reality which this writer confronted was not the one that a smugly "common-sense" view of the world postulates as exclusive and ultimate.

— VI —

WHAT, then, do the French see in Poe? Today, at least, we hear little of the *idéologue* who was of such great interest to Mauclair and Valéry; and not much more of the poet and critic whom Mallarmé and his Symbolist followers took as their master. The Poe who for so many years was revered as one of the great literary martyrs, a man whose life and genius were snuffed out by a hostile and materialistic milieu—this Poe also has been all but lost to view. From two important articles by Arnavon and Béguin which appeared in Paris in the centenary year of Poe's death a rather different set of features emerges. The emphasis now, it seems, is on the Poe of the tales, a writer characteristically American in quality, and a man who in his writing was able to triumph over the conflicting personal and environmental forces that brought so much misery and defeat into his life.

Unlike the stories, the poems of Poe have seldom been carefully examined by French critics, although they have not in the least been reluctant to praise them. It is rather a disappointment, therefore, that in a recent essay on Poe,[55] Cyrille Arnavon preferred not to deal at greater length with this side of Poe's work; for his brief comments on the poetry are possibly the most illuminating that any French critic has made. But Arnavon is aware that his compatriots, insufficiently experienced in English, most of them, have too often passed enthusiastic judgment on material they were not altogether equipped to read. He chooses not to make this mistake, and he leaves the appraisal of the poetry to those for whom English is as native a language as it was for Poe. Arnavon believes, in any case, that the poems of Poe are not his chief claim to remembrance.[56] True, he liked to think of himself as a poet primarily, but the slender volume of his output and his continual work of revision are fairly certain indications of his semi-sterility as a poet. It is the

stories that form the central part of his work, at once
the most copious and the most widely known. Why are
they read? Not, surely, because Poe continued to write
in the vein of some German romantics or English
Gothic novelists. If he had done only this we would inspect his work today as a museum-piece merely, curious, but dated and dead. Nor is Poe's perennial appeal
owing primarily to his skill, ease, and efficiency as a
writer—although these qualities, when present, certainly help. What gives his stories their inexhaustible
attraction, according to Arnavon, is that beneath their
delirious surfaces we find as substratum the experience of humanity in pain.[57] In an essay written at the
same time as Arnavon's, the same point is made by
Albert Béguin,[58] who in speaking of the "profundities"
of Poe's work echoes the very word that Baudelaire
had been the first to use.

It is significant also that Albert Béguin—than
whom no one is better informed on the relation between German romanticism and French literature—
should adopt the view that Poe is essentially an American writer. Béguin sees him as no less American than
Hawthorne, Melville, and James; and he suggests that
it was because of his American quality that Poe was
welcomed in France. The author of *L'Ame romantique
et le rêve* might well have recognized a European tradition in Poe's work, either by emphasizing, as we
have seen others do, the supposedly French calibre of
Poe's mind, or by underlining a similarity between
his imagination and that of a Hoffmann or a Novalis.
But Béguin is persuaded that Poe's rationalistic habit
of mind is peculiarly American, rather than French;
and, as for the imaginary world of his tales: "The
dream realm these tales have opened to us could hardly

have arisen except in the new world. Where else could
be located their landscape of fog and lake, crossed by
sudden shadows, amid which the carefully studied
phantoms of the *Histoires extraordinaires* act out their
disturbing destinies?" [59] Arnavon, too, is ready to recognize Poe as an American, but he declines to believe
that he was an average American. With all those who
take an interest in this writer, Arnavon is appreciative
of the great array of factual information made available in the monumental biography of Poe that was
published in this country some years ago. But with all
those who have responded in more than a superficial
way to the nature of Poe's work, he queries the image
of Poe which that biography presented. He grants that
a romantic legend of Poe—as a long-suffering soul of
great nobility, asphyxiated by an ignoble culture—has
persisted too long in France, and that it is well now to
contract this legend to the less imaginative contours of
reality. But that cannot justify seeing Poe as a commonplace embodiment of conventional middle-class
ideals.[60] The French legend may have been distorted
and exaggerated; it nonetheless reflected a considerable
truth. Out of the lamentable life that was his in America, Poe was able to salvage the victory which his work
represents, a work in which all is lucidity, if not light.
This was his greatness as a man : that he was not defeated either by his own inherent weaknesses or the indifference his native country displayed to the kind of
work he did.[61] America gave birth to Poe and has the
dubious honor of having provided him with many of
the difficulties in which his genius was tempered in its
struggle for realization. But it is France, writes Béguin,
that may rightly claim to have given Poe to the world,
and to America again. Ultimately, this claim should

be made for the man who gave Poe to France originally; and our rediscovery of Poe, if we care to make it,
will be owing to him who was proud to call himself
the originator of the whole affair—"moi, l'initiateur!"
—Charles Baudelaire.

SINGULAR EXCITEMENT
INCREDIBLE SYMPATHY

IN 1846, the year which was to see the beginnings of
his fame in Europe, Poe was engaged in writing a
series of articles on his literary contemporaries. "The
Literati," as he called the series, dealt with such writers
as N. P. Willis, Margaret Fuller, William Kirkland,
Mrs. Osgood—names that are now almost without exception ignored or forgotten, but which at that time
carried a good deal of weight, if only for readers in
the United States. These writers were his colleagues
and rivals, and it was they, rather than Edgar Poe,
who determined the character of the literary milieu
of America in the 1840's. It was with them, therefore,
that Poe had to concern himself. His own career had
been relatively unsuccessful. Only his sensationally
caustic criticism was sure to attract a wide audience,[1]
and so in this journalistic venture he turned his attention to commenting on the personalities and the
work of other writers, most of them with not a frac-
tion of his greatness.

But if his star was on the wane in America, in
France in 1846 it was just beginning to rise. Poe was
to be accepted there in time as a peer among an order
of writers altogether superior to those he was examin-

ing in "The Literati," and his work was later to be
all but incorporated into the body of French literature.
He died too soon to witness this remarkable vindica-
tion of his genius, but three years before his death Poe
did become aware in some fashion that the French
were taking an interest in him. He spoke of this in a
letter to Evert Duyckinck, dated 30 December 1846:
"Mrs. Clemm mentioned to me, this morning, that
some of the Parisian papers had been speaking about
my 'Murders in the Rue Morgue.' She could not give
me the details—merely saying that you had told her.
The 'Murders in the R.M.' was spoken of in the Paris
'Charivari' shortly after the first issue of the tale in
Graham's Mag: – April, 1841." [2] His chief purpose in
writing to Duyckinck was to persuade that important
literary entrepreneur to use the prestige of foreign
acclaim as a device to keep alive the never too firmly
established vogue that Poe was enjoying in America.
Characteristically, Poe saw fit to overstate the case. He
would have it that the success of the "Rue Morgue"
was all but immediate in France. He was in error on
this and on another count: for the *Charivari* made no
mention of Poe or his story in 1841 nor for a good
many years thereafter.[3] It was Duyckinck, evidently,
who had the more accurate information. Very likely
what he told Mrs. Clemm was that he had heard rumors of a lawsuit which had resulted from the publication in Paris of a plagiarized adaptation of "Murders
in the Rue Morgue." Although this was not the first
of Poe's stories to reach a French audience, the con-
troversy which its publication led to did serve to bring
Poe's name to general notice in France.

The story appeared under the title "Un Meurtre
sans exemple dans les fastes de la justice" in the col-

umns of the Paris newspaper *La Quotidienne*, where it
ran as a serial from June 11 to June 13 in 1846. It
was signed with the initials "G. B.," and attributed
to an American author, but the name of Poe was not
given. The translator adapted the story with considerable freedom, omitting the introductory section,
in which Poe demonstrated the reasoning powers of his
detective, Dupin, and adding descriptions which emphasized the Paris setting. The translator's purpose
was apparently to cater to the popular interest in
stories of crime, and so he also invented details that
would make the Rue Morgue murders even more
grisly than Poe had conceived them. If the matter had
ended here, this garbled version would never have become a literary event, and Poe's renown in France
would probably have been owing rather to *La Revue
britannique*, which had published a translation of "The
Gold Bug" in November, 1845, and was to publish a
translation of the Maelstrom story in September, 1846.
For in both instances *La Revue britannique* named
Poe as the author.

But on 12 October 1846 another version of "Murders in the Rue Morgue" was before the readers of
the newspaper *Le Commerce*. This was the work of
Emile Forgues, a journalist with a great deal of talent
for discovering and translating material from English
and American sources that would prove of interest to
the French public. At a very early date, for example,
he had recognized the originality of Poe's stories. His
article on this subject in *La Revue des deux mondes*
(October, 1846) was the first discussion of Poe to be
printed in France, and it was Forgues' version of "A
Descent into the Maelstrom" that had been published
in *La Revue britannique*. But whatever his familiarity

with Poe's work in the original, he was thought, on this occasion, to have contented himself with paraphrasing the version of "Rue Morgue" that had appeared four months earlier in *La Quotidienne.*

The editors of *La Quotidienne* made no objection; but Forgues had enemies on the staff of another journal, *La Presse,* for he had once charged *La Presse* with plagiarism. Now it seemed that Forgues could be proved guilty of the same charge, and *La Presse* made the appropriately pointed remarks. Forgues had his defense ready; both stories, he said, derived from a common source, the tales of Poe. But *La Presse* would not give him a hearing in its pages, and so he brought suit for libel against that paper. Although he lost the case, public interest in the litigation was so great that the attorney for *La Presse* credited Forgues with having made France aware of the new American writer. Let us grant him this distinction; but we may wonder what would have been the reaction of Poe—who in his critical reviews was so often incensed at real and imagined instances of plagiarism—had he known that it was through this same misdemeanor that his name was launched in France.

In January, 1847, six weeks after the Forgues trial, and capitalizing on the interest it had aroused, the socialist daily *La Démocratie pacifique* began to publish translations of other Poe stories. These were the work of Isabelle Meunier, an Englishwoman married to a French disciple of Fourier. By 1853 the first edition of Poe in book form was available—a slender volume containing translations of "The Gold Bug" and "Hans Phaall" by one Alphonse Borghers. Other translations were soon to follow in an unending stream; but the great importance of the Forgues case was that it almost certainly was responsible for bringing Poe to the attention of the one man who was most fully equipped, and almost predestined, to establish Poe's fame in France: Charles Baudelaire.

In the volumes of Baudelaire's correspondence his first reference to Poe occurs in a letter to an unidentified addressee, dated 15 October 1851, in which he asks for copies of Poe's works to be sent him from London. What should be quoted, however, is the account of his first encounter with Poe which he gave in a letter to Armand Fraisse, a literary scholar and critic in Lyon:

In 1846 or 1847 I became acquainted with certain fragments by Edgar Poe. I felt a singular excitement. Since his complete works were not collected in one volume until after his death, I took the trouble of looking up Americans who were living in Paris so that I might borrow files of the magazines which Poe had edited. And then—believe me or not as you like—I found poems and stories which I had thought about, but in a confused, vague, and disordered way, and which Poe had been able to treat perfectly.[4]

This is one of the basic texts in the history of modern literature. Here we find stated or implied the extraordinary relationship that Baudelaire recognized as existing between himself and Poe. And not only that, for the consequences of this relationship were such as to make much French literature after Baudelaire reflect the singular commotion which he says he experienced. In this way the reverberations set up by the impact of Poe on Baudelaire extended themselves beyond France to make themselves felt on modern writers in America and England, writers who, though sharing Poe's language, would be almost loath to admit that they have anything else in common with him.

This letter to Fraisse might therefore well serve as epigraph to more than one large inquiry into the history of literature during the past century. Our interest here, however, is not in all the far-reaching implications of the matter but only in its more immediate results.

Writing several years after the event, Baudelaire is imprecise as to when the encounter took place. Was it in 1846 or 1847? François Porché seems assured that Baudelaire read Forgues' essay on the stories of Poe when it appeared, in October, 1846, in one of the most widely circulated of French periodicals, *La Revue des deux mondes*.[5] The more cautious opinion rests on the contemporary testimony of Baudelaire's friend Charles Asselineau, who recalled that it was the translations of Mme Meunier which brought Poe to the notice of the French poet.[6] The first of her efforts, a translation of "The Black Cat," was published on 27 January 1847 in *La Démocratie pacifique*.

When one remembers the contempt that Baudelaire frequently expressed for democracy, and indeed for politics as a whole, it seems unlikely that a political journal, and especially one with a socialist orientation, would have served as a meeting place for him and the writer he was to recognize as his American counterpart. But in 1847, although Baudelaire himself was by no means in the socialist camp, he had many friends who were; and his sympathies, at this period of his life at least, were broadly humanitarian. He would have been disposed, therefore, to read *La Démocratie pacifique*. "The Black Cat," moreover, is precisely one of the tales which would have stirred in him the singular excitement which his first encounter with Poe brought about. This is a story of Poe which he all but

knew by heart, and which, in an improvised translation, he would retell, or rather recite, to the astonishment of his friends.[7] There is some reason, then, to
agree with Léon Lemonnier that the start of Baudelaire's interest in Poe may be given a very precise date:
January, 1847. He was then twenty-six years of age.

In reconstructing an image of Baudelaire as he was
at the time when this interest began, one must be wary
of drawing a portrait in which the only features that
stand out clearly are those which will bring to mind
the visage of Edgar Poe. One could do worse, of course,
by presenting a sketch in which Baudelaire would appear not simply as Poe but as one of Poe's heroes: a
William Wilson or a Roderick Usher. A fantasy of this
sort once occurred to Baudelaire himself. In his
Journaux intimes there is a curious passage which
reads: "My ancestors, idiots or maniacs, in stately
chambers, all of them victimized by terrible passions." [8] But if life seldom imitates art to quite *this*
degree, there nevertheless exists in the early biography
of Baudelaire a number of details which do something
to explain the great attraction Poe was later to have
for him. On these details particular stress should be
laid. They not only lend substance to the otherwise
vague "affinity" which is said to exist between the two
men; they also serve to make Baudelaire's immediate
response to that affinity seem a plausible and perhaps
an inevitable phenomenon.

Far from being idiots or maniacs in stately apartments, the ancestors of Baudelaire belonged to a class
of people found far more commonly in real life than
in the pages of a story by Poe. The father of Baudelaire came from a family of small landowners in the
province of Champagne. His education was thorough,

and in the circles in which he moved as a tutor of
drawing he acquired the fastidious manners, the almost sublime sense of courtesy, for which his son was
later to admire him. This man, Joseph-François Baudelaire, born in 1759, was married first in 1805, and
then again, as a widower, in 1819, at the age of sixty.
Of this marriage a son was born in 1821. His wife, the
mother of Baudelaire, was scarcely twenty-six. In the
striking disparity between the ages of his parents we
have the first fact about Baudelaire which deserves
particular notice, and it is the poet himself who calls
our attention to it:

I have an execrable temperament, which I blame on my parents. Because of them I am forever disorganized. That's what
happens to the child of a mother of 27 [*sic*] and a father of
72 [*sic*]. An unbalanced marriage, pathological, senile. Imagine, a difference of 45 years! You tell me you are studying
physiology with Claude Bernard. Go ask your teacher what he
makes of the offspring of such a union.[9]

Baudelaire was only six years old when his father
died, but for the rest of his life his memory of this man
remained one of his most cherished pieties. To his
father, as to Edgar Poe and the family servant Mari-
ette, the morning prayers of the poet's later years were
addressed. But towards his mother his attitude was
very different and far more complex; and here is a
second fact about Baudelaire which any sketch of his
character must emphasize. The "perpetual oscilla-
tions" of which his biographer Porché speaks [10] are
nowhere more evident than in Baudelaire's letters to
his mother. To read this correspondence, extending
over almost thirty years, is to participate in a human
drama of extraordinary turbulence and pathos.
Towards her he could be affectionate and hostile, pos-

sessive and sardonic, respectful, condescending, and bitter. There are few possible intensities missing from the emotional spectrum which these letters reveal. What is it that Baudelaire wanted? Perhaps only what he considered his due : love, sympathy, dedication. But he wanted these things to a degree that his mother found it impossible to conceive of, much less to give. The demand was too great, greater than Baudelaire himself was aware of or could bring himself to admit. Thus when he spoke most clearly of this relationship he did so indirectly, in a letter written not to his own mother but to the woman who had so faithfully played that role in the life of Edgar Poe. The first volume of Baudelaire's translations is dedicated to Maria Clemm :

a mother whose greatness and goodness are as much an honor to the World of Letters as are the wonderful creations of her son. I would be a thousand times happy if an errant ray of that charity which for him was the light of his life could make its way across the ocean between us, and descend on me, wretched and unknown, to comfort me with its magnetic warmth.[11]

Mrs. Clemm was not a brilliant woman, but Baudelaire knew that her faith in the genius of her son-in-law was absolute and her loyalty to him boundless. His own mother was similarly lacking in any special intellectual or artistic distinction; yet it was not at all this fact that disturbed him, but rather the conviction, mutely and tenaciously held, that from his earliest years he had been betrayed by her.

"When one has a son like me," he used to say, "remarriage is out of the question." [12] It is not simply an outrageous pride that is finding expression here. A recrimination such as this has a more profound psychological causation behind it. To be caught up in the

ambivalent emotional dialectic in which the passions
of love and hate act as allies rather than opposites—
Baudelaire knew well what this experience was before
he encountered Poe's version of it in "The Black Cat."
For in the year following the death of her first husband Mme Baudelaire married again. From the shock
of this second marriage her son never recovered.

This was the betrayal that remained hidden, a fes-
tering sore, in the great attachment which he felt for
his mother. The betrayal was the more grievous, and
his mother the more culpable, in that she had chosen
as her second husband a career officer in the French
army. M. Aupick, who was later to attain the rank of
general and end his career as an ambassador of France,
was an intelligent and even a generous-spirited man.
But the assumptions and values of a professional
soldier—the emphasis on order, efficiency, punctuality,
decorum—were not those a Baudelaire would find
congenial. Any stepfather, perhaps, would have been
resented as an intruder; this one was in addition a
menace.

Almost at once the unhappy consequences of his
mother's choice were realized. In 1832 Colonel Aupick
was assigned to a post in Lyon, and in that city the
young Baudelaire began his schooling. Not as a day-
student, however. It was no doubt the colonel's decision that the discipline of boarding school was what
his unpredictable young stepson needed. And so for
seven long years it was this discipline that he experienced, first in Lyon, and later at the Lycée Louis-le-
Grand, in Paris. In one of his early poems Baudelaire
alludes to the drab routine of this institutional existence. He describes the *lycéens* at recess, squatting for-
lornly in the courtyard of the school, the sky above

them framed into a square by the building which is at once their home and their prison. We see them

accroupis
Et voûtés sous le ciel carré des solitudes
Où l'enfant boit, dix ans, l'âpre lait des études.[13]

"Solitudes"—a significant word: for the sense of alienation which Baudelaire was only too ready to cultivate as a result of his mother's remarriage was given additional emphasis by the educational regimen which had been considered most suitable for him. Later in life Baudelaire could be the most sociable of men. But his idea of himself was always that of a person set apart, single and distinctive. He took no special pride in this singularity. "Try to understand this one thing," he wrote to his mother, "that much to my own grief I am not made as are other men." [14] This was in 1844. When he made his discovery of Poe a few years later he was as much relieved as astonished to find that his alienation was not altogether complete. He translated Poe, he said, "because he resembled me." [15]

In 1839, when the bitter milk-diet of his schooldays had been finally swallowed, Baudelaire was ready to enter upon some appropriately brilliant career. Or so his parents thought. The prestige and position of General Aupick, together with the evidently unusual gifts of the boy himself, would make this a relatively easy matter. But he would listen to none of the advice they gave him. Instead of responding to their conventional ideals of financial and social success, he remained insistent that his vocation was with literature and nothing else. A disappointing decision for his mother; and for his stepfather a kind of domestic insurrection. But this was a revolt which not even a general could put down. For one thing, it had for too long been left smouldering; and for another, Baudelaire at the age of twenty-one was to come into a modest inheritance from his father's estate. He would then be his own master and could do as he liked. And so during the three years from 1839 to 1842 the conflict of wills remained unresolved. In a nominal sense, Baudelaire gave way: he resumed his studies, ostensibly to prepare for admission to the École des Chartes, where he would be trained as an archivist. His real interests, however, lay in other directions. During his school years he had made his first experiments in poetry. Now he would continue with them. Too long oppressed by the alternating severities of the *lycée* and the Aupick household, he was now, in his eighteenth year, eager for the freedom and the irresponsibility, the complex of new sensations, which were available to a young *littérateur* of promise in the Paris of 1840.

But he went too far. Bad enough that debts began accumulating; but the virtue of thrift was not the only one which Baudelaire gave evidence of despising. It seemed to the Aupicks that their worst suspicions were being thoroughly confirmed. The world of artists and writers was not a world they knew or could even in imagination be in sympathy with. But they had heard rumors of the enormous moral hazards such a world presented, and the truth of these rumors was being brought home to them in more senses than one. Disciplinary action was therefore in order, and, although somewhat belated, when it came it was decisive. In early June, 1841, Baudelaire was packed off on a long sea voyage, on a ship bound for Calcutta. He had neither assented nor objected to his parents' decision. It hardly mattered, for in one more year he

would become of age and then only his own decisions
would be of consequence.

Yet this voyage of ten months, around the Cape of
Good Hope to the French islands of Maurice and Bourbon in the Indian ocean, was a major event in his life.
The desire of Mme Aupick was that this experience
would free her son from his attachment to the cafés
and ateliers of Paris. And perhaps in the mind of the
prudent general, who had hit on this means of cor-
recting the situation, there was the further hope that
the romance of travel and French colonial politics
would exercise a decisive fascination on the mind of
a young and suggestible boy. (And why not? If the
stepson had been Rimbaud such a hope would have
been exactly realized, and we would now marvel at the
psychological sagacity General Aupick displayed.)
What actually took place, however, was that upon his
return to France, Baudelaire was more than ever determined to devote himself to literature. The voyage
had been tedious and uncomfortable, but it had not
in the least shaken his resolve. It had instead, although
he was perhaps not immediately aware of it, served to
enrich his poetic imagination. One can point to "L'Albatros," "A une Dame Créole," and one or two other
poems as literary work which grew directly out of this
interlude abroad. Not a great harvest, certainly, but
then an experience such as this may bear more devious
fruit. The exoticism of the tropics, the new worlds of
sight, sound, and smell which were borne in upon his
consciousness in the southern latitudes, all this was to
become if not an explicit subject matter for his poetry
then something of possibly greater importance: an
added dimension to his sensibility. Out on the open sea
he became aware of other solitudes than those defined

by a "ciel carré" over a *lycée* courtyard, and symbolism of the sea and the long sea voyage plays a major role in his poetry. What had especial appeal for his imagination was the image of a great ship embarking, with all sails set, for a destination distant and preferably undefined. For Baudelaire, "les vrais voyageurs sont ceux-là seuls qui partent / Pour partir." [16] Only those artists and writers who in their work set sail in this way could arouse his interest. Need it be said that he ranked Poe among the greatest of these?

The voyage of Baudelaire was important for another and much more precise reason in preparing him for the day in 1847 when he read "The Black Cat." During his stay on the island of Bourbon he happened to witness a scene which made a great impact on him. A young negress, the servant of one of the local planters, had been found guilty of some slight offense, and in accordance with the antiquated code of colonial law then prevalent she was publicly flogged. At the time, Baudelaire was only revolted by the spectacle.[17] But his memory of the lash falling on the flesh of the half-naked girl was an experience of the special *"frisson nouveau"* which is scored as theme and variations in some of his more notorious poems. The event forced Baudelaire to recognize in himself the existence of strong sadistic longings. He may have deplored this psychological fact—"to my own grief, I am not made as are other men"—but he would not deny its reality; and as a result of his own self-knowledge he was enabled to understand the dynamics of sadism which Poe described in "The Black Cat."

Soon after his return to Paris, Baudelaire reached the age of twenty-one and promptly cut his ties with the Aupick household. He could do this because his

share in the estate left by his father, while not especially large, was large enough to make him financially
independent. He therefore struck out for himself,
found his own lodgings elsewhere in Paris, and settled
down to the business of being a poet.

His life after 1842 falls into two clearly defined
periods. The first, very short, but the only happy
period of his life, was a time of study and apprenticeship. It lasted hardly three years. The second period
takes up the remainder of Baudelaire's lifetime, from
1845 to 1867. These were the years of accomplishment and some measure of fame, but they were years
also of struggle, defeat, and personal miseries, during
which time he was seldom able to get entirely clear of
the shadow of poverty. Of this future he himself was
the architect. The business of being a poet, as Baudelaire conceived it, called not merely for diligence
and study, and called not at all for a hermetic and
ascetic isolation. New experiences had to be sought
after and cultivated, friends had to be entertained and
surprised—an expensive business, requiring a good
deal of capital. The necessities of life were relatively
cheap in the Paris of 1840, but a man who aspired to
be one of the great dandies of his time could not content himself with the mere necessities of living. The
dress of a poet had to be distinctive and elegant, his
house furnished in accordance with a taste both dis-
criminating and opulent. The results were predictable:
Baudelaire lived well beyond his income and soon
found himself deeply and irremediably in debt. His
difficulties were greatly compounded by the fact that
soon after he had begun his new mode of living he
formed his enduring liaison with Jeanne Duval. A
young mulatto girl whom he had discovered in one of

the cheap dance halls of Paris, this "Vénus noire" remained for years a fixture in his life, causing him intolerable anguish and vexation, and yet exercising over him an unwavering fascination that none of his friends could explain. The specious style of affluence in which he had entered upon his first years of independence could not be long sustained. For much of his life after 1845 he was almost literally on the run, moving from one hotel to another in flight from the demands of his many creditors. Perhaps if he had been able to free himself from the incubus of Jeanne Duval and to apply himself with single-minded intensity to the work he was capable of, he would have been able to find a way out of these difficulties. But such a common-sense solution was not available to Baudelaire. He could not rid himself of the perverse attraction his mistress had for him, nor could he submit himself to the long, steady effort that alone would suffice to recapture for him some measure of security. He knew what kind of action was needed, but in the vicious circle in which he found himself he could act only in a way that was counter to his own interests: "Assume a condition of perpetual sloth enforced by a continuous run of bad luck, and along with this a deep hatred of sloth, yet finding it absolutely impossible to throw off because of a perpetual shortage of money." [18] What Poe defined as "perverseness"—the natural instinct by which a man acts in the way that will insure self-defeat—this was a trait which Baudelaire had no trouble in recognizing in the pattern of his own behavior. His life was crippled by this fatality; no wonder, then, that he was ready to respond to the same phenomenon in the hero of "The Black Cat" when he

saw how the hero of that story became the chief designer of his own destruction.

If therefore it was something of an accident that
Baudelaire took up a copy of *La Démocratie pacifique*
and read Mme Meunier's translation of a story by an
obscure American writer, it was much less of an accident that this particular story made a remarkable impression on him. The results would have been much
less sensational if the story had been "King Pest" or
"Loss of Breath." But to "The Black Cat" he could
not be indifferent. The emotional experiences of his
formative years had shaped him in such a way that
he could not but respond with singular fullness to the
vibrations that emanate from this tale.

The point deserves emphasis, because in examining
the record of Baudelaire's career for reasons that
would explain his interest in Poe, one may be led to
construct an alternative theory. Baudelaire was pas-
sionately fond of novelty. Whatever in the realm of art
was new and curious, and least likely to achieve a
widespread popularity, was almost certain to engage
his attention. And if the subject succeeded in arousing
his own interest he would at once set about organizing
a similar response in the minds of as many other people as possible. Always active in the forefront of the
avant-garde, he was eager for his discoveries in literature, painting, and music to reach the notice of the
cultural stragglers who were bringing up the rear. It
was in this spirit that he wrote his art criticism, arguing a case for Delacroix and Daumier at a time
when these painters were getting the cool reception
that is usually accorded any innovation in the arts.
Baudelaire considered that Gautier and Nerval were
being similarly undervalued, and he did what he could

to make their poetry and stories better known. He was
prompt to welcome a radically new work like *Madame
Bovary*, but he was anxious also that a forgotten novel
like *Les Liaisons dangereuses* be brought once more
into circulation. And just as he had held up Delacroix
as the great painter of the nineteenth century, so, after
hearing the first Paris concert of Wagner's music in
1861, he at once began an educational campaign on
behalf of the German composer.

These discoveries were among the triumphs of Baudelaire's critical insight. But by no means all of his
enthusiasms were so solidly based. When we read the
full history of his various artistic and literary passions
in such volumes as *L'Art romantique* and *Curiosités
esthétiques*, we come upon a number of other names
which are now quite without lustre, names of painters
like Hausouiller, poets like Dupont and Barbier. And
yet for them also Baudelaire had very generous praise.
What is especially disturbing is that the rate of turn-
over is so high. As a contemporary witness phrased it:

One day Baudelaire could be seen with a volume of Swedenborg under his arm. . . . In our walks through the Louvre he
would recommend Bronzino, a master of mannerism, as the
greatest painter of them all. On another day, the Pole
Wronski had supplanted Swedenborg. . . . And another time it
was Van Eyck and the primitive painters who had replaced
that fool of a Bronzino.[19]

Is it not possible, therefore, that in Poe Baudelaire had
simply discovered a man and a writer who was of interest because he was new and bizarre; and is it not
also possible that, in the labor he gave to making Poe
a great man in France, Baudelaire was simply engaged
on his masterpiece of developing a popular taste for
an author who would not normally, and on his own

power, have found any considerable following in that country?

There is something to this theory, but at best it is no more than a partial explanation. Baudelaire was certainly always on the lookout for what was new and different, and he took a keen delight in advertising the discoveries he made in this area. His *Salon de 1845* concludes with a statement of this attitude: "Let us hope that in the coming year we will be able to have the singular pleasure of hailing the arrival of something really *new*!" [20] This pleasure he experienced in full once he began to read the work of Poe. And yet surely it was not its novelty alone that compelled his attention. Novelty wears off. To have remained for sixteen years steadfastly dedicated to the task he had elected to perform for Poe, Baudelaire must have been animated by a more permanent motive than that of creating a literary fad.

Whatever the motive may have been, it is clear that the results of Poe's impact on Baudelaire are remarkable enough to stand in no need of exaggeration. Late in life he remarked that Poe and Joseph de Maistre had taught him how to think: "De Maistre et Edgar Poe m'ont appris à raisonner." [21] But the process inevitably took time. However deeply stirred he was by his reading of "The Black Cat," Baudelaire was not a completely changed man immediately thereafter, nor did he at once resolve to devote the bulk of his energies to translating the work of this new writer. That came later. In 1847 he was at the outset of his career, just beginning to be recognized as one of the leading talents of his generation. In two important monographs, the *Salon de 1845* and the *Salon de 1846*, he had established himself as one of the best art critics in

France. He was becoming known also as a result of
the variety of articles, essays, and reviews which were
appearing under his name in the Paris press. And although he was reluctant to publish his poetry—the
first of his poems did not appear until late in 1846—it
was primarily as a poet that he was regarded by those
who knew him.

There was no sudden shift in the literary situation
of Baudelaire in 1847. He went on with his own work
as a critic of art and literature, and since the idea of a
unified volume of poems had for long been active in
his mind, he continued with the poetry that later on
was to make up *Les Fleurs du mal*. He continued also
to be actively interested in the ideological skirmishes
that were taking place in France at this period. His
first contact with Poe shook him up considerably, but
it did not all at once endow him with a new set of beliefs and attitudes. If in 1847 he was disposed to be
friendly to the viewpoint of a socialist paper like *La
Démocratie pacifique*, he did not suddenly change his
mind when he saw how the editors of that paper had
reacted to "The Black Cat." In printing Mme Meunier's translation, these men were not concerned
primarily with its interest *as a story*, nor were they in
any way aware of the impression it would make on
the mind of a man like Baudelaire. For him, "The
Black Cat" was a kind of symbolic case-history in
which he was able to discern a psychological truth that
echoed obscurely but imperiously in the depths of his
own character. For the editors of the paper that published the story, "The Black Cat" was simply a document to illustrate how human nature could be vilified
by a writer who did not share the enlightened philosophical assumptions held by the editors, and presum-

ably by the readers, of such a paper as *La Démocratie pacifique*. In a note prefacing the translation, Poe's story was held up as an object lesson in reactionary thinking and its psychological validity stoutly denied.[22] Baudelaire was one reader on whom this editorial moralizing must have been utterly lost. Then and there he might have seen that he could have no meaningful alliance with the optimistic adherents of the socialist cause and the philosophy of progress. But no break came. Indeed, in 1848, he aligned himself actively with the revolutionary movement. With General Aupick on one side of the barricades, Baudelaire would want to be found on the other. But this was nonetheless a strange move for him to make. Prior to 1848 he had been only contemptuous of active political affiliations, and in his *Salon de 1846* he had specifically singled out the republican faction as "the inveterate enemy of luxury, art, and literature" [23]—the enemy, in a word, of all that he most valued. It would be futile, however, to try to make sense out of Baudelaire's political history. After the revolutionary days of June, 1848, we find him as one of the founders and editors of a short-lived leftwing publication, *Le Salut publique;* and in another surprising reversal of attitude, he is associated late in the same year with a journal dedicated to the conservative cause. Not until 1852 did he give up his erratic political interests. It happens that this was the year in which appeared the first results of his discovery of Poe: an essay, "Edgar Poe, sa vie et ses ouvrages," and translations of four of the tales. But it would be going well beyond the nature of the evidence to infer that it was Poe's aversion to democratic institutions that caused Baudelaire to terminate his excursions into the area of politics.

The discovery of Poe in 1847 resulted in a singular excitement, but it was not a sudden, explosive experience of total illumination. Once his commitment to Poe had really seized him, however, a pronounced change for a while came over his way of life. The portrait which Asselineau gives of Baudelaire is that of a man for whom social activity was an absolute value. Art, books, and ideas formed his dominant interests, but these interests had to be shared, and so at all hours of the day or night Baudelaire was ready to begin or resume the conversational activities in which he was both brilliant and tireless. This came to an end, however, when, around 1852, his attraction to Poe began to take on the proportions of a "possession," as Asselineau describes it.[24] He had been known as a wit, as a man of wide and varied interests. At about this time he must have become something of a Poe bore. The American author obsessed him. He was willing to talk only of Poe, willing to listen only to talk about him. Having resolved to translate his work, perhaps in its entirety, Baudelaire submitted himself to the exacting demands which such a job entailed. He who had formerly lived in contempt of schedules could stay at his desk from ten in the evening to ten the next day. Friends might call—he left the key in the lock—but they would be ignored. He would continue silently with his work, attentive only to what was in front of him: the text of Poe to be finished that day, and the indispensable English dictionary.[25] Always an obstacle to creative writing of his own, the "perpetual sloth" of which he wrote to his mother disappeared entirely in this new undertaking. There were no difficulties that could not be in some manner surmounted. He had a mission to fulfill. It was his custom, as he told Ar-

mand Fraisse, to importune American visitors in Paris
for chance copies of the magazines in which Poe's
work had first appeared. If Poe's idiom at times proved
obscure, he would consult an English bartender in a
café on the rue de Rivoli. No room for false pride in
these matters. In his recollections of Baudelaire,
Asselineau tells of one incident in particular which indicates to what lengths his friend was prepared to go
in order to accomplish the goal he had set himself.
Baudelaire once heard that an American writer who
must have known Poe was staying at a Paris hotel.
He suddenly descended on this gentleman, and found
him occupied in the purchase of a pair of shoes. Ignor-
ing the transaction and the presence of the astonished
tradesman, Baudelaire at once began his inquiries.
But it developed that the American had no interest in
his compatriot, dismissing him as merely a bizarre
writer who was not "con-se-cu-tive" in his conversation. Baudelaire was not interested in hearing this kind
of testimony and he stormed away in a fury. Slam-
ming on his hat, he summed up the situation in a formula which speaks rather well for his knowledge of
how the lines of literary force were drawn in America.
"Ce n'est qu'un Yankee," he shouted.[26]

The translations on which he worked unremittingly
for sixteen years represent a great accomplishment,
and, for a man of Baudelaire's temperament, a heroic
one. It is hardly surprising that the translator himself
seems to have regarded his five volumes of Poe as his
most important single achievement. Even before the
series was half-finished, he wrote to Sainte-Beuve: "So
much has been said about Loève-Veimars [the French
translator of E. T. A. Hoffmann] and of the service
he rendered French literature! Will I not find some-

one brave enough to say the same about me?" [27] Such
was his own view of the enterprise of which the first
results appeared on 15 July 1848 with the publication
in *La Liberté de penser* of "Révélation magnétique."

It does not look like an auspicious beginning. "Mesmeric Revelation" has no narrative interest and pre-
tends to none. In its basic situation it bears some resemblance to "Facts in the Case of M. Valdemar," for
both tales are presented as the records of conversations
held with men who have been hypnotized at the point
of death. They are enabled to speak as it were from beyond the tomb. But in "Valdemar," by emphasizing
the phenomena of physical decomposition, Poe worked
up to one of his most astonishing climaxes. In "Mesmeric Revelation" there is no climax and no action,
but only a rather tedious catechism which anticipates
some of the ideas found later in *Eureka*. In this story,
a Mr. Vankirk, long accustomed to hypnotic sleep as
the sole means by which the pain of his serious illness
is relieved, sends for a mesmerist and suggests that a
series of questions be raised during his hypnotic
trance. Perhaps in this way, he suggests, there may be
discovered more profound truths than are available to
empirical or rational inquiry. The trance is thereupon
induced, and following the lead of his questioner,
Vankirk attempts to explain such problems as death,
the immortality of the soul, the nature of "unparticled
matter," and the "substantive vastness of infinity."
These matters had a compelling fascination for Poe,
and in *Eureka* he endeavored to discuss them with
what fulness and philosophical precision he could
command. But "Mesmeric Revelation" is at best a
curious failure, both as story and as treatise. It seems
odd, then, that Baudelaire should have elected it as his

first exercise in the translation of Poe. So odd, indeed, that one of the earliest commentators on the Poe-Baudelaire relationship, writing in 1893, concluded that the existence of "Révélation magnétique" was evidence that Baudelaire had decided to translate every Poe item he could find, regardless of interest, intrinsic merit, or any other consideration.[28]

The fact is that in 1848 the kind of thing Poe was doing in this story was of very great interest. In America, England, and France, the traditional orthodoxies of religion and philosophy were considered sterile and outmoded by the articulate intellects of the time; and in their search for new verities or for more convincing reasons to adhere to the old, these men took to modes of inquiry with a fervor that strikes us nowadays as both naive and mistaken. In principle, both Carlyle and Emerson would have assented to the motive behind Vankirk's experiment: "I was not long in perceiving that if man is to be intellectually convinced of his own immortality, he will never be so convinced by the mere abstractions which have so long been the fashion of the moralists of England, or France, and of Germany. Abstractions may amuse and exercise, but take no hold of the mind." To fill the void left by the enforced abdication of such philosophers as Newton and Descartes and the supposed bankruptcy of institutional Christianity, recourse was had to a new and motley set of prophets and doctrines. Swedenborg, Lavater, and Saint-Martin were studied with great seriousness. Interest in spiritualism, phrenology, and mesmerism became intellectually fashionable. It is always something of a surprise, for example, to recall that the great realist Balzac, a man whom one would imagine particularly immune to any transcendental sympathies, was

in fact deeply affected by the quasi-mysticism of Swedenborg and wrote several novels under that unlikely
influence. Baudelaire, too, went through this phase; so
much so that his most famous poem, "Correspondances," has been thoroughly glossed as a Swedenborgian document.[29] In translating "Mesmeric Revelation"
for *La Liberté de penser*—a journal whose very title
is indicative of the unsettled intellectual atmosphere of
1848—Baudelaire was not simply capitalizing on an
astute judgment of popular trends in the literary market. He had found in Poe's account of mesmerism and
the arcane spiritualist illuminations made possible
through mesmerism a story to which his current philosophical interests made him personally responsive.

Nor need this opinion rest on inference alone. In an
explanatory note which he wrote as a preface to his
translation of the story, Baudelaire speaks of the nature of his interest in it. He begins by alluding to the
recent flurry of excitement over Poe that was brought
about by the Forgues case and the Meunier translations, four of which had been published by July, 1848.
"There has been much talk lately about Edgar Poe.
And rightly so. He has mainly astonished [his readers]
—rather than moved them or kindled their enthusiasm." [30] The final phrase is important because Baudelaire, for one, *had* been moved as well as astonished by
what he had read of Poe, and in this brief essay his
effort is to instill in other readers some of his own enthusiasm.

His strategy is based chiefly on an association of
Poe with other more familiar names: Diderot, Laclos,
Hoffmann, Goethe, Jean Paul, Maturin, and Balzac.
Each of these men, says Baudelaire, is characterized by
a literary method peculiar to himself, a method which

is either consciously his own invention or the unconscious reflection and coefficient of his own special sensibility. Then, too, they are all more or less philosophical writers. "They all . . . take readings of nature, their own nature," and hence are far more original and interesting than the "merely imaginative writers who lack a philosophic turn of mind and who amass and align details without ever classifying them or bringing out their hidden meaning." [31] An interest in the supernatural is another characteristic of this group. This bent may be the result of a primitive search-instinct, "the roots of which may go back to distant childhood impressions"; or it may be an adult disposition, akin to the scientific fervor of the professional naturalist. In either case an effort is made to understand all phenomena, all experience, as parts of one large and mysterious unity. These writers are moved by a great ambition, therefore; and if their writings provoke astonishment, it is this ambition which is finally causative. Thus with Balzac and Poe:

We recall Séraphitus, Louis Lambert, and a score of passages from his other books in which Balzac—a great mind consumed with the lawful ambition of attaining encyclopedic scope—attempted to establish in one single and final system the different ideas he found in Swedenborg, Mesmer, Marat, Goethe, and Geoffroy Saint-Hilaire. The concept of unity also appealed to Poe, and he was no less industrious than Balzac in his pursuit of this ideal.[32]

Let the readers of *La Liberté de penser* therefore approach this story in a proper frame of mind, with a knowledge of the general context to which it belongs, and with a notion of the daring purpose which its author had in mind. Caviar to the general, perhaps, but a piece which should prove engrossing to readers aware of the less conventional literary and philosophical currents of their time. It was in these terms that Baudelaire spoke of Poe in his first formal discussion of his work.

In accounting for the readiness with which Poe became a popular author in France in the middle of the last century, Léon Lemonnier emphasizes the widespread interest in spiritualism and illuminism which was prevalent then as an interest under which Poe was quickly subsumed. Yes; —but is it safe to go beyond this to say that "for Baudelaire, Poe was an *illuminé*"? [33] This is the opinion of P. Mansell Jones, who, like a number of other admirers of Baudelaire, seems vexed at the French poet's admiration for the American and seems inclined to consider Baudelaire's professed resemblance to Poe as a case of mistaken identity.

It is true enough that in one important respect Baudelaire did err in his comments on "Révélation magnétique." Poe either knew or pretended to know a great many rather obscure and esoteric authors, but Swedenborg does not appear to have been one of them. In this story and in those other dialogues which resemble it, "Monos and Una" and "Eiros and Charmion," Poe was probably relying mostly on his own individual imagination and not on a thorough acquaintance with that tradition of esoteric knowledge in which the name of Swedenborg occupies a capital place. But the error Baudelaire made in assigning Poe to this tradition was all but inevitable: some American Swedenborgians were convinced that what was revealed in "Mesmeric Revelation" was not only congenial with their master's doctrines but was objectively quite true.[34] Baudelaire, of course, did not go this far, and by 1856 he could be sardonic at the expense of those "naïfs illuminés" in France who had taken the story seriously.[35] In short, if Poe had for Baudelaire the character of an *illuminé*, that was true only of 1848 and a few years thereafter. It certainly did not remain as his final, definitive notion of Poe.

Nor was it exclusively in this light that he wrote of him in his brief preface to the story. His comments reveal other things besides this misunderstanding. For one thing, *Eureka* was published in January, 1848, but Baudelaire had no knowledge of the nature of this book until several years later. Yet in this essay, dated July, 1848, he in effect foretold that Poe would write *Eureka* and he could even hint of the kind of quality the book would have. For, as he put it, there must come a time when writers like Poe "become, so to speak, jealous of the philosophers, and they then propound their own account of how the world is made, and do this sometimes with a certain presumption that is not without charm and naivety." [36] In speaking of the supernatural element which occurs so frequently in authors like Poe, Baudelaire provides at least the hint of another unusual insight. He says that this interest may sometimes have its origins in the distant impressions of the writer's childhood. He himself was aware, and to an unusual degree, of how deeply rooted in the experiences of infancy may be the dispositions and the very mode of behavior of the mature man; and if one wanted to collect evidence for Freud's statement that most of his basic discoveries had been anticipated by creative artists, one might well begin with some of the autobiographical reflections of Baudelaire.[37] Here, with regard to Poe, he does not precisely say that this writer's interest in preternatural phenomena was the result of impressions and experience dating far back into his psychical life. But in a subsequent essay this suggestion is clearly made: "As for the ardor with which he often treats horrifying material, I have observed in a number of men that this was often the result of a very large fund of unused vital energy, sometimes the result of an unyielding chastity and of deep feelings kept repressed." [38] In discussing the Poe of "Mesmeric Revelation," Baudelaire anticipates this hypothesis.

What should be noticed, therefore, is not merely the fact that in 1848 Baudelaire saw fit to introduce Poe to France as an "illuminist" writer, but that by this time—only eighteen months after his original discovery—he had arrived intuitively at several striking insights into the nature of his work. He naturally was familiar with other stories besides "The Black Cat" and "Mesmeric Revelation." But it seems far from fortuitous that these two stories are the first that must be named in an account of Baudelaire's relationship with Poe. From the one, which he almost certainly read in 1847, he could draw the inference that Poe was a writer who had for subject matter those unusual states of emotional experience which Baudelaire was acquainted with in his own life. From the other story, which he translated in 1848, he could conclude that Poe was in addition a writer of philosophical interest, in whose craft the intellectual virtues of order and method were of primary importance. Two poles of attraction, therefore; but they acted as one, and under their combined influence Baudelaire was soon drawn into the major activity of his life: the Poe translations.

Enthusiasm, sympathy, admiration—feelings such as these may be taken for granted as animating Baudelaire when he began his tremendous task, and by these feelings he was sustained during the long years of his dedication to it. Nor could it otherwise have been carried through. But however essential this ardor was to the fulfillment of his great program, there were two other important credentials which he also needed. He had to familiarize himself thoroughly with the work of his author, and do this not only in order to formulate some general, leading conceptions in the light of which his individual translations would take shape, but also in order to deal competently with a less imponderable necessity: determination of the texts on which his translations ought to be based. Since Poe had revised his work frequently for subsequent re-printings, the problem here was an intricate one in bibliography, and Baudelaire was not always success-ful in solving it. But he was well aware that he would have, in some degree, to be Poe's editor as well as his translator. The first requirement in either case was to understand exactly what Poe had written. Something more was needed than an intuitive grasp of the texts. Their literal sense had to be thoroughly mastered.

In explaining the character of his translation of "Mesmeric Revelation," Baudelaire proclaimed that he had done his work in as literal a way as possible, and added: "I have preferred a rather painful and sometimes baroque kind of French so as best to bring out the philosophical mode of Edgar Poe." [39] But in 1848 his knowledge of English was not adequate to this purpose, and the original version of "Révélation magnétique" contains a good many slips. For example, Poe wrote: "Thus man is individualized. Divested of corporate investiture he were God." Baudelaire trans-lated: "Ainsi l'homme fut individualisé. Dépouillé de l'investiture corporelle, il était Dieu." This is hardly literal, for the change of tense in the first sentence is unwarranted and the usage of *were* in the second is misunderstood. The English idiom "but for" was also misunderstood by Baudelaire, who translated it with mistaken literalness as "mais, pour." Poe's unusual term *sleep-waker* was read by Baudelaire as *sleep-walker* and rendered in French as *somnambule*. Poe's style is not of the easiest, and in this story in particular his English is itself rather painful and baroque. The difficulties which Baudelaire must have experienced in working with it undoubtedly forced him to admit that if he were to prepare merely competent translations his linguistic endowments would have to be improved.

Hence the long delay between the appearance of "Révélation magnétique" in 1848 and the publication of his second Poe translation, "Bérénice," in 1852. Baudelaire never became absolutely bi-lingual. That rare perfection would be too much to expect. But in this four-year period of apprenticeship he brought his command of English up to a very high level. He had learned the rudiments of the language early in life from his mother, who had been born in England and spent her first years there. She was her son's first teacher, and indeed it was she whom he often later consulted when his translations were in progress. He perhaps had instruction in English during his years in the *lycée*, but if scholastic awards are to be taken as reliable indications of ability it would appear that the language he had a special gift for was not English but Latin. And so when he realized the extent of the work cut out for him by his desire to make Poe a great name in France, he regretted that his abilities in English were not much better than they were. "I had forgotten much of my English," he says of himself in 1852, "*but now I know it well.*" [40] Naturally, Baudelaire became the better equipped for his task the longer he continued with it; but what he says here is not exaggerated. By dint of serious study, carried out not through books alone but pursued actively, wherever he could hear English spoken, he earned the right to act as the authoritative translator of the work of Poe.

He was not, as we know, the first in this field. From a strictly chronological viewpoint, the names of Forgues, Borghers, and Isabelle Meunier must be given precedence over his. Nor was he, once arrived on the scene, alone to occupy it. Two other men had taken up the occupation of translating Poe. One of these, Léon de Wailly, was a negligible rival; but the other, William Hughes, remained in competition with Baudelaire throughout the latter's lifetime.[41] With the publication of *Histoires extraordinaires* in 1856, the superiority of Baudelaire was at once recognized. Hughes thereafter had to content himself with the stories Baudelaire left alone. But the role which Baudelaire had elected to play—"*moi, l'initiateur*"— called for no supporting parts, and the perseverance of Hughes, while never much of a threat, remained for years as a minor annoyance.

It was certainly the least of the worries he encountered. In the *Journaux intimes* we find a significant entry: "The story of my translation of *Edgar Poe*." [42] Baudelaire did not live to begin this project, but his instinct about it was surely a good one. It would have made an absorbing story, not only in casting an authoritative light on the central problem—the way in which he came to identify himself with Poe—but absorbing as well in its recital of the many difficulties, delays, and temporary defeats which plagued him throughout this phase of his career.

Bad luck was with him from the first. In 1852 Baudelaire was well along with what he planned as the first volume of his translations. He had offered some samples of his work to various magazines in Paris, and as a result three Poe stories and "La Philosophie de l'ameublement" were printed in this year. But if a solid impact were to be made, a whole book would be more effective than piecemeal publication. Late in 1852 he had reason to believe this problem solved. A publisher was interested and a contract was drawn up. The book was to go on sale in the winter of 1853. But a very grave obstacle suddenly presented itself: with all the arrangements made, he suddenly discovered that he had lost his precious manuscripts—lost them either to Jeanne Duval, whom he had temporarily deserted, or lost them to one of his creditors, who had appropriated them as security. In either case, he was forced to find enough money to pay their ransom. This was impossible; and so the entire book had to be done over. Feverishly, and under the most uncongenial circumstances, working wherever he could find a place to spread out his books and papers, Baudelaire attempted to meet his deadline. He did; but the results, in his opinion, were deplorable. As soon as he went over the first proofs he decided that his new translation amounted to no more than a very crude first draft. The printer was furious, the publisher took the view that he had become embroiled with a madman, and Baudelaire, who had been paid for his work in advance, was in effect obliged to refund the money in order to pay half the costs of this abortive enterprise.

"Really," he wrote to his mother, "I am going out of my mind. This book was to have been the beginning of a new life for me." [43]

He managed somehow to reinstate himself in the good graces of his disappointed publisher; and, better still, he recovered the cache of manuscripts that had been out of his possession during the crucial months of 1852. The prospects seemed more certain this time; a volume would appear after all. High time, too—for Borghers and Hughes were not delaying in presenting their versions of Poe to France, and in some quarters it was believed that the promised work of Baudelaire would be years in the making. But once more his expectations were defeated. The publishing project was suddenly and inexplicably dropped. So we find Baudelaire in 1854 attempting to place his translations in various newspapers and magazines. This was a tedious business, for not just *one* man had to be persuaded in any given case, but an entire editorial staff, each member of which had mastered to a high degree the art of deferring to the opinions of his confreres. After experiencing in full measure all the exasperating consequences of this systematic timidity, Baudelaire at last succeeded in reaching an agreement with the editors of *Le Pays*. A favorable word from the right quarter— in this case, Barbey d'Aurevilly—proved to be the necessary strategic stroke, and on 15 July 1854 *Le Pays* announced that eleven days later it would begin serial publication of "Histoires extraordinaires par Edgard Allan Poe, traduites par Ch. Baudelaire." [44]

Having borne up for so long in the face of repeated postponements of his hopes, the translator now experienced some dismay as the result of their too precipitate fulfillment. Without warning Baudelaire of a

change in plans, the editors of *Le Pays* began printing
the first installment twenty-four hours ahead of time.
He got wind of what was going on and hurried off to
the paper's composing room. Too late, however, to
undo all the damage: there was the author's name
again spelled *Edgard* Poe and there were some mistakes also in the Dedication to Mrs. Clemm. Baudelaire
was to remain from this time the scourge of printers
and proofreaders, haunting the premises where his
translations were being set up in type, and as often as
not revising his proof sheets into what amounted to
fresh copy.

Remorseless in his desire for perfection, he refused
to consider the *Pays* texts as final even after the entire
series had been printed. On 20 April 1855, with the
appearance of the final installment of "L'Aventure
sans pareille d'un certain Hans Pfaall," publication
was at an end. Baudelaire had been saving the clip-
pings of each translation. He now pasted these columns onto large sheets of paper and commenced the
next stage of his work. The printed texts were of value
to him only as a convenient means of redoing the entire job.[45]

Another laborious task, for he had on his hands by
this time enough material to make up not one but two
sizable volumes. And eventually these two volumes
were published: *Histoires extraordinaires* (1856) and
Nouvelles histoires extraordinaires (1857). Not, however, before a new setback was experienced. One of the
editors of *Le Pays* had organized a publishing firm and
with this man, who still retained his post on the paper,
Baudelaire came to an understanding about "the Poe."
But in June, 1855, *Le Pays* commissioned Baudelaire
to write a review of the Exposition des Beaux-Arts.

When, in the conservative opinion of the editors, he violated this trust by devoting one entire article to praise of Delacroix, his commission was terminated, and the editor who was to have been his publisher would have nothing more to do with him. The large bundle of manuscript translations began to make the rounds of other publishers and eventually came to rest at the offices of Michel Lévy in the fall of 1855. Lévy counted on bringing out the two volumes in November of the same year. But he soon realized that in Baudelaire he had met a man who would stop at nothing in his zeal for a perfect text; and so the usual difficulties about proofreading, plus Baudelaire's insistence on writing a long preface, delayed publication of the first volume until 12 March 1856. Even then the translator was not satisfied. Despite all his caution, the book contained a number of typographical errors. But the publisher had reason to be content: *Histoires extraordinaires* turned out to be an immediate success, and so was its sequel, which went on sale in the following year.

An important year this was in the history of French literature. In 1857 *Madame Bovary* was published, and for Baudelaire it was this year that saw the appearance of *Nouvelles histoires extraordinaires* and of his own poems, *Les Fleurs du mal*. Having first devoted a major part of his time and energy to the career of Edgar Poe, he was ready now to make his own personal claim to immortality. But an entry in his journal is revealing: in a plan for a twelve-hour working day ("TOUS LES JOURS"), we find that he has scheduled five hours a day for his work on Poe and three hours for his own poetry.[46] The entry is undated, but it seems to belong to a time relatively late in his career. With Poe's work successfully established in

France, Baudelaire might well have considered his mission completed. But in fact he neither abandoned his interest in Poe at this time nor let it diminish in any way. Two volumes had appeared; three more were to follow.

The first of these was his translation of *The Narrative of Arthur Gordon Pym*, which began to appear in *Le Moniteur universel* on 25 February 1857. Poe's long sea story involved a number of special difficulties. Since it formed one extended work, there could be no interruption in the sequence of its printing. Baudelaire therefore had to guarantee that he would be on time with his copy and have it in a really finished state before submitting it to the typesetters. Convinced by this time that no proofreaders could be trusted, he moved to the Hotel Voltaire on the Quai Voltaire. The offices and presses of *Le Moniteur* were a few doors down. Thus he would be able to work on his installments until the last possible moment, five o'clock, and then be on hand to supervise the actual printing of the text for the next day's edition. The very nature of the story caused additional problems for him. Although his knowledge of English was by now far from mediocre, Baudelaire saw that the nautical and geographical terms in *Pym* called for a specialized skill in English vocabulary, if, that is, the text were to be accurately translated. He could easily have faked the necessary terms without much risk of arousing his readers' suspicions, and without real damage to the quality of his translation. But for him—except in one striking instance—such an alternative was inconceivable. He therefore attempted to make himself expert on all the technical matters that are brought up or alluded to in *Arthur Gordon Pym*. While Baudelaire was working on this story, his friend Banville recalls, "he could be seen making use of atlases, maps, and mathematical instruments which he kept scrupulously clean. For guided always by his love of perfection (the one rule he did follow!) he was checking up on the nautical calculations of Gordon Pym so as to assure himself of their exactitude." [47] And when Asselineau, who also witnessed it, attempted a joke on the subject of this elaborate discipline, Baudelaire replied: *"Eh bien?* —and what about those readers who will follow the story in their atlas?" [48]

In order to make sure that such readers, following the adventures of Gordon Pym with an eye on their atlas, might find the narrative as authentic as possible, Baudelaire applied his principle of perfection in a very curious way. In Chapters XVI and XVII of the story, Poe's references to compass directions are especially numerous. Baudelaire discovered that three of these references were in error. Rather than let it appear that Poe had become confused, his translator quietly rectified the mistakes. And so three words in the English text, "west," "west," and "north," appear in French as "est," "sud," and "sud." It was Jacques Crépet who first noticed what Baudelaire had done. Here is his comment: "We must confess that this procedure, on the part of him who set no limits to the respect and love he gave his author, seemed to us when we came to notice it more moving than any protestation of the most ardent devotion!" [49]

Hardly less striking evidence of this devotion was his next volume, *Eureka*, on which he began work in 1859 but which was not fully ready until 1863. When promising his mother a copy of it he wrote: "I'll send it to you—simply as proof that this terrible book has been finished; for I doubt that you will be able to read two pages without falling asleep. I even doubt whether there are ten people in France capable of appreciating it." [50] Baudelaire was not counting on any sizable audience for the book—its sales would be small; but what he evidently regarded as his responsibility towards Poe required that this ambitious philosophical treatise be made available in French.

The inevitable delays and misunderstandings that had attended his previous efforts to make Poe known in France arose in new shape this time too. Baudelaire contracted with the editor of a new journal, the *Revue internationale*, published in Geneva, for the appearance of *Eureka* in monthly installments. Starting in October, 1859, sections of the translation were printed for four consecutive months. As usual, typographical errors abounded, for this time Baudelaire could not be on hand to supervise the pressmen in Geneva; and the editor, belatedly aware that he had commissioned a work of only very slight general interest, refused to pay Baudelaire the lump sum that had been contracted for. To crown his disappointment with the project, Baudelaire discovered that the editorial policy of the *Revue internationale* was precisely opposite to the sort that he (or Poe) would have desired. Mere literature was held in much less esteem by these "*canailles de Genève*" than the ideals of Utility, Progress, and Science.[51] So with something over half the translation already published in this paper, Baudelaire brought it to a stop.

His own publisher in Paris, the same Michel Lévy who had realized a windfall in the earlier Poe volumes, was not eager to print a new book so radically different from them. Nor was Baudelaire either. He had developed some new plans—a translation of Poe's poems, and, especially, a de luxe edition of all the prose fiction he had so far translated. But Lévy was not interested; he wanted more new stories translated, for such material would sell. Baudelaire, on his side, could not look for a new publisher since Lévy held absolute rights to all the work Baudelaire had done. Thus both men sought to outwait each other. Lévy's financial position was the stronger, however, and Baudelaire was at length forced to capitulate. For a flat sum of 2,000 francs (or a possible four-year income from one Poe volume) he surrendered all claim to any profits that his subsequent translations might make. This was in 1863. *Eureka* appeared the following year.

The final volume, *Histoires grotesques et sérieuses,* was published in 1865. If Lévy had agreed to printing a new edition of Poe's work, Baudelaire would have regrouped the stories so that these remaining items would find their logical places within the whole. But since Lévy said No to this, the volume simply had to be a repository for the rather varied material that Baudelaire had on hand. Some of this material, as late as 1865, was appearing in French periodicals, for only by such publication could the translator get any new returns on the work he had done. And yet, in spite of the fact that he could expect no income from the sale of the book, Baudelaire was never more painstaking about the accuracy of page proofs than he was in this case. There were formidable obstacles in his way. He was in Belgium, ill and nearly desperate; Lévy was uncoöperative. But the translator's frenzied urgency on the subject prevailed, and Baudelaire was able to give to this final volume all the scrupulous and disinterested care that he had given to the first.

If in fact it was Baudelaire's intention originally to translate everything Poe had written, he must soon have realized that the project was beyond his powers. He had discovered Poe too late, at the age of twenty-six, and for several years thereafter his imperfect command of English was less an asset than an impediment. But above all, the severe standard of excellence which he imposed on himself insured that this work would never be completed in its totality. A more modest ambition had to suffice.

Although a translation of "The Raven" was among his earliest efforts, and although he did translate those poems that are integral to certain of the tales, Baudelaire on the whole avoided the poetry of Poe. This had not always been his intention. For a while, at least, he had plans, and rather precise ones, to bring out a selection of Poe's poems in French. By 1857, however, these plans were unsettled: "a translation of poems so carefully composed and so concentrated is something we can hope for but never realize." [52] In his essays on Poe and in his correspondence Baudelaire attempted to make amends for his deficiencies in this department; and similarly he advertised Poe's claims for recognition as an important critic.[53] But of all Poe's critical writings, only "The Philosophy of Composition" was translated by Baudelaire. He certainly was acquainted with the more important essay, "The Poetic Principle," and yet this he did not translate, apparently preferring such curiosities as "Maelzel's Chess Player" and "The Philosophy of Furniture." There is probably only one convincing explanation for so odd a preference: Baudelaire wanted to give to France a conception of Poe's work that would be fully in keeping with its sometimes surprising variety. The great drudgery necessitated by his work on *Arthur Gordon Pym* and *Eureka* testifies to his desire to make known what he considered the great range of Poe's genius.

In any event, it is quite clear that he was not motivated merely by considerations of financial success. After the publication of *Nouvelles histoires extraordinaires* it became evident that there existed in France a wide and ready market for this kind of book. Four editions of it were printed in Baudelaire's lifetime, and its predecessor, the *Histoires extraordinaires*, was even more successful. Yet Baudelaire turned his attention to a different kind of thing, the long romance of the sea, *Arthur Gordon Pym*, and having completed his version of it and having found that it had less popular appeal, he did not revert to the many short stories of Poe that still remained untranslated. Instead he undertook the fantastic labor of translating *Eureka*. This would round out his work, establish Poe in France as a philosopher, finally, and not alone as the author of poems and stories and literary criticism. After sixteen years and the translation of nearly 1,500 pages, Baudelaire's work was finished, his legacy at last complete, and the final chapter written in this extraordinary story of the devotion of one great writer to another.

4

THE POET AS TRANSLATOR

IN READING the first versions of Poe's tales that became available in France, Baudelaire felt a singular
excitement and an incredible sympathy, and he devoted much of his life to arousing these responses in
others. We have seen how, as translator, he attempted
to do justice to the full range of Poe's work. But inevitably, as the result of his first and deepest attraction,
it was Poe's work in fiction that absorbed most of his
energies. The Edgar Poe whom Baudelaire resolved
to make a great man in France was above all the Poe
of the stories.

When we turn the pages of these translations now,
what should be our attitude? Is this long labor of love
to be regarded as no more than a literary curiosity on
which a French poet was foolish enough to waste a
great many years of his maturity? Or, since that theory seems too desperate, should our hypothesis be that
Baudelaire, in French, succeeded, where Poe, in English, failed? We would have to say, then, that the
stories as Baudelaire tells them *are* literature, whereas
Poe's only aspire to be. If so, it is not really translations we are looking at but re-creations, not transcripts
but originals; for otherwise all of Poe's distressing lia-
bilities would be as much present in the French text

as in the English and function there in the same unfortunate way. Not, therefore, how good the translations are in and of themselves, but how faithful they are to what they pretend to represent: this is a basic issue with which we should be concerned. But not the only one. For in reading these translations we are reading Poe's work as it was seen and understood by Baudelaire. That slight contempt that many of us feel —the result, perhaps, of too early a familiarity with Poe's stories—may it not be displaced somewhat, or even altogether, if we approach the stories now through the medium of a foreign language? There is some paradox in suggesting that a writer may be better understood if we use a less rather than a more familiar route to approach him. But along this less familiar route we shall have Baudelaire as guide, and the foreign language is the French of a great poet. These facts may make some difference.

In the standard "Virginia" edition of Poe's writings, there are five volumes of *Tales*, containing a total of seventy-one titles. Of these, forty-five were translated by Baudelaire. If the one list is compared to the other, it will be noticed that Baudelaire's choices were not made at random. Or, if we examine the shorter catalog of the stories he did *not* translate, we shall find that it is made up almost without exception of stories that have not worn well. For it is true, of course, that Poe's was an uneven talent, or a talent too often forced by economic pressures into a mode of employment quite foreign to its nature. As the author of "The Tell-Tale Heart" and "The Purloined Letter," Poe is universally famous. His reputation does not rest on, or even involve, such stories as "The Business Man" or "Lionizing," and yet he wrote a great many boring trifles of this kind. There are in all about twenty stories of Poe that are widely and deservedly known, and with the possible exception of "The Assignation"—a story which, in my opinion, is less deservedly than widely known—Baudelaire translated all of them. That fact is significant. And on the other side of the ledger we find that he had the perception to choose *Arthur Gordon Pym* for translation rather than the hardly less long but much less interesting "Journal of Julius Rodman." Among the inferior works of Poe, Baudelaire made generally intelligent selections. Poe's satirical and semi-allegorical vein is represented by such stories as "Lionnerie," "Le Roi peste," and "Quatre Bêtes en une." Baudelaire passed by "The Landscape Garden," but he translated two similar sketches, "The Domain of Arnheim" and "Landor's Cottage." He avoided "Mystification," but not "The Balloon Hoax," which is an instance of it. In short, we find represented in the translations of Baudelaire very nearly all (I would say all) of Poe's greatest and most memorable stories, and enough samples of his less successful ones to illustrate the variety of the work he attempted.

In spite of the often extravagant praise which he lavished on Poe, Baudelaire was too discerning a critic to let his personal enthusiasm destroy his sense of proportion; and although it was not part of his strategy to call public attention to the limitations and weaknesses of Poe's work, he was certainly aware that not all of it belonged to one high level of achievement. Thus when he had completed his first large group of translations he had about thirty-five stories ready for publication. He did not issue them pell-mell, as if they were all of equal importance, but instead carefully divided this material into two distinct categories which he described to Sainte-Beuve: "The first volume is set up to entice the public: Hoaxes, speculations, tricks of all sorts. 'Ligeia' is the only piece of importance with any tie to the spirit of the second volume. . . . The second volume treats the fantastic at a higher level: Hallucinations, mental illnesses, the sheer grotesque, the supernatural, etc." [1] And in fact these rather general distinctions between the contents of the *Histoires extraordinaires* and the *Nouvelles histoires extraordinaires* prove to be quite meaningful. It happens that Poe thought of "Ligeia" as his best story [2]—Baudelaire was not aware that this was the author's opinion—and it is somewhat out of place in *Histoires extraordinaires*. But there was good reason, as we shall see, for Baudelaire's placing it where he did. He wrote to an interested publisher: "Here is the table of contents. Just read it through and you will see the scheme behind it." [3] His first two volumes are the result of a thoughtfully ordered plan: taken together they supplement each other; considered separately, each has its own architectural logic.

The *Histoires extraordinaires* begins with three famous tales of ratiocination: "Double assassinat dans la rue Morgue," "La Lettre volée," and "Le Scarabée d'or." They are arranged in that order so that the two stories which illustrate what Baudelaire called "the divinatory powers of Auguste Dupin" will be read as a pair. The next large group comprises seven tales, and these may be described, more or less appropriately, as "hoaxes, speculations, tricks of all sorts." But there are important differences among them, and these differences become obvious if the stories are read in the sequence Baudelaire gave them. Of least interest are the

first two in the group. "Le Canard au ballon," and the
other story of a balloon hoax, "Aventure sans pareille
d'un certain Hans Pfaall." The latter is far too long
and detailed to be successful, but it has some of the
features of the classic "imaginary voyage" and so offers a lead into the next pair of stories, "Manuscrit
trouvé dans une bouteille" and "Une Descente dans le
Maelstrom." In both of these, Poe is engaged in his
characteristic work of exploring the frontier between
reality and fantasy; but his technique in these two
cases is to give particular emphasis to the *realistic* details of the experiences he imagines. They too are
"hoaxes" accordingly, but much less so than the two
stories that precede them. In the three that follow the
same element is present, but in a different way. All
three deal with experiments in hypnotism : "La Vérité
sur le cas de M. Valdemar," "Révélation magnétique,"
and "Souvenirs de M. Auguste Bedloe." By 1855
Baudelaire knew where he stood on the subject of mesmerism, and so he arranged these stories as the final
ones in the "hoax" category. "Valdemar" and "Mesmeric Revelation" had found some readers who were
willing to accept them as authentic reports, but apparently no one was credulous enough to put any faith
in the Bedloe story ("A Tale of the Ragged Mountains"). For the subject here is metempsychosis, and
despite the tone of *vraisemblance* which it shares with
the six other stories of this group, the narrative is well
beyond the border of belief. Metempsychosis again is
the subject of the last three *histoires extraordinaires:*
"Morella," "Ligeia," and "Metzengerstein." The first
and third are among Poe's earliest work and lack the
control that makes "Ligeia" a more successful variation on their common theme. But in both "Morella"

and "Ligeia" the phenomenon of metempsychosis is described as involving two women, and so Baudelaire probably decided to keep these two stories together and let the more wildly extravagant "Metzengerstein" point the way to the second volume. He thus arranged the contents of *Histoires extraordinaires* so that there would be a definite progression from the analytic and rationalistic exercises of the detective stories, through tales that become increasingly less plausible and realistic in spite of their studiously veracious tone, into a final trio which establishes the distinctive imaginative world of Poe. This was the volume that Baudelaire hoped would catch the public attention. It did just that. But its success was in large part the result of his astute selection and arrangement of the stories the book contains. Baudelaire understood very well the nature of the material he had translated.

A close study of the sequence in which the contents of *Nouvelles histoires extraordinaires* are presented would reveal that this volume also was organized with similar acumen. But since there are twenty-three stories in this collection, it will be more convenient to demonstrate the point by a few representative examples.

Almost all of Poe's best work is to be found here: "Le Chat noir," "William Wilson," "L'Homme des foules," "Le Coeur révélateur," "Bérénice," "La Chute de la maison Usher," and so on. But present also are several of his weakest stories: "Le Roi peste," "Le Diable dans le beffroi," "Lionnerie," "Quatre bêtes en une," and "Petite discussion avec une momie." These are placed in the middle of the volume, as if Baudelaire had been guided by the traditional rhetorical principal that the places of importance are the beginning and the end. And indeed the two final stories, "L'Ile de la fée" and "Le Portrait ovale" are, as I hope to show later in Chapter Eight, crucial to an understanding of Poe's imagination. But why did Baudelaire set his version of "The Man of the Crowd" between "William Wilson" and "The Tell-Tale Heart"? In a broad sense he answered this question when he described the make-up of the book to Sainte-Beuve: these are stories of "hallucinations, mental illnesses." However, this general subject matter is found in many of Poe's stories; why the particular grouping we find here? Because the central motif in all three is that of the *Doppelgänger*. The theme of premature burial is present in "Bérénice," "Usher," and "Le Puits et le pendule," and hence these stories also appear as a sequence. After "Le Masque de la mort rouge," one of the few serious moral tales that Poe wrote, Baudelaire placed "Le Roi peste," which is another moral and allegorical story, having much the same point as the other, but treated in what Poe misconceived as a humorous vein. The series continues with four more rather heavy-handed specimens of this type, in the course of which a satirical intention becomes increasingly visible. The interview format of the last of these, "Petite discussion avec une momie," provides a transition to "Puissance de la parole" and two more imaginary conversations. The serious tone of the first stories is thus recaptured and is sustained to the end of the book.

The last of Baudelaire's anthologies was *Histoires grotesques et sérieuses*, in which he assembled the short translations he had found time to do before and after his work on *Eureka*, and which served also as a final repository for something translated many years before, "La Philosophie de l'ameublement." The book is made

up, inevitably, of residual material, but Baudelaire did
what he could to give it some kind of structure. Re-
calling the organization of *Histoires extraordinaires*,
he placed at the beginning two related examples of
Poe's interest in ratiocination: "Le Mystère de Marie
Roget" and "Le Joueur d'échecs de Maelzel;" and at
the end he grouped "Le Domaine d'Arnheim," "Le
Cottage Landor," and "La Philosophie de l'ameublement." This was a set of sketches for which his own
title was "Imaginary Dwellings." [4] He did not, however, make use of this title in the book. Typically, for
he seems to have been very reluctant to avail himself
of even a conscionable editorial freedom. In only one
case did he add something important to the text as Poe
had written it: the various chapters of *Arthur Gordon
Pym* have brief titles in the French translation. This
was no doubt the result of its original publication as a
serial in the columns of *Le Moniteur*. For the most
part, Baudelaire consistently avoided the temptation—
and surely for a creative genius it must have been a
strong one—to revise or enlarge on the Poe texts as
he had received them.

Over-scrupulous? But what other hypothesis can
account for the severe self-restraint with which Baudelaire treated Poe's work? The last few pages may
have seemed distractingly encumbered with citations
of the French titles Baudelaire gave the stories. Yet
the nature of these titles offers an important lesson
about his attitude towards Poe. "The Tell-Tale Heart"
is "Le Coeur révélateur," "The Cask of Amontillado"
is "La Barrique d'Amontillado," and "The System of
Dr. Tarr and Prof. Fether" is just as awkwardly entitled in French: "Le Système du Docteur Goudron et
du Professeur Plume." Modern translators sometimes

give themselves considerably more imaginative lati-
tude. Gide's *La Porte étroite* becomes *Strait is the
Gate;* we know Proust's *Sodome et Gomorrhe* in English as *Cities of the Plain;* and Robert Penn Warren's
novel *All the King's Men* is presented to French
readers as *Les Fous du roi.* The effort, it seems, is to
find something flashy, a title that will be just a little
more resonant and suggestive than the title the author
devised. This was not Baudelaire's procedure, although
one may well believe that it was not because he was
unable to improve on at least a few of the English titles
Poe gave the stories. Nor was it because this practice
of renaming a work in translation is a peculiarly modern phenomenon. Baudelaire's contemporaries were
acquainted with it. The Forgues version of "Murders
in the Rue Morgue" was elaborately renamed, and to
his version of "The Tell-Tale Heart" Hughes gave the
more explicitly ominous title "Le Coeur mort qui
bat." [5] Baudelaire's choices, however, are the result of
a very cautious literalness. In only two instances did
he really vary from this standard: "The Gold Bug" he
entitled "Le Scarabée d'or," and "The Imp of the Perverse" appears in French as "Le Démon de la perversité."

Thus in the very nature of the French titles which
Baudelaire provided for the stories of Poe there is an
implicit promise that these translations will be faithful
duplicates of their English originals. An exhaustive
analysis of how well this promise is kept would neces-
sitate a formidable study all to itself, one so thick with
tabulations and quotations, and with so much wearisome duplication of evidence, as to be all but unread-
able. A definitive study of this sort would be worth
the trouble, but this is not the place to attempt it. For

it is quite possible to reach tenable conclusions about Baudelaire's technique as a translator if the inquiry, although ranging over a variety of texts, is limited to illustrating representative instances of his work.

In comparing what Poe wrote to the version Baudelaire made of it, one is struck first of all and most of the time by the astonishing fidelity of the French translation. Very often Baudelaire's text conforms to Poe's word for word and phrase for phrase:

My name is Arthur Gordon Pym. My father was a re-
Mon nom est Arthur Gordon Pym. Mon père était un re-

spectable trader   in   sea-stores   at
spectable commerçant dans les fournitures de la marine à

Nantucket, where I was born. My maternal grandfather was
Nantucket, où je suis né.   Mon aieul maternel

an attorney in good practice.
était attorney, avec une belle clientèle.[6]

Baudelaire might have begun with the more usual French formula: "Je m'appelle Arthur Gordon Pym." Or, with greater dramatic force: "Mon nom? Arthur Gordon Pym." Instead, he gives a meticulous transcription of Poe's purposely simple and straightforward sentences. He thus captures not only the sense of these lines but their tone as well. He could do this with equal success when faced with a rather more difficult problem in tone. "Some Words with a Mummy" concludes in this fashion: "As soon, therefore, as I shave and swallow a cup of coffee, I shall just step over to Ponnonner's and get embalmed for a couple of hundred years." Baudelaire brought "Petite discussion avec une momie" to an end in the very same style: "C'est pourquoi, une fois rasé et mon café avalé, je vais tomber chez Ponnonner, et je me fais embaumer pour une couple de siècles." [7]

However, a more typical example of Poe's style may be found in "The Masque of the Red Death," in a passage which describes the ominous clock that reverberates through the apartments of Prince Prospero:

Its pendulum swung to and fro with a dull, heavy monotonous clang; and when the minute hand had made the circuit of the face, and the hour was to be stricken, there came from the brazen lungs of the clock a sound which was clear and loud and deep and excessively musical, but of so peculiar a note and emphasis that, at each lapse of an hour, the musicians of the orchestra were constrained to pause, momentarily, in their performance, to hearken to the sound.

Compare Baudelaire:

Son pendule se balançait avec un tic-tac sourd, lourd, monotone; et quand l'aiguille des minutes avait fait le circuit du cadran et que l'heure allait sonner, il s'élevait des poumons d'airain de la machine un son clair, éclatant, profond et excessivement musical, mais d'une note si particulière et d'une énergie telle, que d'heure en heure, les musiciens de l'orchestre étaient contraints d'interrompre un instant leurs accords pour écouter la musique de l'heure.[8]

A study of these two texts is particularly rewarding. In keeping with the heavy atmosphere of drugged slumber that pervades the story, Poe's sentence takes the form of a long and drowsy undulation. To carry off this general effect in French, as Baudelaire does, is no small triumph. The syntactical problem would have been greatly simplified for him if he had taken the much more convenient course of breaking up the passage into several units, each one of which could then be handled in a single sentence. But he does not do this, nor is there any attempt to sidestep the very

words and phrases Poe used. The "brazen lungs" of
the clock are presented as exactly that in French. Poe's
phrase "were constrained to pause" is retained in the
passive voice, and there are other scrupulously faithful resemblances as well.

But in a few details the passage is somewhat different from the English version. *"Tic-tac"* is not "clang,"
nor does Baudelaire's concluding phrase coincide precisely with Poe's "hearken to the sound." These are
highly illuminating differences. They enable us to recognize that although Poe's meandering sentence succeeds very well in general effect, some of its details
are strangely haphazard. If the clock were actually
clanging, for example, the music of the orchestra
would be constantly interrupted, and not only when
the hourly chimes began. A clock with lungs of brass
—this is an original image, but Poe mistakenly uses
the adjective *brazen*. The more immediate associations
of this word are altogether out of place at this juncture. The same indifference, or perhaps unconscious-
ness, with regard to language is evident also in his
choice of *stricken* as a past participial form. *Struck*
would be much the better word here, for the other involves the inappropriate connotations of *smitten*,
wounded. On the other hand, his sentence is especially
fine in its concluding phrase: "the musicians of the
orchestra were constrained to pause, momentarily, in
their performance, to hearken to the sound." As we
read, impeded by the commas, we experience, through
the halting rhythm of the prose, the feelings of hesita-
tion and doubtful expectancy that assailed the musicians when the hourly striking of the clock reached
their ears.

We notice that in his translation of the passage Bau-

delaire diminishes *clang* to *tic-tac*, and of course the
associations of the English word *brazen* are happily
absent from his phrase *poumons d'airain*. His final
lines, however, are not quite so effective as Poe's. Over-
looking the significance of Poe's faltering rhythm, he
ends his translation in one smoothly fluent line. But
if unaware of the precise *means* by which Poe gained
his effect, Baudelaire was fully responsive to the effect
those means produced. He makes an effort to capture
it by stating what is left implied in the rhythm of the
English prose: the musicians are forced to interrupt
their own music for the threatening and more imperi-
ous music of the clock. To sum up, then, the French
version of Baudelaire, while avoiding two pitfalls in
Poe's diction, manages to echo remarkably the spirit
and structure of the English passage. The innovation
at the end is a brilliant attempt to seize what Baudelaire recognized as latent and elusive in Poe's text.
A translation of this excellence is hardly less than a
tour de force.

It represents an excellence that he had to work for
and that he could not invariably sustain. Of his early
work, "Révélation magnétique," which we have already considered, is characteristic. And though after
completing it Baudelaire was silent for four years,
preparing for his career as Poe's translator, the first
harvest of this industry was not without a good many
tares. One passage in "The Balloon Hoax" proved especially troublesome: "We passed over innumerable
vessels of all kinds, a few of which were endeavoring
to beat up, but most of them lying to." Not many English readers are competent to arrive at more than a
very general impression of what is meant here, and
Baudelaire, who did not master nautical terminology

until he began work on *Arthur Gordon Pym*, found himself in even worse plight. In his original effort, as published in *Le Pays*, he translated this sentence in the form : "Nous passâmes au dessus d'innombrables navires de toute espèce, dont quelques-uns essayèrent de lutter avec nous, mais dont la plupart se resignèrent à leur infériorité." [9] Another equally grievous blunder occurred in the *Pays* printing of "La Chute de la maison Usher." In order to calm the nervous excitement of Roderick during the fatal night of storm at the Usher mansion, the visitor to the house reads aloud from a medieval romance entitled "The Mad Tryst." Baudelaire's name for this work : "Le Fou triste." But Yves Le Dantec, who calls attention to these two cases in his essay on the Baudelaire translations, observes that Baudelaire's progress in English was so rapid that when the stories appeared in book form almost all the errors that had originally marred them had been noticed and corrected.[10] *Les Aventures d'Arthur Gordon Pym* was very nearly perfect in its first appearance in *Le Moniteur*.

But some mistakes inevitably remained. The Baudelaire translations as we have them now are astonishing in many ways, but they are not altogether flawless. A few of the flaws are very simple ones. For example, in "Berenice," the phrase "He pointed to my garments" is translated "Il regarda mes vêtements." And in the same story "I spoke not . . ." appears as "Sans dire un mot, il me prit . . ." A misreading of a more complicated sort occurs in the French text of "Ligeia." Poe wrote : "And, indeed, if ever that spirit which is entitled *Romance*—if ever she, the wan and misty-winged *Ashtophet* of idolatrous Egypt, presided, as they tell, over marriages ill-omened, then most

surely she presided over mine." And Baudelaire translated: "Et, en vérité, si jamais l'esprit de roman—si
jamais la pâle *Ashtophet* de l'idolâtre Egypte, aux ailes
ténébreuses, ont présidé, comme on dit, aux mariages
de sinistre augure,—très-sûrement ils ont présidé au
mien." [11] His great skill is in evidence in these lines,
but the full sense of Romance is not rendered by the
word Baudelaire employs, and the shift to the plural
in the second half of the passage shows that he did not
read the sentence in the way Poe intended. Again, in
"La Chute de la maison Usher," there is a sentence in
French which is not in accord with what Poe wrote.
"Ce fut particulièrement une nuit . . . fort tard, avant
de me mettre au lit" does not translate "It was, especially, upon retiring to bed late in the night." [12] The
error is the more surprising in that Baudelaire's subsequent text indicates that the narrator *has* retired.

These mistakes were made unconsciously, to be
sure, and it is regrettable that for all his perfectionist
zeal Baudelaire was unable to avoid them. But they
and the others like them have neither the frequency
nor the magnitude to constitute a really damaging im-
perfection. No French reader, for example, will have
misunderstood Poe if deficiencies of this sort are the
only inaccuracies that are there to mislead him. It is
possible, however, that there may exist other reasons
for believing that the Poe of Baudelaire is not the
"real" Poe. In translating the stories, Baudelaire
could have improved or injured certain of their important details in such a way as to alter the focus in
which Poe, the authentic Poe, that is, should be seen.

As a matter of fact, we find that he does both these
things. An earlier quotation from "The Masque of the
Red Death" illustrated how careless Poe could be in

his selection of words—*clang* and *brazen* militate against rather than reinforce the meaning and tone of the passage in which they occur. The French translation does not reflect these two shortcomings. Similarly, in "The Tell-Tale Heart," when Poe is describing the great caution of the murderer as he opens the door of the room in which his victim lies sleeping, the diction gets out of control. Poe writes: "and then I thrust in my head . . . how cunningly I thrust it in!" Baudelaire makes use of a much more likely verb, *passer*: "puis je passais la tête . . . avec quelle adresse je passais ma tête." [13] In "The Man of the Crowd," Poe uses the French word *roquelaire* (*sic*) to describe the specific kind of overcoat the man is wearing, and thus he succeeds only in demonstrating the extent of his knowledge of French. The word *roquelaure* is rare and curious, but it has no function in the story. Baudelaire replaces it with the suitably commonplace *manteau*. On the other hand, Poe's euphemism "women of the town" is made direct and specific in the French version: "des prostituées." Poe's occasionally erratic grammar is also improved. Of three lines of conduct he says: "I am at a loss to know how or why it was that we pursued neither the one nor the other" ("Some Words with a Mummy"). Baudelaire makes the necessary correction: ". . . il se fit que nous n'en suivîmes aucune." [14] Badly written sentences are clarified. In "The Masque of the Red Death," the followers of Prince Prospero seal up the gates of the castle in which they have taken refuge: "They resolved to leave means neither of ingress or egress to the sudden impulses of despair or of frenzy from within." The French translation expands this in the interests of greater force and clarity: "Ils résolurent de se barricader contre les impulsions soudaines du désespoir extérieur et de fermer toute issue aux frénésies du dedans." [15] This does more than straighten out Poe's rather inept English. The careful balancing of "du désespoir extérieur" and "frénésies du dedans" lures attention to the ironical drift of the story. For in sealing up their refuge as an oasis of salvation from the plague, the courtiers are in actuality only sealing in their own doom. Baudelaire's translation conveys just what Poe meant to say but does so with considerably more art.

There are other deviations in the French text which function in the same way. During one phase of his torture, the victim of the pit and the pendulum recalls, he became aware of "wells, of which my imagination now pictured a great many in various positions about the dungeon." Baudelaire reproduces this almost exactly, but he adds a detail that Poe would have appreciated: "puits, que mon imagination multipliait maintenant dans les ténèbres de mon cachot." [16] With the phrase "dans les ténèbres" allusion is made to the fantasy-creating effects of darkness. In the same story another of Poe's sentences is improved in its translation. "The mode and the hour were all that occupied or distracted me" is transformed into "le mode et l'heure étaient tout ce qui m'occupait et me tourmentait." [17] Poe's second verb in English would be hard to justify, and so Baudelaire substitutes a better one and eliminates the useless conjunction *or* in favor of *and*. In his description of Ligeia Poe writes:

I looked at the graceful outlines of the nose—and nowhere but in the graceful medallions of the Hebrews had I beheld similar perfection. There were the same luxurious smoothness of surface, the same scarcely perceptible tendency to the aquiline, the same harmoniously curved nostrils speaking the free spirit.

The French translation is equivalent to this, except that Baudelaire introduces a new phrase before the second sentence. He adds "c'était ce même jet"—it was of the same casting. That is, he makes use of a metaphor to bring into greater relief the earlier allusion to medallions.[18] The trance of Berenice is described by Poe as one "very nearly resembling positive dissolution." But the substantive here is too strong for the context. Baudelaire accordingly reduces this extravagant term to one of greater accuracy: ". . . ressemblant parfaitement à la mort." [19] Changes of this sort, in which the expressions of Poe are either strengthened or weakened, bring about the same result: the over-all tone of the story is made more consistent.

Perhaps one of the best examples of Baudelaire's technical facility occurs in his version of "Morella." There is at least one paragraph in this story which it would seem very difficult to improve on:

But one autumnal evening, when the winds lay still in heaven, Morella called me to her bed-side. There was a dim mist over all the earth, and a warm glow upon the waters, and, amid the rich October leaves of the forest, a rainbow from the firmament had surely fallen.

But Baudelaire is equal to it:

Mais un soir d'automne, comme l'air dormait immobile dans le ciel, Morella m'appela à son chevet. Il y avait un voile de brume sur toute la terre, et un chaud embrasement sur les eaux, et, à voir les splendeurs d'Octobre dans le feuillage de la forêt, on eût dit qu'un bel arc-en-ceil s'était laissé choir du firmament.[20]

In his own lines Poe gives us much, but not quite all
that we find in this translation. The margin of difference is a measure of the greater mastery of Baudelaire,
who saw how Poe's description, finely wrought as it is
in English, could be raised in French to an even higher
level of evocation.

We notice, first, that it is not the winds alone that
are lying still. In the French version, with the whole
sky, the total atmosphere, asleep, a feeling of stillness
is made absolute. Over the earth there hangs not the
"dim mist" of Poe, but "un voile de brume"; and with
the word *voile* we are reminded that this apparently
timeless moment will be transient. That veil will some
time be removed, as will the "warm glow" that rests
upon the waters. Baudelaire, however, suffuses this
glow with an intense and vivid radiance. By "un chaud
embrasement" we are made to see the color of a glowing coal. In this way the contrast between the warmth
of the glow and the coldness of the water beneath it
joins and reinforces the previous image of transience
suggested by the "voile . . . sur toute la terre." It
brings in another suggestion, too: a contrast between
the warmth of life and the chill of death. There are
only autumn leaves in Poe's description, but in that
of Baudelaire the entire forest seems alive with "les
splendeurs d'Octobre," a phrase that evokes, as Poe
nowhere does, the poignancy of the scene and of this
moment in the story. For all the beauty of the setting
—placid, vivid, and alive—will soon be at an end.
Baudelaire is using this image, adapting it and unify-
ing it, so that it will suggest the death of Morella. Accordingly, he revises the final detail, "a rainbow . . .
had surely fallen." Instead of the obvious word *tomber*
he uses *choir*, an archaic term, more suggestive, more

"poetic." The rainbow has collapsed, and its colors now are broken and fragmentary and will soon be extinguished. Baudelaire does one other thing. He avoids Poe's direct statement at the end and writes instead: "et, à voir ces splendeurs d'Octobre . . . on eût dit . . ." If, that is, the scene *could* be visualized. But the implication is that this is impossible, that language cannot convey its rare quality, and that the experience of having seen it must remain unique. The English passage is, therefore, descriptive merely. The prose of Poe, while very accomplished in this instance, remains prose. Baudelaire transmutes it with the resources of a great poet. He makes it alive with metaphor: its details become images, the images are made coherent, and they finally emerge with symbolic force. "Every landscape is a state of mind"—Poe would have approved of Amiel's famous saying,[21] and sometimes his own descriptions provide good illustrations of it. But not here. His paragraph is admirable, but it does not remind us, as Baudelaire succeeds in doing, of Keats's "Ode to Autumn."

One of Baudelaire's modern editors, Yves Le Dantec, after a careful study of the poet's methods as translator, sums up his procedure as follows: first, a literal translation, sometimes quite feeble; then, careful and sensitive retouchings; and, finally, "a masterly transposition onto his own keyboard." [22] The last stage is clearly in evidence in the "Morella" passage, but it would be wrong to assume that this kind of achievement is always to be found in his work. There are details in Poe's writing that are weakened rather than improved in the French translation. If in the French "Morella" a prose picture is made over into a poetic image, in translating "The Masque of the Red Death"

an almost antithetical method was employed. At one
point in the story Poe wrote: "To and fro in the seven
chambers there stalked, in fact, a multitude of
dreams." The insistence on the metaphor is important
here, for the meaning of the story is not grasped unless the reader is given to understand that the drama
is not being played out on any realistic stage. Baudelaire missed this detail in writing: "Bref, c'était
comme une multitude de rêves qui se pavanaient çà et
la dans les sept salons." [23] The verb he uses is an excellent choice, but by reducing Poe's metaphor to a
simile Baudelaire weakens the force of the sentence
and tampers with its significance. It is questionable
also whether he has done justice to a line in "The Pit
and the Pendulum," viz., "After this I call to mind
flatness and dampness." Baudelaire translates *flatness*
by *fadeur*. [24] This suggests insipidity, a flatness of
taste; whereas a more primitive sense, that of touch,
is the one relevant here as Poe asks us to relive the
experience of the prisoner who found himself trapped
in an Inquisition dungeon. In another story, "Berenice," there is an important detail which Baudelaire
misconstrued. Egaeus, the hero of the story, in describing the symptoms of his monomania, tells how he
would "muse for long unwearied hours with [his] attention riveted to some frivolous device on the margin,
or in the typography of a book." Interpreting the
word *device* to mean *motto*, Baudelaire translated the
phrase as "quelque citation puérile sur la marge ou
dans le texte d'un livre." [25] But the mental aberration
of Egaeus is not clarified if *this* is presented as an illustration of it. For the quotation of some motto might
well warrant his long attention; a merely ornamental
curlicue would not. By shifting the meaning in this

way, Baudelaire makes the psychology of Egaeus the less rather than the more extraordinary.

These various similarities and differences between English text and French translation may be brought into sharper focus if we alter the approach somewhat and concentrate simply on a few details from the first page or so of "The Fall of the House of Usher." [26]

In French, the "vacant eye-like windows" of the house are rendered as "les fenêtres semblables à des yeux distraits." This communicates Poe's meaning with greater sureness than he himself did, for Poe provides two adjectives, *vacant* and *eye-like*, the first of which seems more appropriate to eyes than to windows, the substantive it was intended to modify. The English phrasing is awkward; Baudelaire's is not, and yet the full sense is preserved. On the grounds before the house the visitor notices "a few rank sedges" and "a black tarn that lay in unruffled lustre." Here, however, Baudelaire is not so successful. The word *rank* connotes *overripe*, verging on decay, and thus this vegetation is of a piece with the house and the master of it. Baudelaire misses this implication in translating the phrase as "quelques bouquets de joncs vigoureux." His final adjective suggests health, inappropriately; a word like *luxuriants* would have been preferable. So also, in his description of the tarn, Poe is calling up associations of unhealthy radiance, the phosphorescence of decay. Hence *lurid*. Baudelaire's word for this is *lugubre*, which falls short of the effect desired. A little later on, the narrator speaks of the letter he received from Roderick Usher, "a letter . . . which in its wildly importunate nature had admitted of no other than a personal reply." The wording is ambiguous, for one may easily understand it to mean that the narrator himself prepared an answer to the letter; and yet the remainder of the paragraph implies that his reply took the form of a personal visit to the Usher mansion. Baudelaire is aware of the difficulty and straightens it out: "une lettre . . . dont la tournure follement pressante n'admettait d'autre réponse que ma présence même." These four illustrations, taken from the first two pages of one story, point to the same conclusion as that reached by an examination of more widely scattered instances of Baudelaire's technique. There is really no ponderable difference between the English version and the French translation, for on the average the improvements that may be discerned in the latter are compensated for by its deficiencies.

Only in two stories—and those, significantly, in which the titles were noticeably altered—are the effects achieved by Baudelaire in a real sense superior to those we find in Poe. In raising the word *imp* to the power of *demon* in "Le Démon de la perversité," Baudelaire hints that his telling of the story will be weighted with an expressly theological sense of guilt and retribution. Poe's notion of "perverseness" was welcomed by Baudelaire, but he seems to have read into it more meaning than Poe intended it to have. For its originator, the concept was psychological only; for Baudelaire it had primarily a moral significance. He saw it as one of the consequences of original sin, a proof of human corruption.[27] "Le Démon de la perversité" becomes therefore a more sombre and pessimistic fable than "The Imp of the Perverse."

In his translation of "The Gold Bug" there is a similar transposition, the nature of which is indicated by the disparity between the words *bug* and *scarabée*. Nowhere in the story is Poe's word literally trans-

lated, and once, when *beetle* occurs, the French text
gives it as *bête*.[28] The attempt throughout is to enrich
the tone of the story, to deepen its colors, and to make
the actions of the characters more dramatic. In at least
one instance, Baudelaire succeeded in doing this
through ignorance. Jupiter, the negro servant of Legrand, describes his preoccupied master as "pale as a
gose." Mistaking the meaning of the dialect spelling,
Baudelaire translates the cliché with startling freshness: "pâle comme une oie"—white as a goose.[29] An
accidental hit, but a very good one. Baudelaire does not
try to duplicate in French the dialect speech of Jupiter,
and this omission, for modern taste, amounts to a genuine improvement. At one point in the story Poe falls
victim to the fatally easy device of so-called humorous
writers by making as pronounced as possible the abyss
between the elegant speech of his narrator and the
nearly unintelligible speech of the Negro. This elementary kind of comedy is not present in "Le Scarabée
d'or." On the positive side, it is in his management of
the scenic values of the story that Baudelaire excels.
For example:

In this manner we journeyed for about two hours, and the
sun was just setting when we entered a region infinitely more
dreary than any yet seen. It was a species of table land, near
the summit of an almost inaccessible hill, densely wooded
from base to pinnacle, and interspersed with huge crags that
seemed to lie loosely upon the soil, and in many cases were
prevented from precipitating themselves into the valleys below, merely by the support of the trees against which they
reclined. Deep ravines, in various directions, gave an air of
still sterner solemnity to the scene.

Poe is clear and detailed enough, but a bit perfunctory.
Baudelaire, in the style of Delacroix, prefers a scene
that will be more menacingly suggestive:

Nous marchâmes ainsi deux heures environ, et le soleil était au moment de se coucher quand nous entrâmes dans une région infiniment plus *sinistre* que tout ce que nous avions vu jusqu'alors. C'était une espèce de plateau près du sommet d'une *montagne affreusement* escarpée, couverte de bois de la base au sommet, et semée d'énormes *blocs de pierre* qui semblaient éparpillés *péle-mêle* sur le sol, et dont plusieurs se seraient infailliblement précipités dans les vallées inférieures sans le secours des arbres contre lesquels il s'appuyaient. De profondes ravines *irradiaient* dans diverses directions et donnaient à la scène un caractère de solennité plus *lugubre.*[30]

The italics indicate the original brushwork of Baudelaire. He makes the hill a mountain and clears up Poe's rather misleading usage of *crags* by using the phrase *blocs de pierre.* But all the other words of interest in the French passage add an atmosphere of peril, gloom, and mystery to a landscape which Poe was satisfied to present merely as wild and difficult of access.

The character of Legrand in the same story is transformed in a similar way, made more intense, more individual. Poe has him utter a "loud oath," which becomes "un terrible juron" in French.[31] When calm, he speaks with a kind of grave pomposity in such phrases as: "When you first made this assertion. . . ." An unusual verb and the platitude is made original, sardonic: "La première fois que vous lâchâtes cette assertion . . ."[32] The effect of these and other details is cumulative, resulting in a story which has evidently a richer texture, and therefore a greater interest, than the story Poe originally wrote.

But the difference, discernible as it is, remains one merely of degree. "Le Scarabée d'or" is not in any sense a new creation. It opens up to the reader no new order of experience, provides no illumination, moral,

imaginative or otherwise, that bears the distinctive
stamp of Baudelaire rather than Poe. There is less care
and less craft in "The Gold Bug," and in translating
the story Baudelaire took the opportunity to rewrite a
few of its details. But this he did in the spirit of Poe.[33]
The surfaces of "Le Scarabée d'or" are more carefully wrought; there is no intrinsic change.

If in translating this story in such a way as to
heighten its quality Baudelaire did not manage to
leave Poe far behind—for, in a word, he only gave
to "The Gold Bug" the atmosphere that belongs to
"The Fall of the House of Usher"—then it would be
mistaken indeed to conclude that his translations as a
whole represent a decided improvement on their originals. The conclusion this inquiry much rather leads
us to is that the Poe of Baudelaire is the Poe we know
in English. This or that detail may have been overlooked, or improved, or weakened in translation. But
there is no full-scale transmutation. Baudelaire did
not melt down these stories, remove their dross, and re-
cast them in the pure gold of his French. He could
have done so, perhaps. But his admiration for Poe's
work was too intense, his identification with the man
too complete, to allow him even to contemplate such
an experiment in literary metallurgy.

5

"MON SEMBLABLE, MON FRÈRE!"

OF ALL the factors that helped make Baudelaire's translations the nearly perfect things they are, it was his identification with Poe that counted most heavily. Study and diligence, important though they be for a work of this sort, would not have been enough to insure the kind of success which Baudelaire achieved. Nor can this success, visible in almost every feature of his work, be attributed to chance, good luck, or to something equally extraordinary: a state of permanent inspiration. Certainly he worked hard, was patient and meticulous; certainly some of his best strokes were fortuitous rather than planned; and it is evident also that his great poetic sensibility was often engaged in a task that he might have seen through simply as an economic expedient on a plane no higher than hackwork. But in fact there was something more. So great was his response to Poe that in translating his work he found an avenue for his own self-expression, and he explicitly stated as much: "Do you know why I so patiently translated Poe? Because he resembled me. The first time I opened one of his books I saw, to my amazement and delight, not only certain subjects that I had dreamed about but SENTENCES that I had thought

135

of and that he had written down twenty years before." [1]

What makes this statement especially remarkable
is that there was in fact a more solid basis for it than
Baudelaire himself was aware. In the essays he wrote
on Poe he gives evidence of having had only a general,
and sometimes inaccurate, acquaintance with the facts
of Poe's life. He says, for example, that Poe was born
in 1813, that both Poe's parents died in Richmond,
that the merchant John Allan adopted him, that after
leaving the Allan household Poe went to Greece, then
to Russia; and so on.[2] All errors, but Baudelaire can
hardly be blamed. Only in this century, and at a relatively recent date, have the legends and lies about Poe
—some of which he himself fostered—been finally
dispelled. Yet if Baudelaire in some respects relied too
heavily on hearsay, he had intuitively far too keen a
feeling for his subject to be misled by the calumnies of
a Rufus Griswold: "This pedagogue-vampire defamed
his friend at length in a long, dull, and vicious essay,
printed at the beginning of the posthumous edition of
his works. Can it be that America has no ordinance
prohibiting dogs from entering cemeteries?" [3] That
says it well enough. But imagine how resolute in his
opinion Baudelaire must have been to have given the
lie direct, as he does here, to a man whom he knew
Poe had appointed his literary executor. The charge
which Baudelaire in effect leveled against Griswold—
that he had concealed some facts and distorted others
—has been fully sustained. If part of Baudelaire's
method as a biographer was to check the statements
made by presumed authorities against his own feeling
of what Poe's motives were and of how he must have
acted, he did well to do so, for the method was often

successful. At least he could pounce on a slander when he saw it, although mistakes of fact, naturally, he could not infallibly recognize. But in all that concerned the personality and character of Poe, Baudelaire had a very sure instinct for the truth and knew he had, for the man resembled him.

The resemblance which Baudelaire was struck by was a resemblance on the plane primarily of ideas and temperament. Their careers, too, were somewhat alike. There was little similarity between their personal modes of life. It is the disparity here that has put many people off, puzzled that the lurid and satanic Baudelaire of popular legend could have found any real kinship with the ethereal American poet of "The Bells" and "Annabel Lee." Poe was a drunkard, to be sure, but was not Baudelaire interested in more modish and garish vices? As a matter of fact, when one investigates the lives of the two men, especially during their early years, one discovers that the resemblances between them are uncommonly close, although not, of course, in every particular.

— I —

ONE salient fact in the lives of both is the persistent importance that their mothers had for them. Whatever psychological line one may choose to adopt on this subject, the fact is there, noticed as early as 1893,[4] and one of the principal *données* which a biographer of either man must take into account. Poe presents the harder task, for with Elizabeth Arnold, Mrs. Allan, and Mrs. Clemm enacting successively the mother role in Poe's life, it is the mother-symbol that his biographer must conjure with. But Poe's sonnet "To My

Mother" was written for Mrs. Clemm, and to this woman he was bound during most of his mature life by ties of more than filial piety. In recognizing her importance for Poe, Baudelaire not only grasped one of the chief truths about his life; he also revealed, in the intensity with which he expressed that recognition, something of the importance that Mme Aupick had for him. The *Histoires extraordinaires* are dedicated to Mrs. Clemm in such terms as these:

It is evident that this mother—a flame and hearth kindled by a ray from the highest of heavens—was set as an example to our people, who are too little mindful of self-sacrifice, of heroism, and of anything beyond the plane of duty. In all justice, should not the name of the woman who was for this poet the moral light of his life be inscribed at the head of his works? [5]

On evidence largely second-hand, Baudelaire estimated quite accurately the major significance that Mrs. Clemm had for Poe. He had no access, of course, to Poe's letters; but could he have read them he would have found more than one direct confirmation of what his intuition had revealed. Shortly before his death Poe wrote to Mrs. Clemm: "If possible, oh COME! My clothes are so *horrible* and I am so *ill*. Oh, if you could come to me, *my mother*. Write instantly—Oh *do* not fail. God forever bless you." [6] In a letter to Mme Aupick, in 1855, Baudelaire expressed much the same sentiments, although in a rather different kind of prose: "What emptiness around me! What blackness! What darknesses of spirit and what fears of the future!" [7] If he had been able to see Poe's letter would he not have been reminded of his own, and made the more poignantly aware, by the contrast between Poe's childish, frenzied directness and his own rather empty rhetorical formulations, of his own longing for an immediacy of relationship which was a fact in Poe's life but an aspiration only in his? If Baudelaire had been more fully informed about the early life of Poe, he would also have recognized that his words to Mme Aupick, "I suffer much at the thought of meeting your husband"[8] could equally have been said by Poe to Mrs. John Allan. For not only were Poe and Baudelaire reared in homes of affluence, they were both in addition resentful of the men who made those homes possible. Baudelaire had no correspondence with his stepfather, but in his feelings towards him he had another bond of sympathy with Edgar Poe, although he was unaware of it. For Poe's letters to John Allan are often smouldering with suppressed hatred, and sometimes afire with it.[9]

These are some of the grounds for seeing in Baudelaire's professed resemblance to Poe something more than a curious whim. And there are other grounds as well. Both men very early made up their minds that they would be poets, and in striking off for themselves they were looking for a freedom in which this resolve might be brought to fruition. Poe's life, from the time he left the Allan household until the day of his death, was almost uniformly one of misery and deprivation. Baudelaire's inheritance cushioned him for a while against a fate nearly as sombre, but he too, once he had wasted his modest patrimony, learned what impoverishment was and what it was to be a literary outcast, known as a notorious writer, perhaps, but not a popular, and much less an important one. But no matter what the difficulties under which he lived, Baudelaire saw to it that his appearance was always maintained in the manner which his special distinction as a poet called for. Be informed, he told his mother, "that through all my life, in bad times as well as good,—I have always devoted two hours to my dress and appearance." [10] Thus he displayed his separateness from and his superiority to the common ruck. In Poe he detected a man of similar distinction: "His features, bearing, gestures, the way he held his head, everything marked him . . . as one of the elite." Necessarily so, for the poet, according to Baudelaire, is a man set apart from humanity who under even the most adverse circumstances is at his personal best. "Poe would have known how to transform a thatched cottage into some new kind of palace." [11]

To have recognized that Poe, too, had been something of a dandy was for Baudelaire another proof of their kinship. Himself, he had cultivated this role and all the anti-bourgeois activities that went with it from the time he was able to choose his own wardrobe. There is no "influence" here; he did not pattern his behavior on Poe's. And yet one can hardly avoid the feeling that in one of the final expedients of Baudelaire's career he did take his cue from Poe. The parallel, this time, seems too close to be merely a matter of accident. Writing in 1856, Baudelaire described how Poe in his last years all but abandoned his work as a writer and journalist in order to resort to lecturing. "One knows what these lectures are—a kind of gamble, as if the *Collège de France* were made available to all men of letters, the author holding up publication of his lecture until after he has made maximum profit on it." [12] In 1864 Baudelaire had reason to recall these words. For in that year he went to Brussels with the hope that as a lecturer in Belgium he would be able to earn the money and the recognition that his

own country had been reluctant to give him.[13] The
project began auspiciously, but soon turned into a
fiasco, and Baudelaire resolved to write a mordant
book on Belgian civilization. But his health was failing, and nothing ever came of this project. In 1866 he
collapsed, and died two years afterwards. What was
to have been for both men a final stroke of good for-
tune after so many years of penury and neglect proved
to be for both Poe and Baudelaire only a discordant
and clumsy finale to their lives.

— II —

DURING the two years of his stay in Belgium, all the
contempt which Baudelaire had ever felt for the crude
materialism and optimism, the lack of elegance and
taste, which he was aware of in his age, came to a violent boil. His letters of 1865–66 seethe with an expression of this outrage. The Belgian audiences who
went to hear him speak were looking for some kind of
curiosity, a monster preferably. Instead they found a
man who was polite, detached in manner, conservative in his views, a man who abhorred free-thought,
Progress, "and all modern stupidity." Accordingly,
they refused to believe that this man could have written *Les Fleurs du mal*.[14] "What a collection of riff-
raff!" Baudelaire exclaims. "And I who had thought
France an utterly barbarous country, here I am forced
to admit that there is another country even more barbarous than France." [15] Or perhaps even more than
Poe's America! Following the lead of Tocqueville's
famous book, Baudelaire had emphasized the im-
probability of America's fostering an artistic talent of
any real importance. For Poe the United States must

have been nothing but a vast prison, "a great barbarous realm equipped with gas fixtures," [16] in which he could scarcely breathe, much less find it possible to realize himself as an artist. The wonder is, says Baudelaire, that he managed to bear up as long as he did in such an environment.

It was not, however, the specifically democratic character of the United States that was responsible for the shabby treatment Poe received. In Baudelaire's opinion, all poets were considered *personae non gratae* throughout the contemporary world, whether the particular political system under which they lived was democratic or not. The fate of Poe in America had been matched by the fate of Gérard de Nerval in the France of Napoleon III.[17] Baudelaire alluded to this parallel in 1856; in his final years he must have realized that he, too, with Poe and Nerval, was another instance of the law which he had promulgated in his *Journaux intimes*: "Nations have their great men only in spite of themselves." [18]

But in the meantime, hit back! Hit back against the slogans, and half-truths, and modernist superstitions which had acquired almost universal adherence, but which to a man of taste and intelligence were only revolting and pernicious. Baudelaire took this course, not because he was convinced that his individual counterattack could accomplish very much, but because for him there could be no indifference to or compromise with mediocrity, stupidity, and error. These things had to be fought, and in this fight against many of the most firmly entrenched values of the nineteenth century Baudelaire found that he had an ally in Edgar Poe. Thus, to a striking similarity be-

tween the lives of the two men, there is added another
resemblance, an affinity of ideas.

Especially in his "Notes nouvelles sur Edgar Poe"
does Baudelaire warm to his work of heaping ridicule
on those features of his age which he considered inimi-
cal to art, literature, and all right thinking. Democracy, socialism, the ideal of universal literacy, the
beliefs in Progress and human perfectibility, the obsession with material values—all these are the object
of his trenchant indictment, and in almost every case
he finds it possible to incorporate into his argument
some reference to Poe or some statement Poe had
made.[19] He presents his American counterpart as a
man patrician in mind, a Southerner and a Virginian,
by nature if not by birth an aristocrat; above all, a
poet. Such a person, says Baudelaire, could not be
duped by the cheap ideological nostrums which were
cherished by so many of his contemporaries, as much
in France as in America.

It is with pride, obviously, that Baudelaire associ-
ates himself with the opinions of Poe. And, objectively,
he was right in doing so. In their social and political
thinking the two men were of the same mind. Poe was
never quite so outspoken on these matters as Baudelaire, but he had very definite opinions about them.
These opinions, often obliquely and sardonically
phrased, are strewn throughout his work; collected,
they would add up to a severe critique of his country
and his century.[20] This Baudelaire knew; only in his
effort to get at the basis for this side of Poe's thought
did he go wrong, imputing to Poe a viewpoint which
was really held only by Baudelaire himself: "Let us
note that this author, product of a self-infatuated age,

child of a nation more self-infatuated than any other, clearly saw and imperturbably affirmed the natural wickedness of man." [21] Baudelaire is thinking of Poe's theory of perverseness, but thinking of it in his own way, or at least giving to the theory an inflection which its originator would not readily have recognized. For Poe, devoid as he was of traditional religious convictions, would not have imagined that his theory was a modern restatement of the concept of original sin and its consequences for the human character. But this was the light in which Baudelaire acclaimed it, taking it as proof "that we are all born marked for evil!" [22] Superficially, Poe might have subscribed to the view of life this phrase implies, but the evil, the *mal,* of Baudelaire was of a theological density that was quite foreign to the mind of Poe.

— III —

WITH the term *beau,* however, as Baudelaire defined it, Poe would have been in almost complete accord:

I have found the definition of the Beautiful—of my Beautiful. It is something that is ardent and sad, and somewhat vague, leaving room for surmise. . . . A lovely and seductive head, a woman's head I mean to say, is a head that evokes in a dim, blurred fashion dreams of both sadness and sensual pleasure; and that involves some thought of melancholy, of lassitude, and even of satiety. . . . Mystery, and regret too, are qualities of the Beautiful. . . . I can scarcely conceive of an instance of Beauty . . . where there is not some *Woe* present as well.[23]

This is *his* definition of the Beautiful, written not for publication, but only as an entry in his private diary. Yet there is nothing here—except, possibly, "sensual pleasure" (*volupté*)—that Poe would have objected to, and almost every detail in this passage may be annotated out of Poe's own work. In "The Philosophy of Composition" occur the famous propositions regarding the inseparability of beauty and melancholy, and the necessity that there be in poetry "some amount of suggestiveness—some under-current, however indefinite, of meaning." [24] In the same essay Poe employs his characteristic logic to arrive at the conclusion that of all subjects for poetry the death of a beautiful woman is the most appropriate. Even Baudelaire's example, in the passage quoted, was anticipated by Poe. In "Landor's Cottage" a drawing of a Greek female head is described: "a face so divinely beautiful, and yet of an expression so provokingly indeterminate, never before arrested my attention";[25] and in "The Assignation" another portrait of a woman is described in the same way. Baudelaire was far too close a student of Poe to have missed these details, and yet a definition apparently based on them is nonetheless *his* definition. In such full accord were the two men in their theory of literature and art that Baudelaire did not consider his ideas on these subjects any the less his own for their having been adumbrated years previously by his American counterpart.

If there is one detail which Poe could have wished added to Baudelaire's definition, it would have to do with the relationship which Poe believed existed between beauty and strangeness. "There is no exquisite beauty without some *strangeness* in the proportions" —a dictum which Poe attributed to Lord Bacon, although no one yet has been able to discover the basis for his doing so.[26] But whether Baconian or not, the sentiment was authentically Poe's; and, inevitably, one is tempted to say, it was Baudelaire's as well. In his formulation: *"The beautiful is always bizarre."* [27]

So he expressed himself in 1855, eight years after his discovery of Poe. Influence? Not at all; such a conclusion is reached only by assuming that a simple chronological computation offers a final answer to the whole problem. A taste for the bizarre, an enthusiasm for things strange and extraordinary, was an integral part of Baudelaire's aesthetic long before he had heard of Poe.

Indeed it was this very taste that attracted him to Poe in the first place, just as it had attracted him to Delacroix earlier and was to make him an ardent admirer of Wagner later on.[28] To read Baudelaire's pages on the subject of Delacroix is to see what he looked for and what he admired, whether the occasion was a painting or a poem, a story or an opera. He did not have to wait for Poe to tell him of a relationship between melancholy and beauty; that was something he had already learned from his study of painting. The most remarkable quality of Delacroix, according to Baudelaire, and the quality that makes him a truly modern artist is, precisely, "that peculiar and persistent melancholy which emanates from all his works." [29] The poetic principle, in Poe's summary definition, is "the Human Aspiration for Supernal Beauty." Poe's essay was not published in America until 1850; in his *Salon de 1846* Baudelaire had already written: "Romanticism is just another word for modern art—that is, inwardness, spirituality, color, aspiration towards the infinite, expressed by all the means the arts command." [30] Delacroix was a great painter for Baudelaire because he was a master of these values. The element of *suggestiveness* which Poe emphasized as essential to poetry is the basis for Baudelaire's contrast between Victor Hugo and Delacroix: only the latter invites us to deep imaginative engagement in his work.[31] And it goes without saying that *originality*, on which Poe was to put so heavy an accent, was from the start of Baudelaire's career as a critic one of his enduring criteria.[32]

What calls for special notice, however, is that by 1846 Baudelaire was expounding an aesthetic doctrine which his Symbolist successors seem to have thought of as exclusively Poe's. For Mallarmé and Valéry the hypothesis basic to "The Philosophy of Composition" had all the attraction of a vivifying and revolutionary truth which, if acted on, would add a new dimension to the practice of poetry. Poets needed no longer to depend on inspiration. Instead, a lucid, active, and voluntarist exercise of the mind would suffice (given genius) to produce great poems. The final break with romanticism was thus made possible by this new doctrine.[33] It was not, however, as the Symbolists thought, solely the invention of Poe. He may have provided in his famous essay a full theoretical justification for it; but nearer to home and with no knowledge of Poe's work, Baudelaire had made the very same suggestion. It is one of his charges against an effete romanticism that it enthroned inspiration as alone sufficient to the creation of a work of art.[34] And, with more precision, he enunciates in the *Salon de 1846* the essence of the thesis which Poe advanced and defended in the same year:

Chance has no more place in art than in mechanics. A felicitous detail is the simple result of good reasoning, in which the intermediate deductions are sometimes skipped, just as something wrong is the result of an error in principle. A painting is a machine the component parts of which are intelligible to a practiced eye. If the painting is a good one, everything in it has a reason for being there.[35]

This was exactly Poe's starting point for his demonstration of how "The Raven" was written.

The various points of resemblance between the aesthetic theories of the two men are all but explicitly summarized in the final section of the "Notes nouvelles sur Edgar Poe." The necessity of bringing inspiration to heel, condemnation of the heresy of the didactic, approval of short poems only (but not *too* short), the criterion of totality of effect, poetry as an end in itself, the alliance between poetry and music, between strangeness and beauty—these and the other leading features of what Poe had to say about literary art are all given emphatic statement by Baudelaire. His intention was to outline Poe's aesthetic theory, but his own commitment to the same theory makes its presence felt very quickly, with two interesting results. Baudelaire begins by presenting Poe's ideas, soon veers to a statement of his own beliefs, and through the remainder of the discussion constantly regains and loses sight of the point of view from which he had started. But for him the confusion in viewpoint was of negligible importance: by speaking his own mind on these matters he would, he thought, be giving a faithful transcription of the mind of Poe. Another result is that Baudelaire, in speaking his own mind, often does so by simply translating from "The Poetic Principle" or giving parts of it the thinnest kind of paraphrase. Technically, the word for this is plagiarism.[36] But it would be equally just, and more charitable, to consider Baudelaire's procedure here as proof that he was scarcely exaggerating when he said that some of the very *sen-*

tences which he found written by Poe had been worked out independently in his own mind well before the work of Poe came under his excited scrutiny.

Not a systematic critic himself, Baudelaire was the more appreciative of the way Poe had shaped and co-ordinated the theories the two men shared. And Baudelaire was therefore the more ready to find in Poe's writing support and confirmation for what he already believed. But just as he had attributed to the notion of perverseness a serious moral significance that is lacking in Poe's explanation of it, so in the realm of aesthetic theory he seems to have attributed to Poe an idea which, in its fullness at least, was his alone: the idea of Correspondences. In the "Notes nouvelles," Baudelaire remarks that the instinct for the beautiful is what makes us "consider the earth and earthly scenes as a glimpse into and a correspondence with Heaven." [37] It is the final phrase here that is suspect. For if Baudelaire in writing it meant to speak for Poe as well as for himself he was, most likely, in error. The term *correspondances* had for him a meaning so richly complex that, as we noticed earlier, an entire book has been written merely to gloss the sonnet of which that word is the title.[38] In all of his work Poe makes no use of its English equivalent, nor does he display any interest in or respect for the Swedenborgian *mystique* from which the term in Baudelaire's usage principally derives. As with *perverseness*, so with *correspondence*: Baudelaire imputes to what exists in Poe only as a suggestion, a weight of meaning that the suggestion only potentially contains. An undeveloped hint, a germinal idea, is brought to a full and sudden flowering.

The hint may be found in one of Poe's notes to "Al Aaraaf": "I have often thought I could distinctly hear

the sound of the darkness as it stole over the horizon." [39]
And some of the lines from the same poem—

> Ours is a world of words; Quiet we call
> "Silence"—which is the merest word of all.
> All Nature speaks, and ev'n ideal things
> Flap shadowy sounds from visionary wings—

could not but have impressed the Baudelaire of "Correspondances":

> La Nature est un temple où de vivants piliers
> Laissent parfois sortir de confuses paroles;
> L'homme y passe à travers des forêts de symboles
> Qui l'observent avec des regards familiers . . .

The two poets are alluding in much the same way to synaesthesia, a phenomenon in which one kind of sensory apprehension is experienced through a different sense channel; and by the adherents to the theory of Correspondence this phenomenon was regarded as proof, or at least a corollary, of their major hypothesis.[40] They also took the view, logically enough, that the various arts are so closely related that an effect considered proper to one may be realized by all the others. Thus Baudelaire in discussing Delacroix can speak of the musical quality of his work, on one page, and on the next define this painter's genius as essentially literary.[41] When, therefore, Baudelaire found Poe establishing an integral relation between poetry and music, and assuming that all the arts—including that of the landscape garden [42]—are alike in having the same end in view, he naturally deduced that Poe was in agreement with him on this matter also. Poe's antipathy to allegory—something which Baudelaire never mentions—should have made him more cautious. And there is a remark in Poe's "Marginalia" which nicely clarifies their respective viewpoints:

"The right angle of light's incidence produces a sound upon one of the Egyptian pyramids." This assertion, thus expressed, I have encountered somewhere. . . . It is nonsense, I suppose, —but it will not do to speak hastily. The orange ray of the spectrum and the buzz of the gnat . . . affect me with nearly similar sensations. In hearing the gnat, I perceive the color. In perceiving the color, I seem to hear the gnat.[43]

"It is nonsense, I suppose"—with this qualification Poe undermines the entire statement, as Baudelaire would not have done. For, to Baudelaire, correspondences between sounds, odors, colors, and so on were theoretically as well as empirically true. Poe, however, although he professes to have experienced synaesthesia, seems to doubt that it could *mean* anything. He declines to build on the experience or to derive any consequences from it. Perhaps his lack of interest here was owing in part to his antipathy to the New England Transcendentalists, who set great store by the Correspondence theory and its chief designer, Swedenborg; and perhaps for a mind like Poe's, attempting always, consciously and aggressively, to display a severely intelligent character, this theory smacked too much of the irrational to be worth any investigation. At any rate, despite his native attraction for it, the theory was not assimilated into Poe's thought to anything like the degree Baudelaire assumed.

He was led astray not only because Poe occasionally seemed to allude to some of the tenets of Correspondence but because he found that Poe was at one with him in adhering to the great underlying assumption of that theory: through intuitive and imaginative activity a new realm of knowledge may be discovered. For both men, the imagination was "queen of the faculties":

It is at once both analysis and synthesis. . . . It is the imagination that taught man the moral significance of color and contour, of sound and smell. At the beginning of the world it brought into being analogy and metaphor. It splits up the entire creation, and then, with its materials assembled and arranged in accordance with rules that derive from the depths of the soul, it creates a new world, produces the sensation of the new.[44]

The language of Poe has, oddly enough, a less Coleridgean tone, but his premise is the same:

That the imagination has not been unjustly ranked as supreme among the mental faculties, appears from the intense consciousness, on the part of the imaginative man, that the faculty in question brings his soul often to a glimpse of things supernal and eternal—to the very verge of the *great secrets*. There are moments, indeed, in which he perceives the faint perfumes, and hears the melodies of a happier world. Some of the most profound knowledge—perhaps all *very* profound knowledge—has originated from a highly stimulated imagination. Great intellects *guess* well. The laws of Kepler were, professedly, guesses.[45]

His own *Eureka* was another such imaginative guess. The book has for subtitle "A Prose Poem," and in his preface Poe offers the treatise as "a Book of Truths"—true because of the beauty in it, true as a poem is true. Let it then, Poe concludes, be judged as such. If one is puzzled to explain what motives could have prompted Baudelaire to labor over a translation of this work, as convincing an answer as any may be inferred from Poe's preface. Here was a book offered as evidence that a specifically poetic order of knowledge is possible, that imagination and intuition are also competent,

along with the different disciplines of science and dis-
cursive reason, to investigate the meaning of the world.
Here was a challenge to positivism that was much
more than a verbal assertion of the contrary position.
Eureka was intended as a demonstration that poetry,
in its fullest sense, was a mode of knowledge. Whatever Baudelaire privately thought of the success of
Poe's effort, he could only admire the daring with
which Poe undertook it and applaud the reason for
which it was done. In his own interest in Correspondences, Baudelaire was, for once, the more systematic
of the two men, wondering, for example, whether
some student of analogies had worked out a complete
list of equivalents between colors and emotions.[46] But
that, if done, would only serve to support his conviction that the insights of a poet have their own kind of
objective truth; and in this conviction he was wholly
in agreement with Poe.

He was in agreement with him also on the subject
of how the insights of poetic knowledge became possible. "From the midst of a world gluttonous for only
material things, Poe soared out into dreams," [47] writes
Baudelaire, aware of how Poe had dedicated *Eureka*
"to dreamers and those who put faith in dreams as
the only realities." Calling them realities does not
make them so, however; were not the dreams cultivated by both men less a means of getting at reality
than of escaping from it? But everything depends on
what premise is preferred. If one assumes that the real
is what is factual, measurable, intelligible, and is
therefore identical only with those phenomena which
are apprehended by the senses and analyzed and ordered by the intellect, then it does follow that Poe and
Baudelaire were deluded and that they mistook refuge

and escape for inquiry and engagement. Their assumption, however, was of a different sort, but, it
should be added, one no less unprovable than the other.
It will not be our task, however, to settle the dust that
has been swirling over this problem from the time
epistemology was first thought of, but only to determine with some measure of precision how closely allied were the viewpoints of Poe and Baudelaire on this
issue of dreams as modes of poetic cognition.

Baudelaire first. His was far from the naive view
that dreaming is by definition and intrinsically a
"poetic" activity. As often as not, the normal dreams
of sleep simply give distorted shape to the events and
thoughts of the waking day and thus can contribute
nothing to the "evocative sorcery" that is poetry.[48]
But there are other dreams which act not as cracked
and cloudy mirrors of a reality already known, but as
windows opening onto realms that would otherwise
remain inaccessible. A dream of this type is "the absurd dream, unforeseen, quite unrelated to the character, life, and emotions of the dreamer! This dream,
which I would call hieroglyphic, represents the supernatural side of life." [49] It must be studied as if it were
a new language, of which the indispensable grammar
and dictionary are the doctrines of Correspondence.
The abnormal dreams that are induced by drugs like
opium and hashish may suffice to make the poet aware
that behind the façade of natural experience there exists a vivid and complex realm of being, with "a deeper,
firmer, and more commanding meaning" than any he
knew before.[50] But this is a treacherous means of entry, or rather not of entry, since the poet who relies
on drugs can only sense the existence of this world; he
is unable to take possession of it. Only genius, and an

exercise of the will, can make that possible; and so the false paradises of drugs and intoxicants are but mirages of the "unreal real" which the poet should aspire to master.[51] Thus Baudelaire, as his final meaning of "le rêve," would have us understand nothing like a passive submission to the curious phantasmagoria of slumber, but instead a very active work: poetic composition, in which the imagination is working at maximum efficiency, using and guiding all the other faculties.[52]

If Poe's theory of dream is less complete than this and less carefully shaded, that is because Poe, unlike Baudelaire, did not locate his aesthetic and psychological ideas within the context of the theory of Correspondence. Having done so, Baudelaire was able both to elaborate and clarify his thought on this subject. Again, this is a case of our finding in Poe germinal anticipations that in Baudelaire are found in the form of realizations. Allowance made for this difference in degree, attention reverts to the similarity in kind: on the function and importance of the oneiric element in the poetic enterprise, Poe and his French successor have essentially the same things to say.

In Poe's opinion, imitation, no matter how accurate, is not art. The mere duplication, for instance, of natural beauty is praiseworthy, certainly, but it falls short of the goal which true poetry should have. There must be something more: the materials used by the poet must be reproduced "through the veil of the soul."[53] The example Poe falls back on to illustrate this kind of imaginative refraction suggests a practiced alteration of sensory impressions: a sudden glance at a star reveals more than would a direct gaze, and the green of the grass is seen as more intense if it is looked at with half-closed eyes.[54] The perceptions that result

he calls *fancies*, but only for lack of a better word.
They are intuitive and casual, more psychal than intellectual, but through them a kind of knowledge is
obtained that the reason cannot reach to. These fancies
are of rare occurrence, requiring an intense tranquil-
lity of mind and perfection in bodily and mental
health. But given these conditions, they will arise "at
those mere points of time where the confines of the
waking world blend with those of the world of dreams.
I am aware of these 'fancies' only when I am upon the
very brink of sleep, with the consciousness that I am
so." [55] And in one of his stories, Poe gives this statement the maximum meaning it had for him: "They
who dream by day are cognizant of many things
which escape those who dream only by night. In their
grey visions they obtain glimpses of eternity, and
thrill, in awaking, to find that they have been upon
the verge of the great secret." [56] The word *cognizant*
is an important one here, and the whole passage is a
capital one to an understanding of what Poe was doing. Writing elsewhere, and vaguely, of "ideality,"
and "poesy," he remarks that an integral part of
the poetic impulse is the "unconquerable desire—*to
know*." [57] But here he gives more memorable phrasing
to his conviction that poetry is a mode of knowledge,
and he indicates at the same time the context in which
poetry originates: between dream and consciousness,
when the imagination is most fully at work, although
the other faculties of the mind are not in abeyance.
No more than Baudelaire does Poe recommend trance
as the appropriate mental habit for poetry. Rapture
and abandon there must be, but, in addition, "the most
profound Art (based both in Instinct and *Analysis*)
and the sternest Will properly to blend and rigorously

to control." [58] The true poet is a seer, a *voyant*, but he must necessarily be also an *artiste*.

— IV —

HE IS first of all a man. And from what Baudelaire could learn of the life of Poe, of his ideas on politics and society, of his commitment to art, and of the ambitious ends which Poe conceived art to have, he could only conclude that as man, artist, and *voyant* Poe was his brother. He translated his work, therefore, "because he resembled me."

If Baudelaire's phrase had been taken seriously, or if its truth had been ascertained by an inquiry of the sort just now concluded, there would have been none of the false alarms and excursions that have taken place in recent years over the problems of Poe's influence on the French poet. One finds the Poe partisans bent on computing the extent of Baudelaire's debt to Poe; and, on the other side, with those whose admiration is reserved for Baudelaire only, the contention is made with a good deal of heat that no real debt exists. [59] Whatever may have been the influence of Poe on their hero, it is clear from the great importance this group attaches to originality that Poe strongly influenced *them*. For by no other critic was the gospel of originality preached with more fervent insistence. Indeed, it would be no paradox to say that a solid proof of how little Poe influenced Baudelaire would consist in showing that the French poet did imitate the American, for if he had done this to any major degree he would have run counter to one of his master's most important precepts.

There is a vicious circle here, evidently; and inevitably there must be, since to speak of "influence" and "sources" within the context of so singular a case as that of the Poe-Baudelaire relationship is to assume, contrary to the evident quality it has, that the case was not so singular after all. And thus the relationship is misconceived. Its crucial feature is Baudelaire's claim that in reading Poe he discovered himself. That claim must stand; in the light of it conventional considerations of influence are secondary, if not altogether irrelevant.

They are secondary so far as Baudelaire's ideas on art, poetry, and politics are concerned. They are irrevelant to the really important matter: Baudelaire's achievement as a poet. Perhaps in the one detail we have noticed earlier—the lecture tours of his last years —he patterned his life on that of Poe; and perhaps, negatively, the example of what Poe had done in fiction caused Baudelaire to abandon his early plans for writing stories. (As for the *Petits poèmes en prose,* his point of departure was not Poe but Aloysius Bertrand.[60]) Psychologically he was already formed, his basic ideas on literature and art established, and his characteristic work as a poet begun before he encountered the work of Poe. How could Poe, then, have had any significant and determining influence on him? To be sure, certain specific borrowings may be found. Baudelaire's "Le Flambeau vivant" is hardly more than a free translation of some lines from the less famous of the poems "To Helen." There are also some line-for-line equivalents between parts of "Héautonimorouménos" and passages from "The Haunted Palace." In the preface which Baudelaire intended to write for *Les Fleurs du mal* he was going to acknowledge these borrowings.[61] But they do not add up to

anything consequential, and even when one has studied all the passages that are parallel in idea, tone, or
phrasing, the conclusion must still be that Baudelaire
as a poet learned nothing *new* from Poe. When he
sent a copy of Poe's poems to his mother in 1854,
Baudelaire commented: "A rather curious thing, and
one I can't help noticing, is the deep-seated though not
positively pronounced resemblance between my own
poems and those of this man, allowances made for differences in temperament and climate." [62] In spite of
its qualifying phrases the statement is surprising. One
would find it difficult to justify the term "deep-seated"
(*intime*), and perhaps its presence is the result of
wishful thinking: having found himself resembling
Poe in so many other ways, Baudelaire was reluctant
to see a disparity between Poe's poetry and his own.
On that score, too, he looked for identification. But in
any case the word *resemblance* is the right one. Baudelaire engaged in no sedulous aping, but so similar were
the two men that in their writing they perforce resembled each other.

They did so especially in the two areas in which
each was at his creative best. The stories of Poe and
the poems of Baudelaire are mutually illuminating in
a number of different ways. The themes of death, the
sea-voyage, Platonic love (for that too is present in
Les Fleurs du mal), the alliance between beauty and
strangeness—these are readily visible in the work of
both writers. But the force of the resemblance that
may be demonstrated on these grounds is lessened by
the fact that the resemblance may be extended to other
writers of their time. Something more distinctive
should be looked for, something that has stamped upon
it the peculiar qualities of their minds and their im-

aginations. Let us therefore consider how Poe and
Baudelaire, independently of their great contemporary
Kierkegaard, responded to the phenomenon he described as the Concept of Dread. In Kierkegaard's
definition:

People have often explained the nature of original sin, and
yet they lacked a primary category—dread, which really is its
determinant. For dread is a desire for what one dreads, a sympathetic antipathy. Dread is an alien power which lays hold
of an individual, and yet one cannot tear oneself away, nor
has a will to do so; for one fears, but what one fears one desires. Dread then makes the individual impotent, and the first
sin always occurs in impotence. Apparently, therefore, the
man lacks accountability, but this lack is what ensnares him.[63]

As a rather abstract description of a phenomenon
for which his own life provided all the necessary spec-
ificity, Baudelaire would have seen the point of these
paradoxes. He knew how real a sympathetic antipathy
could be, and how the impossibility of explaining its
existence made submission to it almost unavoidable.
"I am guilty of offenses against myself," he writes;
"this disparity between will and ability is something I
cannot understand. Why is it that when I have so right
and sure a notion of what I ought to do and of what
would be best for me I always do the opposite?" [64] His
subservience to this condition was an important part
of what he called "the horror of life"; [65] and, like
Kierkegaard, he believed that only the traditional religious doctrine of original sin was adequate to account
for this horror as a necessary fact in the condition of
man. Kierkegaard defined the state of Dread as a consequence of the Fall. This too is Baudelaire's thesis,
only with him the idea of the Fall, instead of remaining the moribund metaphor it usually is, at once be-

comes a living image. The Fall of man is a *falling*, an act, an event; and hence in the poetry of Baudelaire we repeatedly come upon the related imagery of downfall and dread of the abyss.

This imagery is recurrent, and apparently spontaneous with him, because Baudelaire *lived* the experience of Dread in the very form of the metaphor which he used to describe it: "In my moral as well as physical life, I have always had the sensation of the abyss [*la sensation du gouffre*], not only the abyss of sleep, but that of action, of dream, of memory, of desire, of regret, of remorse, of the beautiful, of number." [66] This entry in his notebook serves both as introduction to and commentary on the poems, eighteen of them, in which the image of the abyss appears. Of these "Le Gouffre" is the classic instance:

> Pascal avait son gouffre, avec lui se mouvant.
> —Hélas, tout est abîme,—action, désir, rêve,
> Parole! et sur mon poil qui tout droit se relève
> Mainte fois de la Peur je sens passer le vent.
>
> .   .   .   .
>
> J'ai peur du sommeil comme on a peur d'un grand trou
> Tout plein de vague horreur, menant on ne sait où;
> Je ne vois qu'infini par toutes les fenêtres,
>
> Et mon esprit, toujours du vertige hanté,
> Jalouse du néant l'insensibilité.
> —Ah! ne jamais sortir des Nombres et des Etres! [67]

Here it is impossible to separate his fear of the abyss from the attraction it has for him. The antithetical feelings of aversion and longing are fused. For if his awareness of the abyss is fearsome, he knows nonetheless that the abyss provides the only end to the vertigo of living. Hence the cry of anguish in the final line;

the insensibility of nothingness seems to be his only way out. But that too involves a fall, as in the image with which "Le Goût du néant" concludes: "Avalanche, veux-tu m'emporter dans ta chute?" [68] Or when, instead of a despairing nihilism some desperate hope is clung to, the abyss is again the only place where it may be realized. In "Le Voyage" the hope is for the discovery of the new:

> Nous voulons, tant ce feu nous brûle le cerveau,
> Plonger au fond du gouffre, Enfer ou Ciel, qu'importe?
> Au fond de l'Inconnu pour trouver du *nouveau!* [69]

The action of discovery demands a descent into the abyss, the whirlpool or maelstrom. Poe's story of the maelstrom immediately comes to mind, but in another of Baudelaire's poems, "L'Irrémédiable," we find a similar allusion. Once more the image-idea is that of being engulfed:

> Un Ange, imprudent voyageur,
> Qu'a tenté l'amour du difforme,
> Au fond d'un cauchemar énorme
> Se débattant comme un nageur,
>
> Et luttant, angoisses funèbres!
> Contre un gigantesque remous
> Qui va chantant comme les fous
> Et pirouettant dans les ténèbres . . .

Thus the voyager; and what of the ship?

> Un navire pris dans le pôle,
> Comme en un piège de cristal,
> Cherchant par quel détroit fatal
> Il est tombé dans cette geôle . . .

The ship, hemmed in by polar ice, the voyager, pulled down into the maelstrom, these and the other images of "L'Irrémédiable" add to the central theme of dread

of the abyss the related motifs of vertigo and encircle-
ment. Baudelaire's purpose, of course, is not to arrange
a series of analogous disasters for the sake of some
undefined "thrill" they may give rise to. The poem
concludes with an explicit statement of the meaning
these visions have for him:

> —Emblèmes nets, tableau parfait
> D'une fortune irrémédiable,
> Qui donne à penser que le Diable
> Fait toujours bien tout ce qu'il fait.[70]

The evil which this devil represents is, like the omni-
present abyss that Pascal was aware of, an inescapable
condition of life, always present, always at work. Not,
however, as an exterior enemy merely; the evil is a
constitutive part of human nature. Thus, in "La Destruction":

> Sans cesse à mes côtés s'agite le Démon;
> Il nage autour de moi comme un air impalpable;
> Je l'avale et le sens qui brûle mon poumon
> Et l'emplit d'un désir éternel et coupable.
>
> . . . .
>
> Il me conduit ainsi, loin du regard de Dieu,
> Haletant et brisé de fatigue, au milieu
> Des plaines de l'Ennui, profondes et désertes,
>
> Et jette dans mes yeux pleins de confusion
> Des vêtements souillés, des blessures ouvertes,
> Et l'appareil sanglant de la Destruction![71]

This demon is no other than what Baudelaire called
the "démon de la perversité" in his translation of Poe's
phrase "imp of the perverse." It is the force that urges
man to seek his own destruction, to be at once slayer
and slain, victim and executioner.[72] An unaccountable
longing, feared as much as desired, it is the conse-

quence of the first human Fall and the cause of all the
others. Thus in the poetry of Baudelaire the abstract
theological proposition of Kierkegaard is endowed
with the kind of imaginative life that only metaphorical expression makes possible.

In this context, even a cursory reading of some of
Poe's stories will illustrate how much he too was fascinated by the Concept of Dread. To say that the emotion of fear is a fixture in Poe's work is to say very
little, unless something additional is done to define the
kind of fear that is met with in his stories and to establish the significance of the circumstances in which
that emotion is called into play. In a word, the characteristic fear that Poe explores is the "sympathetic antipathy" of Kierkegaard, the "horreur sympathique"
of Baudelaire; the circumstances are those of falling
and entombment.

The motif of the abyss is central to "A Descent into
the Maelstrom," a story which superficially seems to
be a bizarre invention and nothing more. But notice
how Poe has given the story a framework which acts
to reinforce the meaning of its main episode. The actual descent was made by a Norwegian fisherman; his
account of it is told to the narrator of the story when
the two men are at the summit of a great cliff over-
looking the perilous sea. The narrator's fear of falling
from the cliff is counterpointed against both the fear
the fisherman experienced as he made his descent into
the maelstrom and the hope that came to supplant that
fear. It was not a hope of surviving the experience but
of discovering "du *nouveau*" in the course of the fatal
plunge. "I positively felt a *wish*," he says, "to explore
its depths, even at the sacrifice I was going to make;
and my principal grief was that I should never be able

to tell my old companions on shore about the mysteries I should see." [73] In this story it is the lure of the abyss that is predominant.

In "The Pit and the Pendulum," on the other hand, it is the horror of the abyss that Poe is concerned with. But here also the motif is doubled, for the prisoner is already entombed, even though the fate designed for him is a further entombment in the pit which his dungeon contains. Harassed by the pendulum and the contracting walls of the prison, he contemplates for a moment the possibility of accepting this fate. Poised on the deadly brink of the pit, "I threw my straining vision below. The glare from the enkindled roof illumined its inmost recesses. Yet, for a wild moment, did my spirit refuse to comprehend the meaning of what I saw . . . oh! any horror but this!" [74]

This story combines the motifs of the abyss and entombment in a way precisely like that of "L'Irrémédiable"; and the imprisoned ship of Baudelaire's poem is matched by the ship in another story, "MS. Found in a Bottle." This ship also, before its final plunge, is caught in a "piège de cristal," surrounded by "stupendous ramparts of ice, towering away into the desolate sky, and looking like the walls of the universe." [75] Poe does not conclude this story—nor does he conclude the "Maelstrom" or "The Pit and the Pendulum"—in the manner of Baudelaire by explicitly telling his readers that he has given them emblems of human destiny. But are such *post hoc* instructions necessary? In thus failing to provide a key to his work, Poe actually transcends the method of Baudelaire and approaches that of Mallarmé; and here is one more reason why Poe was so much admired by the Symbolists.[76]

When the different stories are read in which the abyss motif is present, it becomes apparent, despite the lack of overt advertisement, that Poe was doing more than describing the thrill of imaginary dangers. It is significant especially that when Poe sought to define his notion of perverseness he once more resorted to the image of the fall, the plunge into the abyss: "There is no passion in nature so demoniacally impatient, as that of him, who shuddering upon the edge of a precipice, thus meditates a plunge. . . . If there be no friendly arm to check us, or if we fail in a sudden effort to prostrate ourselves backward from the abyss, we plunge and are destroyed." [77] Poe nowhere suggests that original sin, the Primal Fall, is responsible for this instinct to self-destruction. There he stands apart from Kierkegaard and Baudelaire. But nonetheless, if in a wholly secular context, he sees this fall as some kind of abdication, repugnant and yet overmastering, and his mode of conveying the Concept of Dread duplicates remarkably that used by Baudelaire. With that imaginative bond between them, Baudelaire was all the more certain that in what he called the "profundities" of Poe's work there was a spirit that answered to his own.

We could well leave it at that; and yet one must question, finally, whether Poe, on his side, would have recognized the kinship by which Baudelaire was so deeply stirred. If only eight years more had been given him to live, Poe could have read *Les Fleurs du mal;* and in that interval his translator would no doubt have made himself known to him. Would Poe have responded with excitement and sympathy to the work of his French contemporary? Or would he, in puzzled consternation, have drawn back from "this atrocious

book," as Baudelaire called it, and in which he claimed
to have put "all my heart, all my tenderness, all my
religion (in travesty), all my detestation"? [78] It is an
absorbing, if idle, speculation; but all the signs point
to a negative response on the part of Poe. This new
French poet, we can hear him saying, has gone much
too far. Occasionally, as in "La Beauté" and "Harmonie du soir," we find a true poetic elevation, ethereal and pure. But far too often we are revolted by the
presence of intense passion in these poems, and passion can only degrade, not elevate, the soul. We will
grant Baudelaire's gifts as a harmonist, and allow also
that he has truly seen what he has chosen to see. For
who can deny that there are indeed moments when
even

to the sober eye of Reason, the world of our sad humanity
must assume the aspect of Hell; but the Imagination of Man
is no Carathis, to explore with impunity its every cavern.
Alas! the grim legion of sepulchral terrors can*not* be regarded
as altogether fanciful; but . . . they must sleep, or they will
devour us—they must be suffered to slumber, or we perish.[79]

Only dimly aware of how he himself had explored
"the horror of life," Poe would perhaps have been
obscurely troubled by *Les Fleurs du mal;* for many of
Baudelaire's poems confront directly and with no hint
of compromise a reality of evil and pain that in his
own poems Poe sought to leave behind. To be consistent with his carefully contrived system, Poe would
have had to deny Baudelaire's achievement as a poet.

He would also have had to ignore the fact that his
grounds for this denial are the same as those he used
to defend his own achievement in fiction. For Baudelaire, like himself, only with a fuller consciousness of
the enterprise, attempted by his art to exorcise the ter-

rors of the soul. But this is a truth which Poe would
not have allowed himself to admit. And therefore it is
Poe, with this denial on his lips, who above all other
men seems to be the one addressed in Baudelaire's
great line:

—*Hypocrite lecteur,—mon semblable,—mon frère!* [80]

6

POE'S IMAGINARY VOYAGE

IF WE ARE ever to see the work of Poe in a way that
will enable us to make sense of the high reputation
which he seems to enjoy everywhere but in his own
country, it is obvious that our orientation must be
towards Europe, and France especially, rather than
towards America. The considerable homage which the
French have accorded Poe during the last hundred
years, the bases for it, and the reasons behind Baudelaire's resolve to make Poe's name a great name in
France—all this is by now a matter of record, a fact
astonishing and probably unique in literary history,
but a fact that may become a value for us only if we
are led to carry the inquiry one stage further, to a re-
reading of Poe. None of his writings better lends itself
to an inquiry of this kind than his *Narrative of Arthur
Gordon Pym of Nantucket*, a book which has been
very differently received and appreciated in the United
States and in France.

Since its publication in 1838 *Arthur Gordon Pym*
has been generally ignored in this country as one of
the least characteristic and least successful of Poe's
writings, and until W. H. Auden included it in the
Poe anthology he edited for Rinehart, it was not readily available except in editions of the complete works.

And yet not altogether ignored. A reconsideration of this book might well start from a hint furnished by Henry James in the first chapter of *The Golden Bowl:* "He [Prince Amerigo] remembered to have read as a boy a wonderful tale by Allan Poe, his prospective wife's countryman—which was a thing to show, by the way, what imagination Americans *could* have— the story of the shipwrecked Gordon Pym. . . ." [1] Be- cause of its memorably trenchant phrasing, James's early blast at Poe in *French Poets and Novelists* (1878) is usually recalled as the final expression of his opinion on this subject. But here in *The Golden Bowl*, twenty-six years later, we find a rather different note. Are we entitled to guess that in the long interim between these two allusions it was his discovery of the French response to Poe that caused Henry James to adopt a less lofty attitude towards him, and perhaps to read him again more sympathetically? It is significant, in any event, that James singles out the "wonderful tale" of *Arthur Gordon Pym*. For almost from the first this story has been regarded in France as one of Poe's major accomplishments. Scarcely available and seldom read on this side of the Atlantic, it has been made accessible in France through no less than four different translations, constantly reprinted in a variety of editions. [2] And whereas in this country only a few scholars have examined it closely, and then only in order to inventory Poe's debt to his sources, [3] two edi- tions of the Baudelaire translation have appeared in recent years carrying prefatory essays by Jules Ro- mains and Gaston Bachelard. This is a convenient measure of the difference in interest the book has had for America and France. *The Narrative of Arthur Gordon Pym* thus provides us with a specific test case for a determination of what it is that underlies and, it may be, justifies, the warmth of the French response to Poe. We may begin where all inquiries of this sort must begin, with the opinion of Baudelaire.

— I —

IT WAS after the appearance of his translation of *Arthur Gordon Pym*, and apropos of it, that Baudelaire, writing to Sainte-Beuve, made another of his efforts to interest that distinguished critic in the work of his American discovery. The request was strikingly phrased: "You, who so love profundities, why not investigate the profundities of Edgar Poe?" [4]

It is the opinion of Baudelaire's great modern editor, Jacques Crépet, that this question was not put with perfect frankness and should not be interpreted as if it had been. In the 1850's a friendly critical review from the pen of Sainte-Beuve could be the making of a newly published book, and Baudelaire, who was largely dependent for his livelihood on the sale of his Poe translations, of course knew this. He was therefore anxious to bring *Les Aventures d'Arthur Gordon Pym* to the presumably cordial notice of an influential critic because of the commercial success that a favorable nod from Sainte-Beuve would insure. Thus the talk about "profundities" was, Crépet argues, no more than a lure, intended to ensnare Sainte-Beuve into reading and reviewing the book.[5] Similarly, Crépet adduces what he calls the pressure of circumstances to explain away another expression of Baudelaire's high regard for the work he had translated. In July, 1857, in a letter to the *ministre d'Etat*, he called *Arthur Gordon Pym* "an admirable novel." [6] But the first edition of

Les Fleurs du mal had appeared two months before, Crépet observes, and it was known that the public prosecutor was preparing a case against it. Naturally Baudelaire was more than a little uneasy about the impending lawsuit. In this letter to an important state official, to whose protection he believed he had some claim, he therefore adopts a distinctly amiable and ingratiating tone. He praises the official publication of the French government, *Le Moniteur universel;* he praises its director and its chief reviewer; and, while he is at it, he also praises *Arthur Gordon Pym,* which had first come out as a serial in the pages of *Le Moniteur.* Behind this profusion of praise, concludes Crépet, there was expediency and nothing else.

But what of the motive behind this special reading of the evidence on the part of Baudelaire's editor? Crépet grants that his own personal opinion of *Arthur Gordon Pym* is far from high:

An admirable novel! This is hardly faint praise. Is it possible that Baudelaire, whose taste in literature was so reliable, could have whole-heartedly admired this youthful work, one which has in it, to be sure, some of the best pages Poe ever wrote, and which attains at times a beauty and boldness he never surpassed—but which also, padded and uneven, encumbered with clumsy "object lessons" and some features of a hoax, is replete with flaws? [7]

One might ask how, in dealing with a literary career as brief as that enjoyed by Poe, it is possible to draw the line between "youthful work" and the work of his maturity. But what Crépet is saying here essentially is that his own evaluation of the book is unfavorable. He therefore declines to believe that the excellent taste of Baudelaire could have been compromised by a differing estimation of it. When we recall that for

many intelligent American readers the whole phenomenon of Baudelaire's infatuation with Poe's work—
and not merely his apparently high praise of *Arthur
Gordon Pym*—gives rise to grave doubts as to the excellence of the man's literary taste, we can appreciate
how strongly personal is the reservation which Crépet
voices here and which he makes the basis for his argument that Baudelaire's praise was more apparent than
real. The entire situation is worth reviewing.

Baudelaire's first reference to *Arthur Gordon Pym*
seems to have excluded it from the singular kind of
work for which he admired Poe. In 1852, in "Edgar
Poe, sa vie et ses ouvrages," he called it a purely
human book, written in a style extremely simple and
detailed. This was faint praise indeed; and yet, five
years later, Baudelaire referred to the story as "an
admirable novel" and urged Sainte-Beuve to take it up
as the point of entry for an excursion into the "profundities" of Poe. Crépet prefers to believe that the
perfunctory comments of 1852 were more genuine
than the enthusiasm that Baudelaire gave evidence of
in 1857–58; and, as we have seen, he explains this
disparity by emphasizing the force of personal circumstances in the life of Baudelaire during the interven-
ing years. But this argument collapses in the light of
the recent discovery that Baudelaire in his first essay
on Poe relied very heavily on John M. Daniel's article
in the *Southern Literary Messenger* of March, 1850.
In his comments on *Arthur Gordon Pym* and in his
long quotations from it Baudelaire was acting as translator rather than essayist. In all likelihood, he had not
read the book in 1852. But by 1857 he had; had not
only read it but translated it and thus had come to know
it thoroughly. This circumstance is sufficient to ac-

count for the warmth of his two later references to *Arthur Gordon Pym*. There is also the fact that of his five volumes of Poe translations this was the third to appear. If Baudelaire's real opinion of the book was as low as the one Crépet wants him to have held, it does not seem likely that its translation would have been undertaken when there still was available other material by Poe of greater interest and of less bulk. For *Les Aventures d'Arthur Gordon Pym* is the longest of all the translations by about one hundred pages. Before Baudelaire set himself so extensive a task he must have had considerable faith in the merits of the book, and he must have had hope as well that the French reading public would be eager to get it. He was wrong there, for the success of the volume was not instantaneous, as had been the case with the *Histoires extraordinaires* and *Nouvelles histoires extraordinaires*. But in spite of this, Baudelaire never later saw fit to exempt *Arthur Gordon Pym* from the praise, both public and private, which he gave to the entirety of Poe's work.

In matters of this kind there can of course be no infallible verdict. But in addition to the considerations of which we are reminded by Crépet there exist a number of others which are at least equally pertinent and which point to a conclusion opposite to his. It might be said, by the way, that very nearly every remark which Baudelaire made about Poe has the extravagant air of overstatement. Why, then, should a special reading be accorded what he said of *Arthur Gordon Pym?* In any event, whether we interpret his praise at full strength, or, with Crépet, see reason to modify it somewhat, the language which Baudelaire uses is certainly intriguing. What is this "admirable novel"? What is the nature of the "profundities" which Baudelaire asserted could be found in it?

— II —

WHEN *The Narrative of Arthur Gordon Pym* was published in book form in 1838, Poe's name did not appear on the title page. The book purported to be a factual account of real experiences undergone by Pym, and, in some measure, actually written by him. But since Poe had already printed two installments of the story under his own name in the *Southern Literary Messenger,* he was forced to explain in his preface to the 1838 edition how that prior publication had come about. In this preface, and in a concluding note, we find Poe doing what he can to surround the story with the air of veracity which he wanted the book to possess. To some degree he was successful in this effort. A number of reviewers in England and America proved gullible enough to be taken in by the hoax.[8] This hardly seems credible now, for if Pym's narrative is almost plausible in the pages that deal with mutiny, shipwreck, famine, and cannibalism, yet when we reach the final section of the story and read of his strange discoveries in uncharted waters near the South Pole, we find ourselves about as far removed from "real" experience as it is possible to get. And even in the earlier sections some of the episodes involve such a degree of the inhuman that, in a cursory reading at least, this quality alone may make itself recognized. We shall find that this story may indeed be read as a true document, but the "truth" it contains is of a very different kind from that which Poe attempted to fake. But the first stipulation should be that this is the work of a highly gifted writer. For all its complexity, and in spite of a good many very obvious flaws, *Arthur Gordon Pym* is remarkably coherent in its management of structure and theme.

The basic element in the design of the book is the pattern of recurrent revolt. Pym's great impulse to go to sea is opposed by his family. This inclination, he says, brought no direct opposition from his father, but it made his mother hysterical, and it caused his wealthy grandfather to threaten disinheritance. But all these difficulties, writes Pym, in a passage very characteristic of him, "so far from abating my desire, only added fuel to the flame." [9] His first and almost fatal adventure at sea, an experience which he recounts by way of prologue to the narrative proper, involves an incident of revolt. Early one morning, with his friend Augustus Barnard, he embarks in a small boat on the ocean off Nantucket. The two boys are drunk, and their craft, the *Ariel*, far from seaworthy. A violent storm comes up, and, as if to insure their destruction, a whaling vessel suddenly bears down upon them in its course towards Nantucket. The ship turns about, however, and a searching party rescues the two adventurers. But this happens only after the captain's authority has been directly challenged. The captain is opposed to making a search, the first mate bent on it, even at the risk of mutiny. "Seeing himself upheld by the men," the mate "told the captain that he considered him a fit subject for the gallows, and that he would disobey his orders if he were hanged for it the moment he set foot on shore." [10]

It is in consequence of this first episode in Pym's career that the major theme is introduced into the story, the theme of deception. In spite of their nearly disastrous experience, the two boys manage to appear in time for breakfast at the Barnard house the following morning. Their appearance "could not have borne a very rigid scrutiny. Schoolboys, however, can accomplish wonders in the way of deception, and I verily believe not one of our friends in Nantucket had the slightest suspicion that the terrible story told by some sailors in town of their having run down a vessel at sea and drowned some thirty or forty poor devils had reference either to the *Ariel*, my companion, or myself." [11] There is nothing portentous about this, certainly; and yet, subdued as it is, here at the very outset of the story is a hint of the importance that deceit, masks, and treacherous appearances will have all through the career of Gordon Pym. One begins to notice also how Poe integrates the theme of deception with the pattern of revolt. These two great recurrent features of the book come simultaneously into play in Pym's successful effort at stowing away aboard the *Grampus*, a whaler under the command of Captain Barnard. Augustus first writes a letter to Pym's parents, signing it with the name of a relative in New Bedford at whose house Gordon Pym was an occasional guest. The forged letter suggests another visit, and the boy's family, taken in by the ruse, permits him to leave home for an absence that will go unquestioned for several weeks. The plot very nearly fails when the two boys, as they approach the Nantucket docks, are met by Pym's grandfather. Pym is recognized at once, but so well does he impersonate a drunken sailor that the old man is soon convinced he was mistaken. Thus the circumvention of parental authority is implemented by two acts of deceit, the letter forged by Augustus and the impersonation carried off by Pym.

On board the ship the stowaway's berth is a coffin-like iron box secreted in one of the holds. The entry to the hold is located in the cabin of Augustus, through a trapdoor in the floor. Below deck the cargo is so badly disposed, and this also by the plan of Augustus, that Pym finds himself concealed in a kind of labyrinth. There he remains entombed for a period of almost two weeks. He is tormented by famine, nausea, and nightmares, and at one point barely escapes with his life when his dog Tiger, unaccountably appearing in the hold, savagely attacks him. This long and nearly fatal confinement below deck is the result of a mutiny aboard the *Grampus*, developing from "a private pique of the chief mate's against Captain Barnard." [12] So savage an affair is it that apart from the mutineers themselves only Augustus survives. He is saved through the whim of one of the sailors, Dirk Peters; but the Negro cook, one of the instigators of the mutiny, orders him handcuffed and thrown into the steerage. Since Augustus alone is aware of his friend's presence on the vessel, his own imprisonment would seem to make Pym's plight hopeless. But not really so. In the desperate career of Gordon Pym the apparent and the actual rarely coincide. And so it is just because he is a prisoner himself that Augustus soon finds it possible to rescue Pym from the hold.

The intervention of Dirk Peters in the fate of Augustus marks the entrance of the third important character in the story. Peters was involved in the original revolt against Captain Barnard, but soon after the success of this mutiny he becomes a leader of a new dissident faction in the ship's crew. The dispute now concerns the plans that have been made for the use of the *Grampus* by those who have gained control of her. These new *de facto* authorities, the chief mate and the Negro cook, are themselves threatened by this fresh uprising. Peters is deserted by his allies, however. But he finds a recruit in Augustus, and, through him, in Gordon Pym; and the three take on the task of overpowering the superior forces of the mate and the cook. Deception is the essence of the stratagem they devise. Pym hits on the idea of "working upon the superstitious terrors and guilty conscience of the mate," [13] for a few days earlier one of Peters' original henchmen was poisoned by the mate and died in convulsions. Pym is therefore made up to impersonate this dead man, and his impersonation is as successful this time as when he encountered his grandfather on the quay. His sudden ghostly appearance throws the mate's gang into confusion. After a short and bloody skirmish, control of the ship is seized from the mutineers and a new overthrow of authority is accomplished.

With a sailor named Parker, the one man of the mate's party who is not killed in the fight, the three survivors begin their agonizing experience of shipwreck. The *Grampus* is theirs, but it is now no more than a hulk, barely afloat: the outcome of the struggle on board and the violence of the tempest raging without.

Yet even in these pages of sometimes excruciating detail Poe manages to reiterate his basic theme, and to do so in terms that accord perfectly with the action of the story. The famished men make repeated attempts to retrieve some food from the interior of the flooded ship. After one such attempt Pym succeeds in bringing up a bottle of wine, which his companions drink as soon as he goes below again for a further search. He is

at first outraged at their treachery, but when he sees
the harmful effects the wine has on them he realizes
that he was actually benefited by their conduct. Twice
the men are led to believe that their rescue is imminent, but their hopes are groundless each time. On
the first occasion the approaching vessel is discovered
to be literally a ship of death. It sails close enough for
them to see that the passengers and crew, despite the
lifelike posture their bodies retain, have been dead for
weeks. The body of a man at the rail of the ship, a
figure whose smile seemed to encourage the men on
the *Grampus*, becomes for them an image of doom
rather than salvation. As the death ship sails past
they see this corpse for what it is: "The eyes were
gone, and the whole flesh around the mouth, leaving
the teeth utterly naked. This, then, was the smile which
had cheered us on to hope!" [14] The sailor Parker draws
a different inference from this vision. It is his fate
later to urge that the men resort to cannibalism, and
he himself dies as a victim to this proposal. But before
this happens another vessel is sighted, about fifteen
miles distant. Once more the men rejoice too soon.
When they study its course more carefully they discover that the ship has apparently reversed its direction and is sailing away from rather than towards
them. Soon after the murder of Parker, Augustus dies
of the injuries he received during the night of storm,
and only Pym and Dirk Peters remain alive. The
Grampus itself now seems to be their only hope. But
it is by this time an almost total wreck, so weighted
with water below deck and so poorly ballasted by its
disarranged cargo that the ship capsizes. This accident, however, proved to be "a benefit rather than an
injury." [15] Because of a thick growth of barnacles on

the ship's bottom, Pym and his companion find themselves with a month's supply of food; and they also
find that their new position on the overturned hull of
the vessel is less precarious than when the *Grampus*
was upright with her decks awash. When we remark
the repetition of such details as these we begin to see
that *Arthur Gordon Pym*, which is so strongly marked
by conflicts of a very evident sort—between man and
man, and between man and nature—is also charged
by an incessant struggle between reality and appearance. Pym is caught up in a life in which nothing is
stable, in which nothing is ever really known. Power
and authority are repeatedly overthrown; expectation
and surmise can anticipate only false conclusions.

In the final chapters, the most memorable of the
story, Poe handles this central theme with remarkable
power. Eventually Pym and Peters are rescued by the
Jane Guy, a ship engaged in exploring the remote
waters of the southern ocean. Once more Gordon
Pym's will-to-disaster asserts itself : although the ship's
captain soon becomes anxious to return home, Pym
urges him to push farther into the unknown south.
Increasingly bizarre phenomena are noticed when the
ship resumes course. A strange *white* animal is encountered, and through the skill and strength of Peters
it is killed and taken aboard the vessel. At last the
Jane Guy reaches the uncharted island of Tsalal, peo-
pled by a strange black race, and geographically unlike any other land the explorers are familiar with.
"The trees resembled no growth of either the torrid,
the temperate, or the northern frigid zones. . . . The
very rocks were novel in their mass, their color, and their
stratification; and the streams . . . had so little in common with those of other climates, that we were scrupu-

lous of tasting them." [16] In spite of these and other
extraordinary omens, the men from the *Jane Guy* are
moved by nothing more than curiosity. And so the
treacherous natives, apparently motivated by an intense white taboo, find it possible to lure them to
destruction. Acting out the role of ignorant and harm-
less primitives, deferential to the superiority of their
white visitors, they invite the ship's company to visit
the interior of the new land. As the men are proceeding through a narrow pass the natives set off great
landslides. Only Pym and Peters, who have strayed
from the line of march into a transverse canyon, escape
this catastrophe in which, once again, friends turn out
to be foes and inferiors masters. The two men thread
their way through a network of caves and crevasses,
come upon curious hieroglyphic markings which they
attempt to decipher, and after several days in hiding
make a sudden dash for the shore. The *Jane Guy* has
already been attacked and demolished. But the two
men succeed in reaching one of the native canoes, and
in it they set off on the ocean once more, steering always to the south. Pym and Peters disappear at last
into a cataract of whiteness falling on a warm and
milky sea. The narrative thus comes to a sudden halt,
but only after recording an astonishing vision: "And
now we rushed into the embraces of the cataract,
where a chasm threw itself open to receive us. But
there arose in our pathway a shrouded human figure,
very far larger in its proportions than any dweller
among men. And the hue of the skin of the figure was
of the perfect whiteness of the snow." [17]

Far from being an aimless welter of merely cumulative horrors, *The Narrative of Arthur Gordon Pym*
is strictly organized and skillfully developed. Its

architecture takes the form of a set of episodes in each of which a revolt and overthrow occur. Like a schematic image of the sea itself, the narrative line of this oceanic adventure follows a pattern of crest and trough, and at each crest the new conflict that has been preparing is resolved in violence. This compositional virtue accounts, in part at least, for much of the force of the story; but, as is so often the case with Poe, a more persuasive explanation of its power must be sought at a less clearly illuminated level than that of conscious plan.

— III —

WE RECALL that when Baudelaire proposed *Arthur Gordon Pym* to Sainte-Beuve as a means of delving into the profundities of Edgar Poe, he had evidently changed his mind about this book. It was no longer to be conventionally—and mistakenly—characterized as a "purely human" story. The difference in the terms which Baudelaire employs derives, in all likelihood, from the recognition on his part that in addition to being a story of adventure, an exciting *yarn*, it is also a psychological drama, involving many of the deepest fears and yearnings of its author. From this point of view the only full discussions the book has received have been written by Marie Bonaparte and Gaston Bachelard. Although neither writes primarily as a literary critic, it seems to me that their explications of *Arthur Gordon Pym* are indispensable to an understanding of this book.

In *Edgar Poe*, Mme Bonaparte devotes one long chapter to it. The chapter is one of her best, but a proviso must be emphasized: the full force of the thesis she develops regarding the mind of Poe cannot be felt by anyone who has not followed step by step her minute elaboration of it. *Edgar Poe* is unique in this way, among others, that it is much less easy to quarrel with the whole volume than with the individual details that make it up. To take one detail, for instance, from what she says of *Arthur Gordon Pym*: Why did Poe choose Nantucket as Pym's birthplace and the starting point for his lurid career? Not simply because it was an important maritime center, but also because it was located in the north, in the vicinity of Boston, where Poe himself was born. According to Mme Bonaparte, his choice of Nantucket was doubly determined: by the external realities of American geography and commerce, and by an internal psychic reality as well. For the story of Gordon Pym—and indeed all of Poe's work—in her reading is nothing else than a palimpsest of the biography and the psychology of its author.[18] Intent always on working out a point-for-point correspondence between what Poe wrote and the facts and inferences that can be supplied for his life, she strains often, as in this case, for interpretations that seem much too particularized to be probable. Especially when they are cited apart from the context which her entire book provides, a good many of her readings, however brilliantly ingenious, must also seem extravagant and grotesque. But after one has edited away the results of her overly ambitious effort at a microscopically diagrammatic proof of her hypothesis, there remains a great deal that is of indisputable interest and cogency.

A good instance of this is her treatment of the passage in *Arthur Gordon Pym* in which Poe prepares the reader for the most terrible episode of the story, the recourse of the four survivors to cannibalism. While the death ship was sailing past the *Grampus*, the men discovered that there existed only a mockery of life aboard her. On the back of one of the corpses there perched a huge sea-gull,

busily gorging itself with the horrible flesh. . . . As the brig moved further around so as to bring us close in view, the bird, with much apparent difficulty, drew out its crimsoned head, and, after eying us for a moment as if stupefied, arose lazily from the body upon which it had been feasting, and, flying directly above our deck, hovered there a while with a portion of clotted and liver-like substance in its beak. The horrid morsel dropped at length with a sullen splash immediately at the feet of Parker.[19]

Although there is nothing here that calls for a specialized psychological decipherment, Mme Bonaparte is too careful a reader to pass over this episode without discerning its significance in the development of the story. The cannibalism theme is introduced. Parker, the only one of the mate's gang who was not killed in the last insurrection aboard the *Grampus*, is the man who will soon be arguing for this last recourse. Ironically, it is at *his* feet that the bird drops the morsel of human flesh. In doing so it suggests the notion of cannibalism to him and at the same time singles him out for this kind of death. When the four men cast lots it becomes Parker's fate to be sacrificed. And Parker, finally, who had been one of the mate's crew, one of the mate's *sons*, is in this way punished for his earlier treachery.[20] A reading of this sort, which analyzes very expertly the narrative art of Poe, requires no special Freudian acumen but only a sensitive response to the literary text; and this response, which is rare enough among readers of Poe, is in evidence throughout the study of Marie Bonaparte.

It is also true, however, that her study is not intended as literary criticism but as a psychoanalytical interpretation of Poe, and its primary interest resides in that special orientation. In spite of the dangers involved in seeking always for a highly detailed correlation between the main events of *Arthur Gordon Pym*, and the traumatic experiences which the author himself presumably underwent, her approach to the book in oneiric rather than realistic terms is certainly a fruitful one. It enables her to see at once that although Poe relied heavily on source materials of a rather pedestrian kind, this fact is by no means adequate to explain the interest and impact of the story as he tells it. Poe followed much the same procedure in his "Journal of Julius Rodman" and produced something altogether inferior. The disparity results from the circumstance that Poe brought himself and the complexities of his personal emotional life into *Arthur Gordon Pym* but not into the other story.

The claim implicit here, that the hero of many of Poe's stories—and those usually his most memorable —is none other than the author himself, requires no elaborate proof for those readers of Poe who have even a general acquaintance with his biography. One does not expect, however, that *Arthur Gordon Pym*, which appears to be in a vein quite different from the one Poe is famous for, will prove no exception to this rule. No matter how one may judge the specific correspondences between the fiction of Pym's career and the facts of Poe's life as these correspondences are adduced by Mme Bonaparte, it seems certain that her psychoana-

lytic method makes possible a number of valuable insights into this unusual story. What better description
of Poe may be written than the passage in which he
describes the psychology of Gordon Pym:

For the bright side of the painting [Augustus' accounts of his
experiences at sea] I had a limited sympathy. My visions were
of shipwreck and famine; of death or captivity among barbarian hordes; of a lifetime dragged out in sorrow and tears,
upon some gray and desolate rock, in an ocean unapproachable and unknown. Such visions or desires—for they amounted
to desires—are common, I have since been assured, to the
whole numerous race of the melancholy among men—at the
time of which I speak I regarded them only as prophetic
glimpses of a destiny which I felt myself in a measure bound
to fulfill.[21]

Like their author, the heroes of Poe's greatest stories
all belong to the race of the melancholy among men.
The "gloomy, although glowing imagination" [22]
which Pym attributes to himself is their disposition and
that of their creator as well. From this personal in-
volvement of Poe in the lives of his imagined characters proceeds the peculiar intensity and anguish
which his best stories convey. When he writes without
this identification the results are merely tiresome and
banal.

Mme Bonaparte calls particular attention to the
presence in *Arthur Gordon Pym* of the obsessive fear
of premature burial, a phobia which recurs throughout
the stories of Poe. The iron box which served as Pym's
hiding-place in the hold of the *Grampus* very nearly
became for him an actual as well as a symbolic coffin.
When Pym discovered that he could not open the trapdoor into the cabin of Augustus, he was immediately
struck by the similarity between his fate and that of

premature burial: "In vain I attempted to reason on
the probable cause of my being thus entombed. I could
summon up no connected chain of reflection, and . . .
gave way, unresistingly, to the most gloomy imagin-
ings, in which the dreadful deaths of thirst, famine,
suffocation, and premature interment crowded upon
me." [23] The same theme appears in the final section
of the story when Pym and Peters barely escape the
fate of their companions, buried under an avalanche,
and are trapped for days in a series of caves and
abysses in the hostile land of Tsalal. When we recall
how frequently death of this kind is a source of terror
in the tales of Poe, the words of Pym seem to be
charged with a dread felt by the author himself: "I
firmly believe that no incident ever occurring in the
course of human events is more adapted to inspire the
supremeness of mental and bodily distress than a case
like our own, of living inhumation." [24]

Interpreting the central meaning of the book as the
passionate and frenzied search for the Mother, seeing
the various mutinies and reprisals as symbolic revolts
against the Father, Mme Bonaparte reads these two
episodes of burial as dreams of death and rebirth.[25]
Characteristically, she goes so far as to say that Pym,
tortured by hunger and thirst in the hold of an unsea-
worthy vessel, is a "clear" representation of Poe's own
prenatal experience, for he was carried in the womb
of a sickly and improvident mother.[26] One need not
acclaim so precise an identification to agree that in
this instance, as in many others throughout her interpretation, a profoundly oneiric drama is going on
in *The Narrative of Arthur Gordon Pym*. All the cus-
tomary paraphernalia of an adventure story are present in this book: the ocean, ships, shipwreck, mutinies,

and an unknown land. But in addition to this normal
and manifest content there exists an undercurrent of
latent meaning in *Arthur Gordon Pym*, and it is this
meaning which Mme Bonaparte seeks to read in psychoanalytic terms.

Starting from the same distinction between manifest and latent content—a distinction which Poe himself found a valuable one in his own analysis of "The
Raven"—Gaston Bachelard has written an interpretation of the story which attempts to give it a wider
range than the narrowly biographical reading which
Mme Bonaparte provides. For Bachelard, a twofold
drama is staged in the career of Gordon Pym.[27] There
is, on the one hand, the human drama of mutiny, shipwreck, and suffering at sea; and, on the other, the
drama of storm and of the constitutive elements of the
physical world itself. Only a double reading, in which
perception is engaged on the two levels of reality and
dream, can make possible an understanding of this
book in something like its full amplitude. Bachelard
asks, for instance, whether the pages which describe
the experience of Pym in the hold of the ship are
simply recording the impressions of a stowaway who
is wedged in among some badly arranged cargo. It is
his theory that despite the precision of the details at
this point the narrative here belongs not to the real
world but to the world of dreams. This is specifically
a labyrinth dream which Poe is presenting; in the concluding pages of the story the same dream recurs.

During his confinement in the hold, Pym remains
alive by subsisting on the meagre provisions which
Augustus has left for him. But the food becomes stale,
a small quantity of liquor arouses rather than quenches
his thirst, and the foul atmosphere of the hold becomes

almost overpowering. These conditions bring on a series of appalling nightmares:

Every species of calamity and horror befell me. Among other miseries, I was smothered to death between huge pillows, by demons of the most ghastly and ferocious aspect. . . . Immensely tall trunks of trees, gray and leafless, rose up in endless succession as far as the eye could reach. Their roots were concealed in wide-spreading morasses, whose dreary water lay intensely black, still, and altogether terrible beneath. And the strange trees seemed endowed with a human vitality, and, waving to and fro their skeleton arms, were crying to the silent waters for mercy.[28]

In this passage, Bachelard observes, Poe fuses the anxieties of the entombed prisoner with the deliria of his deep and unhealthy slumbers. The images of dream and waking life become inextricably confused. These trees, which appear so astonishingly here in a story of the sea, are trees-of-water, waterspouts. Their roots, plumbing the depths of the sea, seize on nothing, are in perpetual movement. In the imagination of Poe, trees walk and glide. This is typical of the kind of life which is present in the natural, the elemental drama of *Arthur Gordon Pym*, recognition of which requires an initial dream-sympathy on the part of the reader. With the scenes of *social* drama, however, as, for example, the account of the mutiny in Chapters IV to IX, a double reading of the kind recommended by Bachelard proves inefficacious. The characters are engaged in a human conflict only and so do not participate in the hidden life of dreamed horror. They are simplified rather than made more complex by their struggle. "Astonishing reversal!" Bachelard remarks; "it seems that in the vision of Poe social man is *less* complex than man-in-nature. Profundity is a function of solitude; our being is deepened in proportion to a more and more profound communion with nature." [29] Unlike the standard imaginary voyages of literature, in which the ocean exists only to be traversed as quickly as possible so that some utopia may take shape for the political and social edification of the reader, the imaginary voyage of Gordon Pym has no definite goal in terms of conscious human life. The adventure which Poe describes is an adventure in solitude. Poe hears the call of the ocean "because this call comes from the most dramatic of solitudes, one in which man has for his antagonist the elemental world itself. There man is alone . . . faced with a universe of monstrous forces." [30]

It is in the final act of the story that Pym, who has from the first been intent on his own disaster, "un naufragé avant le naufrage," as Bachelard so well describes him, contends against both human and material evil. The land of the south exists under the totemic sign of the strange animal which the explorers encounter. With its white coat and its strange red claws and teeth, with its head resembling that of a cat, and yet its ears those of a dog, it makes a curious fusion of fidelity and perfidy. And this same combination of qualities, a synthesis of the familiar and the unknown, exists in the geography of the land itself. The water of its streams has the texture of gum-arabic, with colored and cohesive veins a knife-blade can separate; the rocks are "foreign in their mass, color and stratification"; and the soil is black and soapy in quality. Here in this deceitful organic world the treacherous inhabitants spring their ambush. But this time, Bachelard observes, typically human weapons of the sort that were employed in the struggles aboard the *Grampus* are not brought into play. With his great imagination of disaster, Poe integrates the evil of men and the evil inherent in the nature of the material universe. The perfidious natives make use of the very elements as instruments of destruction, and the men from the *Jane Guy* are killed under landslides of the mountainous earth.

"To be resurrected after such a catastrophe—is this not to take on the stature of certain mythic heroes?" [31] Bachelard follows Pym and his companion in their exploration of the labyrinth in which they find themselves, and in which strange hieroglyphic inscriptions await their decipherment. Thus in a work which remains surprisingly faithful to the simple laws of an adventure story Poe introduces his recurrent concern with premature burial and cryptanalysis. No more convincing proof could be found that *Arthur Gordon Pym* derives from the deepest psychological center of Edgar Poe. "Its final pages," Bachelard concludes,

retain their secret. We would like to re-read, to re-see. It is characteristic of dreams that they would always be entered upon anew. In reading this book we thought we would find distraction, and we learned that the poet sows the seed of dreams that may never be exhausted. We thought also that we were going to see the world. And yet it is the heart of man, that heart tormented and obscure, which lies at the center of it all. *The Narrative of Arthur Gordon Pym* is one of the great books of the human heart.[32]

— IV —

THE psychological drama which is examined in the analyses of Mme Bonaparte and Gaston Bachelard rests on a simple although not immediately obvious equation: Arthur Gordon Pym is Edgar Allan Poe.

It is for this reason, and not simply because this is the sole example of Poe's fiction which approximates the length of a novel, that so much of the thematic material encountered elsewhere in his work is to be found in this one story. To recognize its dream levels, to accept as relevant all or some of the specifications which the readings of Bonaparte and Bachelard offer us, this is, I think, to become aware of the most important feature of *Arthur Gordon Pym;* and to take this step is to recognize at the same time that the book is by no means discontinuous with Poe's more celebrated stories. Specifically, it possesses the additional interest of furnishing the reader of Poe with a surprisingly complete account of his principal themes. Many of his best stories are latent in this one. Hence its title to consideration as the one central and focusing story in the entirety of Poe's work.

We have seen how the experience of premature burial is one of the great physical and emotional trials which Gordon Pym has to undergo. The same kind of experience is repeatedly, indeed compulsively, treated by Poe in "Berenice," "The Fall of the House of Usher," "The Pit and the Pendulum," "The Cask of Amontillado." Nor is this the only link between *Arthur Gordon Pym* and others of Poe's tales. It is only the most evident, the least in need of elaboration.

Perverseness, however, as it is defined in "The Imp of the Perverse" and dramatized in "The Black Cat," is another and less obvious link. When Pym, following the lead of Peters, is descending the face of a cliff during their escape from their last imprisonment, he is overcome by "a *longing to fall;* a desire, a yearning, a passion utterly uncontrollable." [33] This is precisely one of those attacks of perverseness which Poe was later to call "an innate and primitive principle of human action," through which we act "for the reason that we should *not*." [34] How strongly operative this principle was in the character of Gordon Pym may be judged from one of his actions during his entombment in the hold of the ship. Upon discovering that the only food he had left consisted of no more than a gill of liqueur, he found himself "actuated by one of those fits of perverseness which might be supposed to influence a spoiled child in similar circumstances, and, raising the bottle to my lips, I drained it to the last drop, and dashed it furiously upon the floor." [35] It is a revealing coincidence, explicable only in terms of the psychological dynamics of the story, that these two fits of perverseness are both associated with the plight of premature burial. More generally, they may be accounted for in terms of the intense death-wish which is the defining characteristic in the personality of Pym. His flight from home, his desire for shipwreck and famine, in a word his conduct as a whole is nothing else than an illustration on the plane of the life-pattern itself of the instinct which Poe called perverseness.

If these details anticipate such stories as "The Imp of the Perverse," "The Black Cat," and "The Tell-Tale Heart," the book as a whole recalls one of Poe's earliest creations, "MS. Found in a Bottle." In that story the narrator is rescued from shipwreck by being catapulted aboard an enormous vessel manned by a strange and ancient crew. Like the *Jane Guy*, this vessel is navigating in waters near the South Pole; and all the author can learn of its mission is that "we are hurrying onwards to some exciting knowledge—some never-to-be-imparted secret, whose attainment is destruction." [36] Like Gordon Pym, he feels no desire to turn away from the knowledge or the destruction. We recall a great expression of the same motif in another literature, Baudelaire's concluding lines in "Le Voyage":

Plonger au fond du gouffre, Enfer ou Ciel, qu'importe?
Au fond de l'Inconnu pour trouver du *nouveau!*

But this urge, this longing, is also recurrent in Poe's stories. We find in "Eleonora," for instance, a precise metaphor for the dream-experience: it is a kind of voyage, carrying the explorer to "the verge of the great secret." These dream-explorers—and Gordon Pym is surely one of them—"penetrate, however rudderless or compassless, into the vast ocean of the 'light ineffable' and again, like the adventurers of the Nubian geographer, '*agressi sunt mare tenebrarum, quid in eo esset exploraturi*.'" [37] How many of Poe's tales, whatever their overt appearance, seem like nothing so much as manuscripts found in a bottle!

It is of some consequence, by the way, that so evident a similarity exists between *Arthur Gordon Pym* and this story, written four years earlier. Because in its writing he drew on a variety of sources, and because his weakness for "mystification" is as visible in it as in such uninteresting ventures as "The Balloon Hoax" and "Hans Phaall," it is usually assumed that *Arthur Gordon Pym* may be ignored along with those two stories as among the least successful productions of Poe's genius. Neither reason will do. The power of the book was not furnished—it was if anything diminished—by the sources to which Poe helped himself; and the circumstantiality of his procedure in the interests of "mystification," although boring enough in

"Hans Phaall," is as much responsible for the impact of *Arthur Gordon Pym* as it is in the appalling "Facts in the Case of M. Valdemar." To read the longest of Poe's sea stories in the light of the shortest one he wrote, "MS. Found in a Bottle," is to become aware that in both cases a similar emotional and imaginative dynamism is at work.

There is one additional feature of *Arthur Gordon Pym* which relates it in a most important way to many of Poe's other tales. This is the theme of the *Doppelgänger*.

Just as a wave-pattern is formed by the narrative line of the story, as it moves from conflict to conflict, so also a pattern of rise and fall governs the experiences of the chief characters. Pym himself, we discover, dominates the story much less than do his two successive friends. In the beginning, it was Augustus who gave Pym his longing for adventures at sea, who also gave him his first taste of its perils, and who, devising the plan through which the boy's family was deceived, arranged for his concealment in the hold of the *Grampus*. And it was Augustus who rescued him from that nearly fatal imprisonment. After this point, however, the importance of Augustus declines sharply. In the fight against the mutineers he is mortally hurt, and his subsequent death is in keeping with his diminished status as an active force in the story. Meantime a new hero has come upon the scene: Dirk Peters. It is he who begins to dominate the action from the moment the actual struggle for control of the ship is engaged. Peters rescues Pym from drowning when their waterlogged vessel overturns; it is he who kills a strange polar animal in the southern seas; and it is he, and not Pym, who correctly surmises the meaning of the hieroglyphic writing which they find on the walls of the abyss in which they are later trapped. And it is Peters, finally—like Augustus earlier—who saves Pym's life when they make their escape from this symbolic grave. Gordon Pym, throughout all this, is the character to whom things happen. His comrades act; he is acted upon. Only twice in the story, when he proposes the plan whereby the mutineers will be terrorized by his masquerade as a dead man, and when he persuades the captain of the *Jane Guy* to sail farther into the mysterious south, do Pym's actions have a causative function; and even in these two episodes, important as they are, no special emphasis is given to this quality. For the most part, Pym is simply the narrator, the victim, the masochist—and so the more clearly recognizable as Poe himself. The men of action who govern events and save lives by their strength, and whose luck or cunning enables them to solve cryptic writing, these are Augustus and Dirk Peters. In succession they act out the really heroic roles in *Arthur Gordon Pym*, and the nominal hero is related to them only as an important eye-witness who had some share in their achievements.

This unusual bifurcation of the hero, between Pym and Augustus at first, and later between Pym and Peters, is one more indication that *Arthur Gordon Pym*, far from being a perfunctory exercise in imitation of some actual and fictitious accounts of disasters at sea, derives its vitality from the deepest levels of Poe's mind. As we shall see in some detail in the next chapter, the phenomenon of the *Doppelgänger* is perhaps the most characteristic and persistent of Poe's obsessive fantasies. "William Wilson," of course, is the most obvious of his dramatizations of this theme.

But variations on it occur elsewhere, in "The Fall of
the House of Usher," "The Tell-Tale Heart," in
"Ligeia," "Morella," and "A Tale of the Ragged
Mountains," three tales in which metempsychosis is
the motif, and also in one of his most oblique and effective stories, "The Man of the Crowd." But the
Doppelgänger theme is an important one also in the
stories of the detective Dupin, and in "The Gold Bug."
These stories, far apart as they seem to be from *Arthur
Gordon Pym*, are nonetheless related to and illuminated by it.

In these stories we find the narrator cast in the subsidiary role of adjunct and adviser to the heroes Dupin
and Legrand, who in no respect more forcibly resemble
each other than in their common resemblance to Poe
himself. It seems that in all his stories of exploration
and discovery, in which an enigma is to be resolved—
and *Arthur Gordon Pym* may easily be read as a story
of this kind—the same mode of construction is employed. The psychological structure responsible for
this fact may best be explained by Poe's dim awareness of his own divided personality: the gloomy and
glowing quality of his imagination, at one extreme,
and the ratiocinative, analytic power of his puzzle-
solving intelligence, at the other. But can there be any
question that the first of these is the basic and defining
one in Poe's endowment? He could write out of that
layer of his mind directly, employing the first person,
as he does in "Berenice," "Ligeia," and "Morella."
But when intellectual analysis was the dominant interest, or when, as in *Arthur Gordon Pym*, the story
in its most obvious intention concerned a voyage of
discovery in the natural world, Poe evidently felt less
at ease. In these instances he resorted to the device of

the narrator-observer, partaking in the action but failing to dominate it.

It is quite true, of course, that our interest is far more deeply engaged by Pym than it is by the rather colorless friends and accessories of Dupin and Legrand. The role of these narrators is too subservient, too narrowly limited to a simple expository function, to distract our attention from the real heroes. But this is not our experience in reading *Arthur Gordon Pym*. Here the narrator as an actor in the story remains constantly in view. He does so in part because of the mixed character of this book, one of the things about it that contributes to its special interest. Poe has here successfully managed the presentation of a true double-hero. The *Doppelgänger* motif is a major factor in the formal construction of the story. On the one side, there is the relatively passive and ineffective character of Pym; on the other, there are the two energetic and dominating figures of Augustus and Dirk Peters. But these two do not, however, override Pym in importance or dwarf him in any way. Poe prevented this domination from taking place by dividing the specifically active role between two characters. Neither Augustus nor Peters is on the scene long enough to polarize our attention, whereas Pym is always present as the most persistent, if not the most visibly dynamic, agent in the story. There is also a deeper reason. To some extent, *Arthur Gordon Pym* belongs with the classic detective tales of Poe: it is a narrative of exploration; things are to be found out and clarified; a cryptogram awaits solution. In this variety of Poe's fiction the movement is characteristically from darkness to light, upward, from mystery to clarity. And although the sequence of events takes place on a stormy sea and involves brutality and myriad dangers, yet, for all this, the story through most of its length conveys the impression of being an authentic narrative of adventures in a real world. Some of its first readers responded to it in just that way. But from another angle, that suggested by Bonaparte and Bachelard, the story may be read very differently. Behind the straightforward and at times gruesomely realistic prose, and in spite of the recurrence of chapters containing the most arid factual data, there is a potent dream symbolism at work and a power of morbid fantasy that relate this story to those sombre tales of Poe in which the movement is the reverse of the other, going downward this time, from twilight into mystery and darkness. We then realize that in Gordon Pym we have met another of Poe's obsessed and suffering heroes. The connection that can be made between Augustus or Peters, on the one hand, and Dupin or Legrand, on the other, should therefore be balanced by the recognition that Pym is in the same degree a cousin to Roderick Usher. And so we follow his fortunes with the same kind of interest as that which detains us in the house of Usher. In the writing of *Arthur Gordon Pym* Poe effected a remarkable balance between his two major kinds of fiction.

— v —

THUS of all the work of Poe, *Arthur Gordon Pym* is the crucial text because it provides on a large scale an exercise in understanding Poe's characteristic methods. Through a study of this book one learns how Poe should be read. We have seen how many of his recurrent themes are given actual or latent expression in this one long story; and here also we find reflected the two major aspects of Poe's mind, the one obscure in the dark torment of nightmare, the other lucid and enquiring, and eager to explain (all too expansively at times) real and concrete matters of a thoroughly prosaic kind.

A better understanding of this book might eliminate the principal mistake that is made in dealing with the work of Poe, a mistake that results from too heavy a stress on only one side of his talent, and the less important side at that. This emphasis shows up most clearly in the conventional academic question: To what extent does Poe in his stories exemplify the aesthetic principles which he endorses in his criticism? But in such a relevant example as his review of Hawthorne, Poe speaks only as the *raisonneur*, the solver of puzzles, with only the mechanical and intellectual level of his mind engaged. Certainly it is not by virtue of his capacities along *these* lines that Poe is Poe. It is rather the other component of his mind—at the opposite pole from the analytic—which gave him a power the extent of which he scarcely knew himself, to bring up to the surface of consciousness the kind of submerged emotional life that the intelligence prefers to ignore. It is this element in the work of Poe that Baudelaire pointed to when he spoke of Poe's profundities, and it is this element that the critiques of Marie Bonaparte and Gaston Bachelard explore. It is this same element that has been deeply felt, in however mute a way, by successive generations of readers.

For if *Arthur Gordon Pym* is examined from the intellectualistic point of view that Poe himself, in his criticism, aggressively espoused, it must be set down as a failure. If Pym's voyage is not interpreted as a voyage of the mind, then it must appear as just one more sequence of adventures at sea, suitable for the adolescent readers of Stevenson and Verne but hardly worth the attention of anyone else. Mistakes in the story are numerous. At the outset Augustus and Pym are boys in their teens; suddenly they become mature men. The dog Tiger appears from nowhere, and disappears by the same route. At one point Poe lets Pym speak in a way that leads the reader to believe that Augustus too will come through the long ordeal alive. He is dead midway through the story. The several chapters in which, to the fatigue of the reader, Poe goes into detail on such subjects as the best methods of stowing cargo, the nature of the nautical maneuvre known as "lying-to," and the circumstances demanding its use, and in which he expatiates on the flora and fauna encountered by the explorers—all this may be taken as good reason for believing that Poe was simply padding out his narrative. It may also be said that *Arthur Gordon Pym*, when judged by the conventional standards of "realistic" fiction, is simply unfinished, that Poe's ideas for the book were so meagerly developed that he had no goal in mind. Accordingly, after having lured the reader along by many dark promises to the verge of the great mystery, Poe is suddenly brought up short by the realization that he has no mystery to reveal, or nothing in keeping with the clues that led up to it. And so he terminates the story abruptly, and, to smooth matters over, adds a concluding note in which the break in the story is blamed on the untimely death of Pym.

The alternative to accepting these criticisms of *Arthur Gordon Pym* involves no defense of the book as a "well-made novel." All of Poe's work is marred by blunders of a kind which even a modest sophistication will perceive. The limitations that such blunders expose, however, are the limitations that beset Poe as a *conscious* writer, scrupulous about detail and "total effect." It was in this very area that he was poorly equipped, and his demonstrative displays of the talents of an analytic mind serve less as proof that he really possessed them than as evidence of his lack of assurance.

In the main and over all, *Arthur Gordon Pym* is a story with shape and direction, but it is not the work of a meticulous craftsman. Poe's narrative technique is uneven in quality. Relatively simple problems in narration he could not solve, perhaps did not even see. Yet the major problem is handled with ease. With no apparent discontinuity Pym's voyage begins at Nantucket and ends in nirvana. We move along with him from the most pedestrian of beginnings to the most strangely memorable of endings. "My name is Arthur Gordon Pym." This is our starting point, in substance and tone dry and factual. How altogether different are are the final, cadenced lines of Pym's narrative: "But there arose in our pathway a shrouded human figure, very far larger in its proportions than any dweller among men. And the hue of the skin of the figure was of the perfect whiteness of the snow." Between these two passages Poe moves from the bare level of fact and routine human life to the level of dream and its haunting illusions. This is Poe's characteristic movement and direction. How is it managed in this story? Poe evidently understood that the illusion of dream-life, if it is to be captured in narrative at all, must not be presented directly, as something seized and given to the reader. Instead, he starts with the banalities of real life, insists on them, and later weights his story with a heavy load of informative factual material. But it is exactly because of this non-narrative ballast that the concluding chapters succeed in thrusting beyond any experiences that might be recognized as real. For once the ballast has been cut loose, the story acquires an impetus which carries it with extraordinary force into a realm that has no relevance to any data which the conscious intelligence can understand. This is the justification, and a sufficient one, for the strategy Poe used, although it should also be said that his particular mode of employing it was something short of consummate. He let this part of his work, the part that is most firmly anchored in the actual, get out of hand. And in this fact there lies an important lesson about Poe. What should have been easiest for him to manipulate and control, what would have involved only minor problems for a more conventional writer, is precisely the kind of thing that causes him the most difficulty!

One further justification may be suggested for the presence in this story of so much attention to the details of navigation and to digressive summaries of things seen. In a work in which the dominant preoccupation is with deceit, with the masking and unmasking of the real world and the treacherous play of appearances, is it not appropriate that a heavy emphasis should be laid on the circumstantial? Granted that Poe exceeded the limits proper to this kind of thing, his instinct had grasped the artistic necessities that were involved in this story. For *Arthur Gordon Pym*, which on the surface is an episodic tale of improbabilities, is fundamentally, at the submerged level of intuition, a truly *imaginary* voyage. All the factual apparatus which Poe made use of is there in the book to deceive the reader who will be taken in by it. Thus the motif

of deception exists not merely as a theme which may
be abstracted from the story but is integrally present
as well in its construction and subject matter.

A dangerous device, and it is Poe's rather crude use
of it that, for many readers, will seem to render it inefficacious. The heavy burden of concrete detail may
prove too much to allow any imaginative response to
get under weigh. It may act as a lodestone, pulling
back into the real world whatever imaginary and emotional impulses are on the point of being freed. If this
technique is found unsuccessful, it is so not because of
any inherent deficiency but because of Poe's awkward
use of it. The dangers of compounding fact and fiction
are not entirely avoided by him, and this was one great
lesson which Melville may have learned from *Arthur
Gordon Pym*. For in *Moby-Dick* we find at least an
equal amount of digressive encyclopedic information
in the chapters on whales and whaling. Melville, however, perhaps profiting by Poe's mistakes, was able to
float this factual apparatus in his book with greater
success than that attained in *Arthur Gordon Pym*.

— VI —

PERHAPS Melville learned this lesson in literary construction from Poe's story, and, again perhaps, he may
have learned other things from it as well. The doubt
must be underlined, for there exists no direct and explicit evidence that he was acquainted with *Arthur
Gordon Pym*. But if direct evidence—and the lack of
it—are to be considered conclusive one way or another
in matters of this kind, then literary history would be
forced to register the improbable verdict that Melville
never read a line of Poe before 1861.[38] Nowhere in

his books or published letters does Melville allude to his American predecessor. So studied a silence on the part of a man who was profoundly interested in a national American literature, and who could have found in Poe's long story a work singularly germane to his own deepest concerns, has a kind of ambiguity that invites some speculative inquiry. Such silence may be interpreted as an indication of knowledge rather than ignorance—knowledge of a sort which Melville sought systematically to conceal. He was ready enough to cite the names of those books and authors who provided him with the factual and encyclopedic information which he could put to imaginative use. Thus we hear, and from Melville himself, of such a work as Owen Chase's *Narrative of the Most Extraordinary and Distressing Shipwreck of the Whale-Ship Essex, of Nantucket;* [39] whereas of *The Narrative of Arthur Gordon Pym of Nantucket* we hear nothing. But should we expect to? For a consciously professional author like Melville the veracious accounts of actual experience which Chase and men like him drew up were fair game—"loose fish," as Melville would have called them. The imaginative work of another creative writer is, however, something else. Inspiration drawn from this quarter is less freely advertised, and for obvious reasons. What would be our astonishment if, in a gloss on such a chapter as "The Quarter Deck" in *Moby-Dick,* Melville had invited attention to the Shakespearean parallel which he evidently had in mind! The kind of *literate* reading through which one work is illuminated by another, is the kind of reading we must do ourselves. It so happens that there exists copious proof that Melville was well acquainted with Shakespeare's plays. But the relevance of Shakespeare to

Melville would be just as much of a certainty if this confirmatory evidence were not available. By the same token: although there is no external proof that Melville was familiar with Poe's work, to take up *Moby-Dick* after a reading of *Arthur Gordon Pym* is to be struck by the similarities between these two books. Coincidences these similarities may be. But with Poe's reputation in nearly full eclipse in this country it is time a word was said about the kinship between his imagination and that of Melville.

To begin with, there are the opening sentences: "My name is Arthur Gordon Pym," and "Call me Ishmael." That the two principal characters should introduce themselves in this way, and, on the same level, that they should both embark from Nantucket—these are trifles which may properly be disposed of as merely fortuitous resemblances. And the important difference in tone between these two sentences stamps Melville's as one of the great gambits in literature. Or one might think of bringing together the scenes in which characters in both stories ponder hidden meanings: Pym and Peters confronting hieroglyphs on the walls of the caves of Tsalal; the crew of the *Pequod* attempting to decipher the significance of the gold doubloon which Ahab had nailed to the mainmast. But this also is a trifle, and if the only collocations that could be made were on as distinctly minor a plane as this, then the work of establishing a meaningful relationship between Melville's sea story and Poe's would prove eminently futile. However, it is precisely because the two books bear much more than a superficial resemblance to each other that such trifling details take on more significance than they could otherwise be thought to have. Why, for example, did Gordon Pym reject the future of comfortable security which mere compliance with his family's wishes would have guaranteed for him, choosing instead the career of nomad on the seas? Not through any dilettante desire for "travel" and romantic adventure. His visions were of "shipwreck and famine: of death or captivity among barbarian hordes . . . in an ocean unapproachable and unknown." The motives which drove Ishmael to sea derived from similar visions:

Chief among these motives was the overwhelming idea of the great whale himself. Such a portentous and mysterious monster roused all my curiosity. Then the wild and distant seas where he rolled his island bulk, the undeliverable, nameless perils of the whale; these, with all the attending marvels of a thousand Patagonian sights and sounds, helped to sway me to my wish. With other men, perhaps, such things would not have been inducements; but as for me, I am tormented with an everlasting itch for things remote. I love to sail forbidden seas, and land on barbarous coasts.[40]

Acting under the compulsion of such urgencies as these, Pym and Ishmael abandon the circumscribed stability of the land and human society for the mystery and perils of the unknown sea. In their very motives is foreshadowed the experience of disaster to which they both have dedicated their lives.

Both Poe and Melville compound this initial sense of foreboding by adding to the self-revelations of Pym and Ishmael the scenes of action which serve as prologue and prophecy for the tragic climaxes that must ensue. Gordon Pym and his friend Augustus miraculously escape death when their small boat is run down by a whaling vessel during a night of storm. Ishmael visits a whalemen's chapel in New Bedford and studies the memorial tablets of men who had perished at sea;

his steps are followed by a stranger who forecasts the doom awaiting the *Pequod;* and he learns of an ominous accident which befalls Captain Ahab shortly before the ship departs. But all these presages of evil deter him no more than did the nearly fatal experience of Gordon Pym, who "never experienced a more ardent longing for the wild adventures incident to the life of a navigator than within a week after our miraculous deliverance." [41] Before we are very far along in either story we realize that the ships these men are to sail on will never return to port.

This sound of doom, dominating the overtures of the two narratives, will reverberate again. The vessel on which the survivors of the *Grampus* set their hopes of rescue proved to be, as it passed them by, literally a ship of death and an omen of the fate that was in store for them. In *Moby-Dick* the various ships encountered by the *Pequod* have, most of them, only tales of disaster to tell. Yet Ahab refuses to be moved from his purpose, although "all his successive meetings with various ships contrastingly concurred to show the demoniac indifference with which the White Whale tore his hunters." [42] In the same chapter in which Melville describes Ahab's indifference to this evident lesson, he adds a detail which readers of *Arthur Gordon Pym* will hardly fail to recognize. When Ahab goes aloft to act as lookout for the whale, a sea hawk swoops down on him and seizes his hat. The bird "flew on and on with it . . . and at last disappeared; while from the point of that disappearance, a minute black spot was dimly discerned, falling from that vast height into the sea." [43] In Poe's story a carnivorous sea-gull carries a morsel of human flesh over the deck of the *Grampus* and drops it at the feet of Parker, the man who will urge recourse to cannibalism and who becomes soon after the victim of this proposal. The *auspices* are clearly legible in those two episodes; but the prognostic birds of Poe and Melville foretell events through symbolic action.

Gordon Pym and Ishmael are the witnesses and recorders of these events. The great decisions in the stories they tell are not theirs to make, and they both endure, rather than initiate and control, the great actions which their narratives describe. They are the narrators rather than the heroes of these two oceanic dramas: just as Ishmael is dominated by Captain Ahab, so Gordon Pym's role is subordinate to that of his successive companions, Augustus and Dirk Peters. In Queequeg, the pagan harpooner, Ishmael also has his companion. To this redeemed cannibal, frightful as he is with his "dark, purplish, yellow" skin and the black tattooing on his bald, purplish head, the fate of Ishmael is as closely linked as that of Gordon Pym to the bald and deformed half-breed Peters, "one of the most ferocious-looking men I ever beheld." In making their escape from the hills and caverns of Tsalal, Pym and Peters descend the face of a cliff, Peters going first, sustained by a makeshift rope which Pym holds secure at the brink. In "The Monkey Rope" chapter of *Moby-Dick*, in which we find Ishmael similarly tied to Queequeg as the latter is engaged in the dangerous work of "cutting-in" on the whale, Melville characteristically gives expression to the symbolical values that are implicit in this episode. Queequeg appears to Ishmael then as his own "inseparable twin brother," to whom he is united by "an elongated Siamese ligature." [44] And just as Peters is instrumental in rescuing Pym from the caverns of Tsalal, so in

Moby-Dick the coffin which Queequeg has constructed for himself becomes the life-buoy which saves Ishmael in the final disaster. Thus through a corresponding pattern of narrator-and-comrade both Poe and Melville dramatize this theme of death and rebirth.

The pattern of revolt and overthrow, which acts as the articulating principle in *Arthur Gordon Pym* is not present in the same way in *Moby-Dick*.[45] The crew of the *Pequod* is too much under the sway of Ahab to undertake mutiny against him. They can only *hear* of a revolt against a captain's authority, as when they learn the story of what happened on the *Town-Ho*. Ahab himself is so completely the rebel that all the possibilities for action of this kind are exhausted in his character alone, and Ishmael is never more fully assimilated into the crew of the ship than when moved by the feeling that Ahab's quarrel is his own.

Not least among the complexities which make up Ahab's rebellious purpose is his determination to break through the "pasteboard masks" of appearances into knowledge and mastery of the real. It is he who discerns the appropriateness of using Queequeg's coffin as the ship's life buoy and who discovers what depths of wisdom are concealed beneath the insanity of the cabin boy Pip. He is dominated by the conviction that things are not what they seem, that the whale, especially, is not the blind, dumb brute Starbuck calls him but the conscious agency of some inscrutable force that must be challenged and unmasked. In his struggle against the deceits and limits of the human condition Ahab is certainly a far more heroic character than any in *Arthur Gordon Pym*. But the difference between Melville's story and Poe's is, in this respect, a difference only of degree. When Melville describes the Pacific as calm-seeming, but teeming in its depths with sharks and whales, and providing the stage for violent storms; when he writes,

Warmest climes but nurse the cruellest fangs; the tiger of Nepal crouches in spiced groves of ceaseless verdure. Skies the most effulgent but basket the deadliest thunders,[46]

he is adopting as his own the principle which governs all the conduct of Ahab. And he is also stating in these words the meaning of the theme which lies implicit at the heart of *Arthur Gordon Pym*.

Because Melville so very often brings up to the level of direct statement the kind of thing that Poe leaves latent and inferential, one is able to speak of the "meanings" of *Moby-Dick* with greater sureness than is possible with *Arthur Gordon Pym*. Set side by side in this way, the two books provide an instructive lesson in the difference between the use of direct and indirect symbols. Although we recognize the two as stories of quests, we are never in doubt as to the goal of the quest in *Moby-Dick*; whereas, in Poe's story, for all its headlong movement and action, the goal is never defined. We are simply confronted at the end with the enigma of Pym's final vision. Again, in both books, we realize that the water on which Pym and Ishmael sail is more then merely ocean. Melville takes care to clarify its symbolic values: for him it is associated with meditation; it suggests the unconscious life, where evil is to be met. Poe is not so explicit. But though he never directs our attention to the dream level of Pym's adventure, it needs no great acumen to see that the water in this story is the element of chaos and disaster. It alone can serve as the proper stage for the drama that will grow from the intense death wish of Gordon Pym.

In one respect above all this difference between the technique of Poe and Melville is plainly visible, but it is so, once more, because of the remarkable similarity which exists in the material they start from. Both are fascinated with *whiteness*. In his imaginative anticipations of the experience that awaits him on his whaling voyage, Ishmael conjures up "endless processions of the whale, and, midmost of them all, one grand hooded phantom, like a snow hill in the air." [47] The White Whale is already afloat in his vision. But what in this passage will arrest the reader of Poe is its curious echo of the final lines in the account of Gordon Pym: ". . . a shrouded human figure, very far larger in its proportions than any dweller among men. And the hue of the skin of the figure was of the perfect whiteness of the snow." Throughout the last vertiginous chapters of his story Poe multiplies the details which culminate in this cryptic apparition: thin vapors seen on the southern horizon, strange white animals, the white taboos of the black natives, the precipitation of whiteness from the sky, and the pallid waters of the far Antarctic. But at no point does Poe stop to read these signs. They retain the clouded complexity of dream images, composite of dread and longing. Melville, however, is not content to deal with this motif in so mute a way. Not only does he dramatize his meaning objectively—as in the scene in which Starbuck's crew retreats from the horror of a giant white squid; he also meditates in an entire chapter on the meaning of the whiteness of the whale. It was this aspect of Moby-Dick that above all else fascinated and appalled Ishmael, and to search out the reasons for this "vague and nameless horror . . . mystical and ineffable," Melville devotes some of the supreme pages in his book. Collecting instances of whiteness from the most diverse sources, he attempts to fathom the radical ambiguity of this phenomenon. "But in a matter like this," he adds, "subtlety appeals to subtlety, and without imagination no man can follow another into these halls." [48] After pondering the final pages of *Arthur Gordon Pym*, one finds it virtually impossible to read "The Whiteness of the Whale" and not feel persuaded, however total the lack of external evidence, that in his exploration of these halls Melville was following the lead of Edgar Poe.

Lacking such evidence, it would be a tedious business to insist shrilly on Melville's "debt" to Poe. This much is clear: if Melville did not long and seriously ponder the essential drift of *Arthur Gordon Pym* then the similarities that exist between that book and *Moby-Dick* must be accounted one of the most extraordinary accidents in literature.

If it is not to be quite beside the point, however, any talk of debt or influence at this juncture demands the important qualification that the bearing of Poe on Melville is as hypothetical as that of Poe on Arthur Rimbaud. The two cases are curiously alike. More than one commentator on the poetry of Rimbaud has found it legitimate to speak of the influence of Poe's sea story on "Bateau ivre." [49] They do so although there is no certain knowledge that Rimbaud read *Arthur Gordon Pym*, nor is there any immediately convincing evidence in the poem itself that he had this story consciously in mind. But none of them would go so far as to claim that he wrote it with Poe's text open on the table before him. The influence they speak of is not evidenced by the kind of artful plagiarism which a literary sleuth can document and cross-reference.

What is carried over is not a set of particular details but the living thing, the essence and flavor of the whole story. It is *assimilated*, and this, surely, is the kind of influence that really counts. So, if the impact of this book was felt by a schoolboy of genius in an inland town in France, is there not as much and more reason for believing that the young Melville was responsive to it? In any event, it is not the least important quality of *Arthur Gordon Pym* that its contextual site is with the two masterpieces of Melville and Rimbaud. And with that latter name this discussion wheels back full circle to its initial assumption and fundamental point: an examination of the French response to Poe necessarily implies a reappraisal of his work and of his place in American literature.

7

"THAT SPECTRE IN MY PATH"

I N DESCRIBING what he calls the visionary mode of
artistic creation, Carl Jung makes an observation
relevant not only to *Arthur Gordon Pym* but to a good
many others of Poe's stories. By this kind of literature,
Jung says, "we are astonished, taken aback, confused,
put on our guard or even disgusted—and we demand
commentaries and explanations. We are reminded of
nothing in everyday life, but rather of dreams, nighttime fears and the dark recesses of the mind that we
sometimes sense with misgiving. The reading public
for the most part repudiates this kind of writing . . .
and even the literary critic feels embarrassed by it." [1]
The author himself may share this feeling of embarrassment, or find it expedient to say he does. When Poe,
for instance, in writing to a reviewer who had called
Pym "a mass of ignorance and effrontery," concedes
the point and alludes to his story as "a very silly
book," [2] he may have been sincere, or he may have
made this concession out of considerations of prudence.
How are we to know? In the same letter Poe remarked:
"You will find yourself puzzled in judging me by ordinary motives." When, on another occasion, he was
called to task for having written so gruesome a story
as "Berenice," he at once, in effect, repudiated it. In
216

a letter to Thomas W. White, editor of the *Southern Literary Messenger*, Poe wrote:

A word or two in relation to Berenice. Your opinion of it is very just. The subject is by far too horrible and I confess that I hesitated in sending it you especially as a specimen of my capabilities. The Tale originated in a bet that I could produce nothing effective on a subject so singular, provided I treat it seriously. But what I wish to say relates to the character of your Magazine more than to any articles I may offer. . . . The history of all Magazines shows plainly that those which have attained celebrity were indebted for it to articles *similar in nature—to Berenice*—although, I grant you, far superior in style and execution. . . . In respect to Berenice individually I allow that it approaches the very verge of bad taste—but I will not sin quite so egregiously again.[3]

Two American commentators on Poe, Napier Wilt and W. F. Taylor, have gladly taken these remarks at face value and offer them as proof that Poe wrote such stories as "Berenice" merely because he thought that they could easily be sold; and this letter to White is waved about as if it were ample refutation of any effort at "psychologizing" the man and his work.[4] But even to deplore "psychologizing" is perforce to indulge in it. Wilt and Taylor take it upon themselves to judge Poe's motives in this letter to White, and the decision they reach, by inspection presumably, is that Poe intended to and did define the "real" attitude he had toward his tales. In a word, he didn't *mean* them; they were written to formula. Poe would be an easier subject for literary criticism if this theory could be demonstrated. But Poe's own assertion of it is assertion only. In his deferential and defensive letter to White, as Krutch very convincingly puts it, "a genius who was also mentally sick strives with painful unsuccess to reconcile what he thinks of himself with what he hopes will recommend him to others." [5] And thus, in some embarrassment, Poe backs away from one of his most effective stories.

Astonished, taken aback, confused by such things as "Berenice," critics and scholars in this country have tried to explain Poe's stories by explaining them away. The visionary mode of artistic creation seems to be, as Jung suggests, the mode that particularly evokes reductive commentary. The unknown must be forced into familiar shape, and what is extraordinary must be tied to the commonplace. So far as Poe himself is concerned we have by now a mass of information about him, including such "human interest" details as that he once set a broad jump record of twenty-one feet, six inches, and may at one time have worked in a brickyard.[6] One scholarly study attempts to show that Poe was affected by the ideals of "Greek reason, critical thought, and moderated judgments" presumably prevalent at the University of Virginia during his one year there; but grants, in a memorable phrase, that "unlike the Greeks he was moody." [7] Do we think of Poe's writing as apart from everyday reality? Another scholar reminds us that in his work there are allusions to "cabbages, cucumbers, turnips, onions, celery, cauliflower, Irish potatoes, corn, parsley, pumpkins, watermelons, milkweed, and purslain." [8] Surely the implicit purpose of this list is to establish Poe not as an unusual, much less singular, writer, but as one of the common, or garden, variety.

Lately more sophisticated efforts have been made to much the same end. Poe's stories have been explained as the work of a born actor, and as elaborate allegorical jokes.[9] Either way it is implied that they lack intrinsic seriousness, and we are urged to see through them rather than into them. And of course for years now we have been invited to look behind them, to the sources Poe used in writing his tales. It may be merely because Poe is one of our standard authors that so much source-research has been done on him. But there may also be another reason for all this industry. The evident individuality and strangeness of his stories give them an enigmatic quality that is not readily analyzed. And hence the hope develops that if sources can be found, if accordingly it can be shown that Poe did not create only out of his own imagination, then perhaps the elusive strangeness can be fixed somehow, or better yet, dissipated entirely. In actuality, though, this procedure fails to work. It is as true of Poe as of any writer worth reading that his work cannot be reduced to the materials he started from and the hints he used. This should be obvious, and yet the American scholars who have investigated the sources of *Arthur Gordon Pym* go about their task as if for all the world Poe's story were intrinsically of no greater interest or merit than the travelogues from which it in part derives. And similarly with the stories involving situations like those in the derivative Gothic fiction that was proving popular in *Blackwood's* and other magazines in the 1830's. It is not enough to point out that some precise borrowings exist. They do; but Poe chose to borrow some things and not others, and his stories have had lasting success whereas his presumed models have not. These are the very considerations that lend point to source-research, but they are usually ignored so that only the simplest conclusion may be upheld. Because of the popularity of *Blackwood's* with the reading public, writes Edmond Jaloux, one of our critics has claimed that Poe wrote his fantastic stories only to make money, and just as if he were out to win a bet or settle a business problem. As proof of Poe's insincerity this man alludes to the humorous "How to Write a Blackwood Article." But the mystification in this case, if there is any, consists in fooling the reader who is willing to believe that Poe was writing under false pretenses. What mystifiers especially enjoy doing is to present what really interests them under the guise of ruse and farce.[10]

In the attempt to account even approximately for the permanent strength of Poe's best work it is not his sources, in the academic sense, that matter nearly so much as do his resources. Evidence of the latter kind, internal rather than external, should prove more enlightening. This is a probability which for Baudelaire amounted to a certainty. "The characters in Poe," he writes, "or rather the Poe character, the man with hyper-acute faculties, the man with ice-water in his veins . . . this is Poe himself. And his women . . . they too are Poe." [11] If this insight is valid it leads us not to the books Poe read but to the mind that read them. Our attention should be given to what that mind produced. Thus Baudelaire directs us to the stories themselves. In this chapter, developing a point suggested in the discussion of *Arthur Gordon Pym*, we will examine a group of stories in which the theme of the Double appears. We will try to see what significance this theme has in the work of Poe and how relevant it is to our understanding of him.

— I —

IN THE expressly psychological literature which deals with the phenomenon of the *Doppelgänger*, "William Wilson" has an important place. Indeed for Thomas

Mann it is the classic story of this kind.[12] But it seems to be thought of as unique among Poe's work, his single venture with this sort of material. This is true only in the sense that "William Wilson" is the most explicit of his treatments of the Double-theme. It would be surprising, though, if it were the sole story of its kind from an author who is distinguished more than most by the small variety of his fiction. Poe wrote a great many tales, but if no two are very much alike there exists nonetheless a considerable degree of uniformity among them—certainly among those on which his reputation now rests. Thus, in spite of the fact that "William Wilson" is not matched by any other of his tales, it may be considered in one way as an exemplary story, illustrating the motif and providing the key to a reading of a number of others.

"William Wilson" is a first-person account of a man's struggle with, evasions of, and final disastrous victory over, his own conscience, the spectre in his path.[13] Once the introductory pages are written, Poe confines himself to presenting the principal scenes of the conflict. He does so in a highly dramatic way, by giving Wilson a double and by limiting the action to the essential stages of the contest between them. Except for the word of the hero himself, there is no evidence that a second William Wilson exists. The double is a mental projection and only that. In speaking of his family Wilson says, "I am the descendant of a race whose imaginative and easily excitable temperament has at all times rendered them remarkable." [14] We infer accordingly that the second Wilson is a phantasm only, the product of the kind of temperament described. Poe here, as in so many of his stories, is holding a delicate balance between realism and fantasy. On the realistic side, for instance, the story has a series of quite specific settings, chiefly a boarding school in England, and then Eton, Oxford, and Rome; and so there are witnesses to the presence of a second Wilson. But within this context the vein of fantasy appears when Poe, via his narrator, says that "our identity of name" helped to set the rumor going that the two Wilsons were brothers. He cites the one fact that would refute the rumor. Frequently, in Poe, an ostensibly realistic detail becomes meaningful only when inverted. The two Wilsons *are* brothers, but only in the special sense of being *âmes-frères*. It is a psychological condition that the story dramatizes, but in order to show its complete reality for Wilson himself and to make the presentation of his condition as compelling as possible, Poe objectifies the other half of Wilson's soul. Since Wilson is both hero and narrator, only his version of the events is heard, and only what he recalls, in the way he recalls it, is material for the story.

He recalls it as if it were a dream. "Have I not been living in a dream? And am I now not dying a victim to the horror and mystery of the wildest of all sublunary visions?" Poe suggests by these words that the story may be read as an account of dream experience; and it is worth notice also that Poe, who was not a little expert in such matters, describes the apparition of the *Doppelgänger* as "the wildest of all sublunary visions." One might deduce from these words how strong a fascination this form of psychological disorder had for Poe, and how likely, therefore, that he would exploit it more than once. There is confirmation for this idea in the fact that "William Wilson" is in part directly autobiographical. The elaborate description of school and village with which the story begins was ob-

viously drawn from Poe's recollections of his schooldays in England. The name of his schoolmaster is retained; the birthdates of Wilson and of Poe himself
correspond almost exactly. Indeed, the month and day
are exact. The opening pages of the story scarcely
function in a narrative sense, but they have their own
special interest in showing how personally important
to their author was the theme of the divided personality. It is not altogether by chance that Poe makes his
fullest use of autobiographical materials in a story of
this kind.

From "William Wilson" it is possible to go on to the
other stories in which we find variations on the theme
that is paramount in this one. There are, actually, two
directions that might be taken. On the one hand, there
are the tales of ratiocination, "The Gold Bug" and
the like; and, on the other, the tales in which terror
takes precedence over the element of puzzle or mystery. These are the two large categories under which
all of Poe's best stories may be subsumed, except for
Arthur Gordon Pym, which is a kind of résumé of
almost all the other fiction he wrote.

Now it strikes us at once, when we turn to the detective tales, that the theme of the *Doppelgänger* will
not be an important one in this division of Poe's work.
For in these stories Poe attempted to exercise the rational, puzzle-solving bent of his mind, that level of
his intelligence that was, in its way, scientific, logical,
and systematic. On this plane, the mind is turned out-
ward, as it were, to the light of an objective logic. A
kind of game is involved, for the purpose of which the
chief player renounces his ego and submits his judgment to the impersonal laws of evidence and probability. The "area" of the story is not, therefore, the

shadowland of psychology, but instead the well-defined
field of rational inquiry. In the detective stories we
seem to be following the operations of an enlightened
and delicately working intelligence, and not—as in
such stories as "Berenice" and "The Black Cat"—the
convolutions of a deranged and tortured mind. Dupin,
in whose character Poe created the archetypal detective, solves the crime; Roderick Usher, however, is the
criminal, and it is Usher who typifies the damaged
soul.

Dupin *vs.* Usher: that there is this basic disjunction
in Poe's work is significant of more than his conform-
ity to a conventional social-ethical outlook. For if there
is no explicit glorification of the criminal-as-hero,
there is no overt moralizing either. By thus avoiding
the easy moral inference, Poe revealed which of his
two antithetical heroes he more nearly resembled.
There can be little doubt that we find the author in
Usher rather than in Dupin, an indication that, despite his pretensions to a universal sort of mind, Poe's
true bent was towards the darker regions of the psyche
and not towards the clear and level areas of logic. In
the stories of psychological terror it is the author himself who speaks as the criminal hero; whereas in the
detective stories it is Dupin or Legrand who is the real
hero, and Poe as narrator takes on a quite subsidiary
role. He apparently found it impossible, writing in the
first person, to project himself clearly as the efficiently
reasoning detective. Perhaps, for one reason, he instinctively withdrew from so severely intellectual a
role; and perhaps he avoided it also because, aware
that the deepest dispositions of his nature were tinged
with evil, he could not imagine himself as the solver

of crime. Poe could not be the detective, the hunter, for he was too radically the criminal, the prey.

It is in the "dark" tales of Poe that the *Doppelgänger* theme is of special importance, but it is present also in his stories of detection, although so much on the visible surface, so much a part of the telling itself, that it may easily escape attention. In "The Gold Bug" we are told the story of Legrand's ingenuity by a narrator who is himself dense rather than ingenious and who partakes in the work of the discovery only with a good deal of reluctance. So also in the three famous stories in which a crime is solved, "Rue Morgue," "Marie Roget," and "The Purloined Letter," a similar narrative procedure is used. The essence of the procedure is to have the story told by the confidant of the detective, and the regularity with which this technique has been employed by the long line of detective story writers that proceeds from Poe is evidence that Poe developed the formula that is artistically right for this kind of fiction. By means of a confidant-narrator a bridge is established between the often uncanny acumen of the sleuth and the much less gifted intelligence of the average reader. It would be rash, however, to attribute Poe's sure handling of this kind of material to a sort of unerring instinct for what would most satisfactorily "go," for Poe's instinct about artistic rightness in his work is one of the most erratic things about him. Behind his choice of the confidant-narrator device, there was a psychological as well as an artistic necessity. The two happened to correspond. But as a general rule, Poe's failures and limitations, as well as his successes, derive much more directly from the nature of his personality than from the nature of his endowment as a conscious artist.

It is obvious, for example, that in those stories that
have given Poe his world fame the range is very limited. His capacity to work out variations on his themes
was extraordinary, to be sure, but the themes are basi-
cally two : analysis and obsession, especially the latter.
Poe had a great genius for plot, but for characteriza-
tion in the traditional sense he was very poorly
equipped, as any reader can testify who has attempted
to differentiate among the strangely blending features
of such heroines as Ligeia, Morella, and Eleonora, and
such heroes as Usher, Egaeus, and William Wilson. In
a real sense, Poe's heroes are all doubles, one of another, and the physical and mental lineaments of Poe
are what they all have in common.

So also in the detective stories, Legrand shares more
with Dupin than the French character of his surname.
Both come of illustrious families, are found in strait-
ened circumstances, are interested in book-collecting,
and have a "wild fervor" and "vivid freshness" of imagination. Behind such details it is not hard to detect
the mélange of fact and fantasy that constituted the
self-knowledge of their creator. Legrand merges with
Dupin, and Dupin with Poe. In the introductory pages
of "The Murders in the Rue Morgue," we are told by
the narrator :

I could not help remarking and admiring (although from his
rich ideality I had been prepared to expect it) a peculiar analytic ability in Dupin. He seemed, too, to take an eager delight in its exercise . . . and did not hesitate to confess the
pleasure thus derived. . . . His manner at these moments was
frigid and abstract; his eyes were vacant in expression; while
his voice, usually a rich tenor, rose into a treble which would
have sounded petulantly but for the deliberateness and entire
distinctness of the enunciation. Observing him in these moods,
I often dwelt meditatively upon the old philosophy of the Bi-

Part Soul, and amused myself with the fancy of a double Dupin—the creative and the resolvent.[15]

This doubleness in Dupin is precisely that of Poe also, who in this passage affirms a link between his character and himself that transcends a merely surface resemblance in romantic mien or affectation. Dupin is Poe, the resolvent Poe, the analyst who wrote "The Philosophy of Composition," and who professed to have no trouble solving the trickiest of cryptograms.

But however close this similarity between character and author, it should be noticed that Poe does not permit himself a direct identification. He stands off, as it were, from his detective-hero, and in the role of narrator observes him and looks up to him. The analyst whose activities he reports is that self of Poe's which he tried to cultivate, the mask he tried to wear. The "creative" self, however, was quite different from the pattern of rational sagacity we find symbolized in Dupin. That other, deeper, self, whose twisted fears and agonies we read about in such stories as "The Tell-Tale Heart" and "The Black Cat," is his own narrator. In the telling of these stories no intermediary is brought into play; the identification here is direct and unambiguous. When the deeper regions of his mind were involved, Poe dispensed with a narrator. Thus, at the climax of both "MS. Found in a Bottle" and "A Descent into the Maelstrom" the same motif is present: a plunge into the gulf. But in the one case Poe tells the story in the first person, while in the other his technique is to report the experience of someone else. Why this difference? Is it not because the first was a fatal plunge and the other was not? When fatality was at stake Poe preferred to speak for himself.

When analysis was his theme or pretext, he is in the story in the subsidiary role of narrator. Thus the "I" who writes "The Gold Bug" and "Rue Morgue" is merely a spectator and reporter of the successes of the real hero. The "I" who narrates such a story as "The Black Cat" is writing his own confession of disgrace and failure. Poe could record the triumphs of a hero only indirectly, but there is no discernible distance between him and the victims he writes about. They are Poe in a much fuller sense.

— II —

IN THIS way, the elementary difference that exists between the two chief narrative methods of Poe both illuminates his fascination with the theme of the Double and is in turn illuminated by it. An apparently casual difference in technique helps bring into focus an important aspect of Poe's work and the internal pressures from which it derived. In the detective tales primarily, but also in *Arthur Gordon Pym*, his preoccupation with what he called the bi-part soul manifests itself most evidently on the plane of narrative technique; and these stories accordingly offer some collateral justification for a tentative hypothesis regarding Poe: to such a degree was his mind divided and his personality split that the supposedly conscious and controlled operations of narrative method were thereby affected.

If this phenomenon in his own nature could make its presence felt on the plane of literary form, it is likely that it should find expression in content as well. The *what* will be affected, as well as the *how*, and indeed much more so. "William Wilson" has been alluded to already as an instance of how this may happen. But there are several other stories in which the *Doppelgänger* theme is involved, less clearly so than in the classic presentation of it in "William Wilson," but functioning as a submotif, or as a lesser chord which is not the less present for having a secondary status. This is true of such stories as "The Tell-Tale Heart," "The Fall of the House of Usher," and "Morella." However, in one story less well known than these Poe gave to the Double theme perhaps the most ingenious treatment it has ever had. "The Man of the Crowd" presents no such direct conflict between the self and its alter ego as there is in "William Wilson." The two halves are disjunct to such an extent that the very simultaneity of their existence is doubtful. The point of the story suggests a future rather than a present context, for in "The Man of the Crowd" a kind of Dr. Jekyll foresees the Mr. Hyde he will become.

The story is a brief one and may be quickly summarized. The narrator is looking through the window of a London coffee-house one evening, absorbed in his contemplation of the moving crowd outside. From among the people who are passing before him he singles out an old man for particular study. Fascinated by his terrible face, he determines to follow him. All through that night and the next day, as the old man wanders about the city, compulsively seeking to mingle with a throng of people, the curious pursuit goes on. At last, wearied of the chase, the narrator finally approaches the old man directly and stares him in the face. But this move evokes not the least response from the stranger. "This old man," the narrator concludes, "is the type and the genius of deep crime. He refuses to be alone. *He is the man of the crowd*. It will be in vain to follow; for I shall learn no more of him, nor of his deeds." [16]

Now the meaning of this story seems to be that the narrator encountered and failed to recognize a prophetic image of his future self. But this meaning is nowhere directly stated. Perhaps no other of Poe's stories proceeds so much by indirection and faint clues as this one. Yet the clues are there, and when they are read aright the reason for Poe's reliance on implication rather than straightforward exposition becomes sufficiently clear.

The important thing to notice is that "The Man of the Crowd" is not a realistic story. Its time-span is virtually impossible. If the pursuit began around eight in the evening of the first day, it continued uninterrupted through the next twenty-four hours, for it was not abandoned until "the shades of the second evening came on." It would be possible for such a pursuit to last through one night, but that it should continue through the following morning and afternoon is most improbable. And since the narrator remarks at the outset that he has only recently recovered from an illness, the probability of so extended a chase is nil. Another odd detail is that the pursuer consistently manages to avoid being seen by the man he is following. Six times mention is made of this. More surprising still, when he finally does confront the old man, no notice is taken of him: "he noticed me not." If taken realistically, this would be another baffling detail. But the significance of the episode is that the narrator, facing his future double, fails to see and recognize himself.

It is the irony inherent in this crucial recognition

scene that dictates the indirection with which the whole story is told. The narrator misses the essential point. He is not aware of the ironic appropriateness of the epigraph he selected, La Bruyère's remark: "Ce grand malheur, de ne pouvoir être seul," nor of the German phrase which he uses at the beginning and end of his narrative: "es lässt sich nicht lesen—it does not permit itself to be read." William Wilson might have quoted La Bruyère's words with a sardonic sense of their application to his own plight. But the narrator here is not aware of what relevance they have for him, nor of the way in which the German motto sums up the experience he has had. That some things may not be read, some things may not be told—this, he thinks, has application elsewhere, to a "certain German book," and to the old man, "the type and genius of deep crime." Obtusely sententious, he concludes the story: "The worst heart of the world is a grosser book than the 'Hortulus Animae,' and perhaps it is but one of the great mercies of God that *'es lässt sich nicht lesen.'* " Having failed to discover the occult significance of his experience, the narrator fails to see that the motto bears directly on his own life. It is perhaps one of the great mercies of God that the human heart is obscure and unpredictable, and that, in consequence, a man cannot foresee his own future. This is the meaning of "The Man of the Crowd," but it is not a meaning Poe's narrator is conscious of.

As its author, however, Poe was presumably conscious of what this story means. It is too expertly managed, its details too finely controlled and mutually sustaining, to permit of any other conclusion. Furthermore, the evident reflections of Poe's own character that are found in "The Man of the Crowd" make it

unlikely that he did not work this story out very carefully as a parable of his own life. Is it not significant,
for example, that with what we are told of the narrator and the old man we could fashion a recognizable
portrait of Edgar Poe? The narrator describes himself:

For some months I had been ill in health, but was now con-
valescent, and, with returning strength, found myself in one
of those happy moods which are so precisely the converse of
ennui—moods of the keenest appetancy, when the film from
the mental vision departs—and the intellect, electrified, sur-
passes as greatly its everyday condition, as does the vivid yet
candid reason of Leibnitz, the mad and flimsy rhetoric of
Gorgias. Merely to breathe was enjoyment; and I derived positive pleasure even from many of the legitimate sources of
pain.[17]

Here is a partial self-portrait in which one notices
several psychological traits that are characteristic of
Poe. The personality is keyed up, but still within the
shadow of sickness; it is animated by what seems to be
an abnormal spiritual energy; it is aware of this condition and aware also of a perverse disposition towards
masochism. What the narrator later reads in the face
of the old man proves to be in large measure the disastrous fulfillment of the qualities that he felt latent
in himself: "There arose confusedly and paradoxically
within my mind, the ideas of vast mental power, of
caution, of penuriousness, of avarice, of coolness, of
malice, of blood-thirstiness, of triumph, of merriment,
of excessive terror, of intense—of supreme despair." [18]

To read "The Man of the Crowd" in conjunction
with "The Tell-Tale Heart" is to become aware immediately of a number of resemblances between them.
In the latter story, too, there is an old man; only this
time it is not he who is "the type and the genius of deep

crime," but rather the narrator himself. The narrator is the criminal; the story is an account of his crime and its discovery. If the pursuer of the man of the crowd had grasped the significance of what he had witnessed, and, in the insane hope of circumventing his destiny, had killed the man he was following, then all the essentials of "The Tell-Tale Heart" would be present. For this story is one more exploration of the psychology of the bipartite soul.

Living alone with an old man, the criminal-hero develops a profound hatred for him. This hatred he cannot explain, but it seems to him that the eye of the old man is somehow the cause of it. He resolves to murder him, and for a week he goes to the door of his room every night at midnight. At last the victim is awakened by a chance noise made by the madman, who then opens the shutter of his lantern so that a beam of light falls on the hateful eye. Believing he hears the sound of his victim's heart, and alarmed lest this become so loud as to rouse a neighbor, he enters the room and kills his enemy. After making sure that the heart has stopped, he hides the corpse under the boards of the floor. Soon after, the police arrive, and in the conviction that his deed cannot be found out, he leads them to the very room in which it was committed. But soon the murderer begins to hear a recurrence of the heart beats, and convinced finally that the police can hear them too, he shrieks his confession of guilt: "Villains! . . . dissemble no more! I admit the deed! —tear up the planks! —here, here! —it is the beating of his hideous heart!" [19]

What so brief a synopsis fails to clarify is the devices by which Poe makes this powerful story something more than a vivid melodrama. One device, al-

though not of major importance, is the manner in
which the insanity of the narrator is conveyed. When
Baudelaire's translation of "The Tell-Tale Heart" first
appeared in the French press he gave it a subtitle,
"Plaidoyer d'un fou." He later suppressed the phrase,
and rightly so, for the repeated and heated denials of
insanity with which the story begins are wholly adequate indication of the mental state of the speaker. The
cunning with which he went about his work was proof,
for him, that he was not mad. But the cunning was far
from perfect. Otherwise he would have had the foresight to oil the hinges of his dark lantern. That he
should have neglected so essential a preparation re-
futes, on the level of his actions, what he too vehe-
mently protests in his words.

But the engrossing interest this story has depends
less on the general fact that the hero is mad than on
the particular kind of madness that his case involves.
What was the nature of his crime? He had no hatred
for his victim. Quite the reverse: "I loved the old
man." And so he casts about for a reason, a convincing
motive: "I think it was his eye! yes, it was this! He
had the eye of a vulture—a pale blue eye, with a film
over it. Whenever it fell upon me, my blood ran cold;
and so by degrees—very gradually—I made up my
mind to take the life of the old man, and thus rid myself of the eye forever." [20] A simpler solution, but one
which the criminal apparently did not consider, would
have been to leave the house, a house of which we are
told that only the two men lived there. That this solution did not occur to the murderer is one more indication of his mental derangement; but, more than this,
it carries a suggestion of the strange relationship in
which the two characters were involved. Thus the feel-

ings of the old man when he awoke to discover his executioner at the door were feelings that the executioner could identify himself with:

He was still sitting up in the bed listening;—just as I have done night after night, hearkening to the death watches in the wall. Presently I heard a slight groan, and I knew it was the groan of mortal terror. It was not a groan of pain or of grief —oh no!—it was the low stifled sound that arises from the bottom of the soul when overcharged with awe. I knew the sound well. Many a night, just at midnight, when all the world slept, it has welled up from my own bosom, deepening, with its dreadful echo, the terrors that distracted me.[21]

He carried a lantern but had no need of it. Without its aid he was able to see the old man as he lay on his bed, although the time was midnight and the room was "black as pitch with the thick darkness." He could see him well enough with the mind's eye, Poe is implying here; for the act of murder in this story took place on a psychological as well as a physical level, and the nature and meaning of the crime must be sought in the psychology of the hero rather than in the immediately visible external details of his actions.

The murderer identified himself with his victim: "I knew what the old man felt, and pitied him, although I chuckled at heart." But what he did not know was that through this crime he was unconsciously seeking his own death. The shuttered lantern in his hand chanced to symbolize the thing he hated, the pale blue eye of the old man, the eye with a film over it. Whenever that eye fell on him, his blood ran cold. Thus he used the lantern to project a beam of light that filled the old man with terror, and in this way executioner and victim exchanged experiences. But so closely had the madman identified himself with his adversary that the murder he committed also brought on his own death. With unwitting irony he later tells the police that the scream heard during the night was his own, "in a dream." Objectively, this is false, for the scream was uttered by the old man. But subjectively, in the unconscious merging of himself and his victim, that cry was his own. And then at the end of the story another sound is to be identified, the beating of the telltale heart. By an amazing stroke, Poe brings in a detail that makes the story, if taken on a literal, realistic plane, patently absurd; but which, if interpreted for its psychological significance, becomes a brilliant climax to the hidden drama that has been unfolding. The ever-louder heartbeats heard by the criminal, are they, as he says, the sound of the beating of the old man's heart, that old man whose corpse has been dismembered and concealed under the planking in the room? Certainly not—on the plane of realistic and objective fact. It is the "hideous heart" of the criminal himself which he hears. But if we remember that the criminal sought his own death in that of his victim, and that he had in effect become the man who now lies dead, then what he tells the police is true. His conscious purpose was to lie to them about the earlier scream, but then, unconsciously, he told the truth. Now, consciously, he attempts to tell the truth, and this time he is unconsciously in error. And inevitably so. For his consciousness, his very being, had become intrinsicate with that of the man he killed, and with the extinction of his victim the power to separate illusion from reality became extinct in him and his madness was complete. How appropriate to this case, therefore, are the words of Wilson's murdered double: "*In me dids't thou exist*

—and, in my death, see by this image, which is thine own, how utterly thou hast murdered thyself." [22]

If Madeline Usher could have spoken when she returned from the burial vault to confront her brother, she too might have used these words; for "The Fall of the House of Usher" is also based on the *Doppelgänger* theme.

All we learn of the strange situation in this extraordinary house we learn through the eyes and the emotional responses of the narrator. He is at the same time both the author of the story and, as spectator of its events, the audience as well. We react as he does. When the final catastrophe is imminent, we share his revulsion: "From that chamber, and from that mansion, I fled aghast." [23] But there is an additional complication: the narrator is also curiously linked to the chief character. Although he cannot explain precisely why he is terrified in the house, the narrator seems to feel some kinship with Roderick Usher. Perhaps Usher's malady is not so singular as to be exclusively his. It may sometime overwhelm his visitor. The fatal events that lie ahead for Usher may also lie ahead for him. Thus when he enters the house and sees the "carvings on the ceilings, the sombre tapestries of the walls, the ebon blackness of the floors"—these prove to be "matters to which or to such as which, I had been accustomed from my infancy"; and he "hesitated not to acknowledge how familiar all this was." Familiar because he had been a boyhood friend of Usher and had come in that way to know the interior of the Usher mansion; or because the house of his own family was decorated in a similar fashion? It is probably for the latter reason. The setting in which he now finds himself is not foreign to his own mode of life, and the force of the horror which he will increasingly experience derives from his discovery of how in such a familiar setting there should be so much gone wrong. The house is underlaid with the most baffling ambiguities; not an action nor a motive has a self-evident purpose. This much at least the visitor will learn. But even as he makes his entrance he cannot clearly account for the origin of his sensations. The mist of the unknown has drifted around all he sees, and around his own mind as well. He can make things out, still recognizable, but blurred and shifting.

This is his experience from the very outset of the story. He is unable to explain the "insufferable gloom" he feels when he first comes in sight of the house. The building itself, with its vacant, eye-like windows, the rank sedge, and the dead trees—these objects should not, in themselves, oppress him. So he reasons, and in an effort to dispel this effect he studies their reversed images in the tarn that lies before the house. But this experiment only deepens his sense of gloom and foreboding. Unable to resolve the mystery here, he enters the house, in which a more complex enigma awaits him.

The two puzzles are actually very closely linked, however. Through the narrative technique he is employing in this story, Poe aligns the reader with the consciousness of the visitor to the House of Usher. Both will participate in the experience of undefined, ambiguous, and yet very palpable evil. Usher's guest never penetrates beyond the appearances; he *lives* this experience; its significance eludes him. But the reader need not be bound by such ignorance. Poe is careful to provide details of a sort that will elucidate the mystery of the House of Usher. In other words, the open-

ing scene of the story not only serves to establish the
atmosphere of doubt and misgiving, but also to suggest
the moral and psychological sources from which this
atmosphere emanates. What perturbs the narrator in
the appearance of the house and its grounds is that he
is faced with a vision of decay. It is not the condition
of death which he sees, but that of death-in-life. The
house, of course, is the man, an obvious representation
of Roderick Usher; and of his sister also, who in her
subsequent cataleptic state is neither living nor dead.

Poe uses a strikingly paradoxical figure to describe
the impression which this opening scene makes on the
narrator. He calls his depression of soul a sensation
comparable only to "the after-dream of the reveller
upon opium—the bitter lapse into every-day life—the
hideous dropping off of the veil." But the narrator of
this story does not come upon the conditions of everyday life at Usher's house. Rather the reverse: he has
left everyday life behind him when he enters upon a
scene in which decay and death are the presiding elements. His lapse is into a dreamlike state, and a hideous veil has been let down rather than removed. However, it is only through the wrenching effect of
paradox that the baffling complexities of his state of
mind may be conveyed. Poe uses another device to reinforce this point. When the narrator looks into the
"black and lurid tarn" and sees reflected in it the
house, the sedge, and the decayed trees, he experiences
a "shudder ever more thrilling than before." Why? Is
it not because the unreal image, the mere reflection,
seems to him more real and more threatening than
the actual three-dimensional house, sedge, and trees
which he has just observed before? Of the two images
available, it is the shadow rather than the substance

that proves to be the more terrifying. How else, except through a flat, directive statement, which would dissipate altogether the essential tone of the story, could Poe indicate that "The Fall of the House of Usher" concerns the terror of the soul, and that its visible realities are of importance only as clues to the forces concealed within that are engaged in a fatal conflict?

The reflected image of the house in the water acts also as a kind of prophetic picture. The final scene of the story, in which the waters of the tarn swallow the House of Usher, is foreshadowed in this introductory episode. The house in the water has a further and more important meaning, one which relates to the almost explicit equation that is later set up between Usher and his ancestral mansion. The narrator soon becomes deeply alarmed at the appearance and conduct of his friend, but the true horror of his case is not in evidence. It resides rather in the submerged being of Usher, which is here symbolized by the reflection of the house in the water; and it is for this reason that the narrator is terrified more by the reflected image than by the actual, physical building. Thus Poe implies that the evil influences operative in the story derive from the recesses of Usher's mind. In those depths developed the impulses that led to his undoing.

"The Fall of the House of Usher" is usually alluded to, or dismissed, as a famous "atmosphere" story, and so it is; although to say only that about it is to miss more relevant sources of its rare power. To get at those sources something more is needed than the general term *atmosphere*. To be more specific, it is an atmosphere of decay, corruption, putrescence, which pervades this story. It is this that the narrator dimly becomes aware of when he raises his eyes from the tarn to the house. He sees it enveloped in "an atmosphere which had no affinity with the air of heaven, but which had reeked up from the decayed trees, and the gray wall, and the silent tarn—a pestilent and mystic vapor, dull, sluggish, faintly discernible, and leaden-hued." [24] This atmosphere *exists*. At the climax of the story the narrator will discern it again, unmistakably. Now, with the "hideous dropping off of the veil" he speaks of, he finds it possible to make out this aura of decay. And when Poe writes that this atmosphere had no affinity with the air of heaven, he suggests that its affinity is with hell and that the inhabitants of this house are damned.

All Poe's great strokes are accomplished by implication, by suggestion. Especially in such a story as this, in which so much is staked on translucence, ambiguity, and doubt, indirection is the essence of his method. But the details are there and they are not haphazard. As the narrator examines the building more closely, he is amazed to perceive a contrast between, on the one hand, its antiquity and the crumbling condition of the individual stones, and, on the other, "the still perfect adaptation of parts." This reminds him of the "specious totality of old woodwork which has rotted for long years in some neglected vault, with no disturbance from the breath of the external air." The transition here is from stone to wood, reminding us of those decayed trees standing on the ground before the house, the trees to which he has already three times referred, and which now begin to stand as emblematic of the family line of the Ushers. All the images in this first part of the story are images of sterility and rankness. Dry rot is the fused image, now introduced through the reference to old woodwork.

Like the house which represents him, Roderick Usher also seems to emanate an atmosphere of death. The further the narrator succeeds in penetrating into the depths of Usher's mind, the more he realizes "the futility of all attempt at cheering a mind from which darkness, as if an inherent positive quality, poured forth upon all objects of the moral and physical universe, in one unceasing radiation of gloom." [25] In the impromptu which Usher composes, "The Haunted Palace," he is represented as a "radiant" palace, although here, of course, the radiance of health is meant. And in the painting by Usher—a prophetic painting that forecasts the subterranean vault in which the body of his sister will be placed—the phenomenon of radiance is also present: "No outlet was observed in any portion of its vast extent, and no torch or other source of artificial light was discernible; yet a flood of intense rays rolled throughout, and bathed the whole in a ghastly and inappropriate splendor." Through the repetition of this detail Poe succeeds in charging the "atmosphere" of the story. This is not for macabre décor. The effect of Poe's insistence on this detail is to lend symbolic force to the phenomenon. Usher himself is aware of it. His explanation is that the very stones of the house are sentient, and together with the decayed trees, the network of fungi on the exterior of the building, and the reduplication of all this in the stagnant waters of the tarn, the unholy atmosphere has been engendered. During the night of the storm Usher shows his friend the full extent of this miasma: "A whirlwind had apparently collected its force in our vicinity. . . . But the under surfaces of the huge masses of agitated vapor, as well as all terrestrial objects immediately around us, were glowing in the unnatural light of a faintly luminous and distinctly visible gaseous exhalation which hung about and enshrouded the mansion." [26] By now, the appropriateness of *enshrouded* is quite clear. The House of Usher is not just yet a house of death, but it is shortly to be one. Its stones are sentient, half-alive; and Usher himself is correspondingly half-dead. The house is a house of almost total decay. And the decay which it contains is not only physical, but, with Usher, mental and moral decay too, of which the image of dry rot is an all but precise formulation.

For what but a psychological and moral enormity could exist as the motive for Usher's burial of his sister? On a problem of this sort Poe is silent. He provides no direct indications, and, through the device of having the story told by a narrator who barely half-understands the phenomena he encounters, Poe frees himself of any responsibility for illuminating the most complex of the enigmas in the House of Usher. It is not that his almost obsessive fascination with crime suddenly ceased at the borders of the unnatural and perverse. On the contrary, this territory was of great interest to him. But, whatever may be the reason for his reluctance, he did not *directly* explore the moral issues that this area of his work involves. In this respect above all his method is implicative, and so powerfully is this method used in the story that the unnatural atmosphere which permeates the Usher mansion becomes finally redolent of moral corruption. Usher's burial of his still living sister goes beyond sadism. His act seems to culminate a relationship that in intention if not in deed was incestuous.

It is as a result of the whole contextual quality of the story, the special kind of details that are named, and those also that are not, that the relationship of Roderick and Madeline as twins takes on a sinister significance. The story is most readily intelligible as another fable of the split personality. The fissure which ran down the façade of the house and which the visitor first noticed when he made his approach to it, is a clue not only to the instability of the mind of Roderick Usher but to this particular kind of mental disorder. Roderick and his sister are the sole survivors of the Usher line; they are the House. Their deaths are simultaneous, and soon after this takes place the physical house divides from top to bottom and collapses in the waters of the tarn. In that tarn, we remember, the narrator's view of the reflection of the house caused an impression of horror on him more profound than that occasioned by the sight of the actual building. Similarly, the shadowy Madeline proved more terrifying to him than did Roderick, whom he could see clearly and to whom he could speak. He was not even aware that Madeline was in the same room with himself and Usher until "she passed through a remote portion of the apartment, and, without having noticed my presence, disappeared. I regarded her with an utter astonishment not unmingled with dread—and yet I found it impossible to account for my feelings. A sensation of stupor oppressed me, as my eyes followed her retreating steps." [27] The two experiences correspond in a way that suggests an analogy between Madeline and the house-in-the-water. The two, the twin sister and the reflected house, represent the dark, under side of Usher's mind, the depths which cannot plainly be "read," and which are nonetheless forcibly felt to exist. And therein also is the source of the man's fatal malady. Considered in

this way, "The Fall of the House of Usher" is a reversal of the Double motif of "William Wilson." Wilson was haunted by his conscience and finally killed it,
and so himself. The warfare taking place in Roderick
Usher is waged by his consciousness against the evil
of his unconscious.

But it is obvious that his final effort in this struggle
comes too late. The corrosive effort of the evil has gone
too far to be withstood now. The arrival and continued
presence of his friend succeed to some extent in weak-
ening the dark side of the conflict, for Madeline suc-
cumbs soon after Usher's friend has arrived at the
house. To this degree, Usher's plea for help is successful. However, his malady is too far advanced, do what
he will, to permit of a cure. He hastens to inter his
sister's body in an underground vault, thus fulfilling
the desire of which his painting was the prophetic,
and almost surrealistic, representation. But he cannot
thus rid himself of what is so integrally a part of his
own nature. This is the explanation for his ambiguous
solicitude regarding the body of Madeline. He does not
want autopsies by the "medical men," and therefore
the body is interred in secret; and it is interred within
the house so that there will be no risk of ghouls' prying
open the coffin—something which might happen if
the coffin were placed in the "remote and exposed situation of the burial ground of the family." His decision to keep the body in the house is also formed "by
consideration of the unusual character of the malady
of the deceased." But this reason nullifies the other
two. For if Madeline were not really dead the doctors
might be able to hasten her return to life, and a rifling
of the grave might also serve the purpose of a resurrection. Usher, however, must have it both ways: do away

with the body, and yet not do away with it altogether. For it is an integral part of himself that he is trying to dispose of. The death of Madeline, he dimly realizes, would be his own death, as it is finally. And so, during the time of her entombment, he undergoes a significant change:

His ordinary manner had vanished. His ordinary occupations were neglected or forgotten. He roamed from chamber to chamber with hurried, unequal, and objectless step. The pallor of his countenance had assumed, if possible, a more ghastly hue—but the luminousness of his eye had utterly gone out. . . . There were times, indeed, when I thought his unceasingly agitated mind was laboring with some oppressive secret, to divulge which he struggled for the necessary courage.[28]

Usher's secret is at last revealed: "We have put her living in the tomb!" But his crime involved more than an attempt, strangely mismanaged, at murder. In bringing about the premature burial of his sister, who was his twin and counterpart, he was, like the madman of "The Tell-Tale Heart," seeking his own death. His condition is accordingly like that of his sister, as she lies in the vault, midway between life and death. She returns from her grave only to take him with her and to complete the total extinction of the House of Usher. When Baudelaire described the "perversity" so often encountered in Poe's stories as the quality by which a man may be simultaneously and always the slayer and the slain, the victim and the executioner, he defined exactly the character of Poe's most famous hero.

— III —

"IN READING his poetry," Poe once remarked of Coleridge, "I tremble, like one who stands upon a volcano, conscious, from the very darkness bursting from the crater, of the fire and the light that are weltering below." [29] It makes an excellent description of what we experience in reading any writer whose power is generated at levels that lie below the surfaces of consciousness. The Coleridge who wrote "Kubla Khan" and "The Ancient Mariner" was such a writer; Poe was another. But what he says here of Coleridge's poetry applies much more fully to his own stories than to his poems, and the differences between what he achieved in these two areas of his creative work will establish a further significance that the *Doppelgänger* theme had for the mind of Poe.

In "The Fall of the House of Usher," so that even his most superficial readers will not miss the symbolical drift of the story, Poe introduces the stanzas of "The Haunted Palace":

I

In the greenest of our valleys,
    By good angels tenanted,
Once a fair and stately palace—
    Radiant palace—reared its head.
In the monarch Thought's dominion—
    It stood there!
Never seraph spread a pinion
    Over fabric half so fair.

II

Banners, yellow, glorious, golden,
    On this roof did float and flow;
(This—all this—was in the olden
    Time long ago)
And every gentle air that dallied,
    In that sweet day,
Along the ramparts plumed and pallid,
    A winged odour went away.

III

Wanderers in that happy valley
  Through two luminous windows saw
Spirits moving musically
  To a lute's well-tuned law,
Round about a throne, where, sitting,
    (Porphyrogene!)
In state his glory well befitting,
  The ruler of the realm was seen.

IV

And all with pearl and ruby glowing
  Was the fair palace door,
Through which came flowing, flowing, flowing
  And sparkling evermore,
A troop of Echoes whose sweet duty
  Was but to sing,
In voices of surpassing beauty,
  The wit and wisdom of their king.

V

But evil things, in robes of sorrow,
  Assailed the monarch's high estate;
(Ah, let us mourn, for never morrow
  Shall dawn upon him, desolate!)
And, round about his home, the glory
  That blushed and bloomed
Is but a dim-remembered story
  Of the old time entombed.

VI

And travellers now within that valley,
  Through the red-litten windows, see
Vast forms that move fantastically
  To a discordant melody;
While, like a rapid ghastly river,
  Through the pale door,
A hideous throng rush out forever,
  And laugh—but smile no more.

Now there is nothing in the least obscure about
Poe's general intention in this poem. He wanted to
present an image of man-as-palace, and to contrast
states of mental health and mental sickness. Thus, as
Gustave Kahn suggested, "The Haunted Palace"
should convey, through the superior concentration of
verse, the general theme of the story in which it appears. This was the intention, no doubt, but the intention succeeds only in so far as the poem is successful,
and "The Haunted Palace" is not a successful poem.
Poe's heavily allegorical equations are all too minute,
in some instances, and all too clumsily vague in others.
This fair and radiant palace, for example, "reared its
head." The man's mind or brain is the subject of the
allegory, and hence the word *head* is appropriate in
this sense. But what are we to see as the "head" of a
palace? In "the ramparts plumed and pallid" we have
a reference to Usher's pale brow, festooned with his
gossamer hair. The "two luminous windows" are his
eyes, of course; later they are to be "red-litten" (blood-
shot?). His mouth and teeth are the doors of the palace,
"all with pearl and ruby glowing." But a poem put
together in this way is unsatisfactory from the outset,
oscillating violently from the overexplicit to the imprecise. The reader is forced to scramble from one level
to the other in accordance with the poet's inability to
sustain his performance throughout on either level.
When we are offered point-for-point analogies between teeth and pearls, eyes and windows, words and
echoes, and so forth, we naturally wonder about the
other analogies that should obtain but which the
author has left unspecified. What of the ears, for instance; and should we understand by "plumed" ram-

parts that the head is crowned with a tonsure?
Throughout the poem the impression grows and per-
sists that Poe has neither control of what he is doing
nor any suspicion that he lacks this control. He is too
easily the victim of the sketchiness of his original idea.
In this sense, the poem writes itself. It seems that the
ramparts are described as "pallid" only for the sake
of alliteration with "plumed," and because the word
offers as close a rhyme as Poe could find for "dallied."
But "pallid," connoting primarily a sickly pallor, is
as wrong a word as could be used at this point in the
poem. Similarly with the "vast" forms that move
"fantastically." The adjective has no merits except
the specious one that it may be echoed in the adverb.
The hideous throng that rushes out at the end is said
to laugh—"but smile no more." This phrasing implies that at some prior time this same throng did
smile, but this implication runs counter to the meaning
of the final stanza.

These are the obvious defects of "The Haunted
Palace," a poem which serves small purpose in its appearance in the story except to make the house-man
correspondence more evident than need be. What is
especially worth notice, however, is that the clumsy
use of language which renders this poem an inferior
production is more in evidence *in the poem* than in the
prose of the story as a whole. For the most part, in
the "House of Usher," Poe's rather archaic style, with
its profusion of polysyllabic words, its unusually intricate phrases, is a successful means of realizing the
effect he wants: a sense of oppression and irresolution
before the complex and abnormal phenomena which
confront the narrator. We are moved out of the "real"
world of everyday conversation and stock vocabulary

by prose such as this: "I could not help thinking of the wild ritual of this work, and of its possible influence upon the hypochondriac, when, one evening, having informed me abruptly that the Lady Madeline was no more, he stated his intention of preserving her corpse for a fortnight (previously to its final interment), in one of the numerous vaults within the main walls of the building." The narrator seldom says that he *was* in any given place; his expression is usually that he "found himself"—within view of the house, in a large and lofty room, or crossing the old causeway; and this expression, implying the uncertainties of nightmare, corresponds exactly with his experiences in the house of Usher. The master of the house is described as having an "inherent positive quality" of darkness, which he seemed to pour forth in "one unceasing radiation of gloom." Thus when Usher appeared on the final night, his air, the narrator says, "appalled" him; the verb is precisely right.

On the other hand, there are enough verbal miscarriages in the writing to make it doubtful that Poe was intentionally using words with this kind of precision. What "shades of evening" can there be on a day described, in the opening sentence of the story, as dull and dark, with clouds hanging oppressively low in the heavens? The phrase is there merely for its cliché value. The word *singular* is drained of its meaning through excessive use. And we experience a curious jolt, one on which Poe certainly did not plan, when we read: "the valet now threw open a door and *ushered* me into the presence of his master." We are similarly obliged to suppress the implications of the words when we read that Lady Madeline was entombed "in the maturity of youth." No; the evidence of the prose is not nearly strong enough to sustain the conviction that Poe measured his words with care or that the effectiveness of the story is to a major degree the result of Poe's conscious art.

It was on his poems that he lavished his art, and that is precisely the trouble with them. Concentrating on technique, he succeeded sometimes in writing a *tour de force*, but more often failed to achieve even this. As a poet he attempted to be fully conscious of what he was about, and in order that his consciousness might be given full play he contrived for himself intricately difficult problems in stanza forms, rhymes, and meters, and set to work solving them with something of the same skill and interest that he brought to the puzzles of cryptanalysis. The theory behind "The Philosophy of Composition" is therefore quite characteristic of Poe's interest in poetry: a poem must be planned with the same elaborate foresight that is required in the preparation of a perfect cryptogram. Although it is doubtful that Poe was utterly in earnest when he wrote that famous essay, there is strong internal evidence in "The Raven" that the poem actually was composed in the way which Poe described. Such a highly engineered performance could owe to "inspiration" no more than its initial idea. The actual working out of the idea is all a matter of control, efficiency, and verbal mechanics, all so demonstratively managed that "The Raven" seems now an elaborate piece of grill-work, a minutely arabesqued façade, with not a thing behind it.

One feels more certain that there is a real experience behind "Ulalume." In this poem something is straining for expression. But again, Poe bore down so hard on his *means* of expression, made them so prominently the be-all and end-all of the poem, that attention is perforce held up by these means and is unable to penetrate beyond them. With so much machinery the poem is static and dead, overborne by its own technical weight. The overripe rhymes and the clockwork metrics which are the hallmark of these poems seem to be in a very literal way the devices which Poe's conscious intelligence developed in order to bring poetry to heel. By employing them he was giving evidence that the movements of his mind were amenable to the strictest governance, that even in poetry—where an effusive welling-up of emotional life would seem to be legitimate and quite in order—he was the assured master of his soul.

But how persuasive is this evidence? As a poet and as a critic of poetry he installed calculation, clarity, and consciousness as the reigning values in the poetic enterprise. Yet in his own work he was not conscious enough. Had he been so, he would have realized how one-sided was the methodicity he was himself able to employ. For Poe it was enough to control only the external and evident details of his poems, and this he did—with a vengeance. When he attempted most rigorously to write as a conscious artist, as he did in his poetry, he got no further than artifice.

In writing his stories, however, Poe did not feel constrained to work so carefully. Within the wider and looser confines of prose fiction, his great natural powers were exercised with much more freedom. The experiences which haunted him were given room for expression, and proceeding in this area with much less analytic self-awareness Poe was able to give these experiences the shape that so successfully conveys them. In his stories, in other words, he did not try so hard

to govern and impose on his material. The reins are
loosely held, and what he has to say finds its expression, its imagery and cadences, with far more spon-
taneity than we ever meet with in his poems. Poe was
thus at his best when he relied on intuition more than
on analysis; and so it is that his stories, and not his
poems, are genuinely intense and richly suggestive.
When in his verse he made a conscious effort to achieve
these qualities he missed them almost every time.

The theme of the *Doppelgänger* was all but obliga-
tory for the imagination of Poe. In his own character,
as well as in his hero Dupin, the psychology of the "bi-
part soul" was manifest, and the split between his own
creative and resolvent faculties is responsible for the
difference between what he achieved in his stories, on
the one hand, and in his poems, on the other.

The same dichotomy provides the basis for seeing
in Poe one of the major predecessors of Surrealism. It
is perhaps the most striking characteristic of Surrealist
painting that though its thematic material would seem
to belong to the chaos of dreams and the unconscious
life, the *technique* with which this material is rendered
is most extraordinary. What is especially fantastic in
the fantastic art of Tchelitchev, Berman, Dali, and
the like, is exactly this contrast between the apparently
uncontrolled and irrational character of the subject
matter and the nearly incredible control with which it
has been transferred to canvas. It is in just this way
that Poe's work prefigures Surrealist art. He too sought
to find the formal structures that would communicate,
with something like their original intensity, the experiences of the unconscious mind. The terror he knew
was of the soul. But uneasy, evidently, about the
strange nature of this enterprise, Poe felt compelled

to show proof that, for all appearances to the contrary, he was among the most lucid and rational of men. Particularly in his criticism, but in most of his poems, and in some of his stories, too, this proof was put on display. The result is that most of his poems are failures. In them he overplayed his hand to such an extent that the essential *données* are drowned out in the whir of the technical manipulation. But in his best stories Poe hit on the necessary, vital balance. And so powerful are the images he presents, so immediate and fluent are the arrangements he makes among them, that despite blunders which a normally conscious writer— and a poet especially—could scarcely make, we are moved by our response to the living psychological perceptions which these stories communicate.

Or, more exactly, we *may* be moved. For the disposition and assumptions of the reader have a good deal to do with the kind of response any writer may evoke. But it seems possible that in our own time Poe may find more responsive readers than he did in his own, and that our relatively recent rediscoveries of Hawthorne and Melville will be matched by a rediscovery of Poe. For these men, too, in their own day and later, were unable to command the public that their work deserved. The implications of what they wrote were not of a kind which the United States in the nineteenth century wanted very much to hear about. Emerson was found a more congenial spokesman. At least his thought lent itself to attractively resonant emphases on self-reliance, human goodness and human power, a beneficent tendency in the whole cosmos. These affirmations, with the aura of "success" about them, seemed ideally suited to the tempo and assumptions of American life. But Poe, like Hawthorne and Melville, had a rather different vision of how things are or may be; and despite the indirectness of its presentation this vision was one that could be felt and responded to. A young and extrovert America turned away from it. In Europe, however, an older and wearier culture had prepared an audience that was ready to recognize the validity of the special insights which are dramatized in the visionary creations of Poe.

8

THE POOL AND THE PORTRAIT

IN AN early classic of the French cinema, *La Chute
de la maison Usher* (1928), the director Jean Epstein permitted himself a good deal of freedom in
working with Poe's most famous story, but in spite of
some almost reckless revisions he was able to translate
into the language of the motion picture much of the
elusive quality that belongs uniquely to Poe. As we
witness this fascinating movie we are surprised to discover that Epstein has not retained the brother-sister
relationship of Roderick and Madeline, but has instead presented them as man and wife. We discover
also that Madeline's burial place is not, as Poe speci-
fied, within the house itself, but in the family vault,
which Epstein locates on a small island in a lake on
the Usher property. In the film version, the climax of
the story involves not only the reappearance of
Madeline but the burning of the house, a detail for
which there is no basis in the text. And, most surprising of all, Epstein is rash or foolish enough to bring
his version of the story to a relatively happy ending.
For Roderick and Madeline do not die in each other's
arms, as Poe would have it, but, with their guest, escape from the flames and at a safe distance watch the
burning house sink into the waters of the tarn.

Yet the remarkable thing is that Epstein's deviations from the scenario as the author wrote it do not
impair the great impact of this movie. One retains
the conviction that it does succeed in capturing in
visual terms at least some of the essence of Poe's genius.
In accounting for this feeling, one recalls especially
the skill with which Epstein's camera realized the
clouded landscape and the baroque, decaying house as
Poe must have imagined them. Outside, all is gray,
barren, unkempt and hostile; within, we are oppressed
at the scale of Usher's mansion and at the tokens of
its former luxury, now only half visible in the gloom
and decay that have overtaken them. The wind causes
vast undulations in the draperies that cover the
enormous windows, and down the long corridors a
camera skims at floor level, as if it too were one of the
dead leaves which a sudden gust has stirred. Such
images of speed and action are balanced against
images of languor, as, in slow motion, huge bookcases
tumble over, and their shelves of ancient volumes fall
in great symmetrical waves to the floor. Details like
these do more than "save" the picture. They bring
home, as only a full and profound visualization can,
all the dreamlike grandeur and ruin that pervade the
house and the soul of Usher.

And so one recognizes anew that there may be more
than a little foundation for the theory that Poe found
his true audience not in his own country but in France.
Whatever considerations may have prompted Epstein
to make his curious alterations in the plot of "The
Fall of the House of Usher," the losses that these alterations involve are more than redeemed by his triumph on a more difficult and more important plane.
The atmosphere, the tone—however we are to call it

—that Poe communicates in his story are most exactly and movingly communicated by Epstein's movie.

Nor is it simply because of its visual rendition of mood that *La Chute de la maison Usher* may be regarded as an interpretative criticism of the Poe original. By means of an ingenious addition to the basic plot this movie reminds us of the continuities that are present in Poe's fiction. For in presenting the two main characters as man and wife Epstein made use of another of Poe's tales, "The Oval Portrait." That the substance of this little known story can be integrated as a detail within the framework of perhaps the most characteristic story Poe ever wrote, this also comes as something of a surprise. But it is the surprise of recognition, for so well do the two stories fuse that we are conscious of not the least discontinuity between them. This fact alone is evidence of Epstein's unusual insight into Poe's writing. Not only do the successes of his treatment of the Usher story more than offset the odd flaws it contains; it may be said that the film as a whole does what any piece of criticism is supposed to do—it returns us to the original work with our perceptions reawakened and our capacities for understanding enlarged. Starting with the suggestive hint given us in Epstein's film, we will find it possible to go on from such an apparent trifle as "The Oval Portrait" to a general view of many of Poe's other stories. In doing this we become increasingly aware of how closely linked these stories are, and aware of how the relationship that exists among them helps to clarify Poe's perplexing genius. This final chapter is an effort at defining the nature of the Poe imagination.

The narrator who relates the history of the oval portrait tells us, by way of introduction, how he and his valet were forced to seek refuge one night in a deserted chateau in the Appennines. They established themselves in a room that had recently been in use as a picture gallery. For a while, as the servant slept, his master lay awake, examining the pictures and reading a catalogue which described them and gave an account of their origins. After several hours of this, he chanced to shift the position of the bedside candelabrum in such a way that its light made visible a portion of the room that he had not observed before. He was immediately struck by the portrait of a young woman, a portrait the lifelike quality of which was so pronounced that its effect was to startle and appall him. Turning again to the catalogue he learned that the portrait was that of a young wife; it had been painted by the girl's husband, an artist who had "already a bride in his Art." [1] As his work progressed, his model became increasingly weak in health and spirit. It seemed as if the very colors which he put on the canvas were being drawn from the living body of the woman; yet he failed to see what was taking place. At last the portrait was finished, and, "for one moment, the painter stood entranced before the work which he had wrought; but in the next, while yet he gazed, he grew tremulous and very pallid, and aghast, and crying with a loud voice, 'This is Life itself!' turned suddenly to regard his beloved :—*She was dead!*" [2]

In the Epstein movie this is the way in which Roderick Usher brings about the death of Madeline. But let us take this story now just as it stands and wonder for a moment about the meaning and possible intention that lie behind it. One is reminded at once of the allegories of Hawthorne, of such stories as "The Birthmark," or even "Rappaccini's Daughter," but especially of "The Prophetic Pictures." That story and this one by Poe would both seem to be moral tales, the point of which is that the artist, by virtue of his special gifts, does not share in the normal interests and responsibilities of the rest of mankind, and so possesses a great, unconscious power for evil. This idea, a recurrent one in Hawthorne's work, would appear to be basic to "The Oval Portrait." But in considering the matter further one becomes less sure that these grounds will sustain a genuine *rapprochement* between Poe and Hawthorne. It is not merely that the characteristic Poe décor—the gloomy chateau, the Italian mountains, the sumptuously furnished apartments—is so very different from the kind of setting that Hawthorne usually favored. Nor is it of the first importance that in this story Poe evidences none of the hesitancy that so often conditioned Hawthorne's treatment of the preternatural. A more significant difference is that there is no explicit moralizing—or even moral tone—in "The Oval Portrait"; it is this fact that most clearly demarcates these two writers. For it is generally true that Hawthorne tends to point up and expatiate on the meanings of the tales he tells, whereas Poe's procedure is as a rule far more indirect. In this particular case, however, the basic difference is less one of technique than of intention and substance. In "The Oval Portrait" Poe is doing something that Hawthorne never attempted. The interest that lies at the heart of this story is a typical Poe interest, and it has no relevance to moral ideas.

It is an index of how closely related Poe's stories are that the real interest in "The Oval Portrait" may be most effectively described if we approach it through another of his tales in which there occurs a brilliant variation on the same theme. Our guide this time is Baudelaire, who so arranged the contents of the *Nouvelles histoires extraordinaires* that the French reader of Poe would begin "Le Portrait ovale" immediately after "L'Ile de la fée." These are the last two stories in that volume, and although much less pretentious than some of the others Poe wrote they serve admirably to bring into final focus what well may be the defining quality of this writer's imagination. Earlier, in Chapter IV, we remarked the rationale of the sequence which Baudelaire gave to his Poe translations. Here we have the culminating instance of his editorial ability. For "The Island of the Fay," read together with "The Oval Portrait," illuminates with rare clarity the kind of thing that Poe was doing in much of his fiction. Examined separately, however, "The Island of the Fay" does not seem impressive. Apparently a random mixture of philosophizing, some descriptions of scenery, and a final section of fantastic whimsy, it is read, if read at all, only as a trifling "sketch," since no story is narrated, no plot is involved.

Poe begins with some reflections on his preference for the aesthetic pleasure which may be experienced in solitude. Especially does he value solitude when the pleasure it affords is associated with the contemplation of natural scenery. For him, however, such contemplation involves a realm that lies deeper than the aesthetic. "I love, indeed," he writes, "to regard the dark valleys, and the gray rocks, and the waters that silently smile, and the forests that sigh in uneasy slumbers . . . I love to regard these as themselves but colossal members of one vast animate and sentient whole—a whole whose form (that of the sphere) is the most per-

fect and most inclusive of all." [3] These rather animistic
considerations are followed by an account of what he
witnessed during one of his "lonely journeyings, amid
a far distant region of mountain locked within mountain, and sad rivers and melancholy tarns writhing or
sleeping within all." [4] Coming upon a rivulet and island in this region, he stopped to rest and to observe
the scene before him. As the sun began to set, the
western end of the little island was bathed in light,
the trees and grass there radiant and endowed with
life. But at the eastern end all was shrouded in gloom,
the trees dark and mournful and the grass funereal in
hue. In his reverie it seemed to him that this was an
enchanted island, the retreat of the few Fays that were
still left in the world. And on the water at the western
end of the island there did indeed appear a Fay who,
in a "singularly fragile" canoe and with a "phantom
of an oar," began to circle the island. Each time, as her
progress took her through the darkened region, more
of her life ebbed from her, for her shadow fell into
the ebony water and was absorbed into its blackness.
When the sun finally set, the Fay, "now the mere
ghost of her former self, went disconsolately with her
boat into the region of the ebony flood, and that she
issued thence at all I cannot say, for darkness fell over
all things, and I beheld her magical figure no more." [5]

The relevance of this fantasy to the "event" described in "The Oval Portrait" is unmistakable. But
there is a further passage in "The Island of the Fay"
which presents even more vividly the basic idea of
these two stories and is relevant as well to "The Fall
of the House of Usher" and to others of Poe's tales.
It is, in fact, one of the indispensable Poe texts:

The shade of the trees fell heavily upon the water, and seemed to bury itself therein, impregnating the depths of the element with darkness. I fancied that each shadow, as the sun descended lower and lower, separated itself sullenly from the trunk that gave it birth, and thus became absorbed by the stream; while other shadows issued momently from the trees, taking the place of their predecessors thus entombed.[6]

Thus, just as the mirror-like water not only reflects the trees but in doing so absorbs their shadows, so, in "The Oval Portrait," the painting not only reflects the woman but in coming into being has also absorbed her life. In his work the painter had mirrored his wife, had transferred her shadow-in-color to the canvas—and with this outgoing shadow went the substance of life itself. The theme of "The Oval Portrait" is that both construction and destruction may inhere in the same process—even in the specifically creative process of art. We recall also that in "The Fall of the House of Usher" the dark tarn which caught the shadow and reflected the image of the fated house was working all the time at its dissolution. When Roderick and his sister, the two living remnants of the Usher family, collapse in death, the tarn actually and symbolically swallows up the house they lived in.

Once we become aware of the central meaning in "The Island of the Fay" we are prepared to understand more exactly the orientation which characterizes the imagination of Poe. Well does he say, elsewhere in the same story: "These fancies, and such as these, have always given to my meditations among the mountains, and the forests, by the rivers and the ocean, a tinge of what the everyday world would not fail to term the fantastic."[7] But for him they were much more than that, as the introductory paragraphs of this story—so different in their philosophic texture from the fantasy proper that follows—were intended to show. The imagination of Poe could not content itself with the superficially startling hypothesis that inorganic matter may conceivably possess some kind of organic existence. He goes beyond this to the astonishingly particularized notion that trees "grow" shadows as they do leaves; and, as the leaves die and fall, so do the shadows, drowned in the water that reflects them. In the everyday world, shadow is explained in the simplest of terms, as the absence of light. But for Poe the phenomenon of light and shadow is not a simple fact of elementary physics. It is rather a mystery of vitalistic biology.

It happens that in "The Island of the Fay" we can define with unusual precision the shift in focus which accounts for the strange quality of Poe's imaginative vision. The story is an invaluable one for that reason. But what Poe does here is what he is essentially doing in a good many of his stories. In his letter to White, in 1835, Poe describes the nature of stories like "Berenice": "You ask me in what does this nature consist? In the ludicrous heightened into the grotesque . . . the singular wrought out into the strange and mystical." [8] What is emphasized is the transformation of one category—or mode of vision—into another. As we read Poe's stories our perceptions are swerved out of the channels in which we are accustomed to have them move, and as we follow him down new lines of sight we become aware of strange contours in all that we thought we knew.

Poe's treatment of death is another case in point. The problem here calls for more than the assertion, correct as it is, that Poe was "fascinated" by death.

So was Whitman; so were a great many writers whom we would never confuse with Poe. But how, in *his* treatment of this subject, is Poe's special signature to be traced?

We know that death may be adequately defined as the sudden cessation of life; we think of it ("for all practical purposes") simply as the absence of life, just as shadow is the absence of light. But the death of the Fay and the death of the painter's wife are experiences of an altogether different kind. Their deaths consisted in a laborious and anguished emanation. And more than this: in the living economy of matter as Poe conceived it, the Whole—"vast animate and sentient"—continues always to exist, although its parts die in feeding one another and in so bringing about new living structures. In "The Oval Portrait," the life of the woman was drained from her body, but instead of being dissipated this life was transferred to her portrait. The quantity of life remains constant. This principle is as basic to the story as it is to the cosmological treatise *Eureka*. It thus can scarcely be wondered at that when Poe modulates our assumptions about the real world into conceptions that surpass any conjecture we could make, a great many of his readers will remain in ignorance of the extent to which realities are being transformed in front of them. To some degree, depending on their initial sympathy with this kind of literature, they may feel the *effect* of what Poe is doing; but its cause and the mode of its realization remain, as Poe intended them to be, obscure.

To see the organic in the inorganic—this is one of the typical modulations in our experience of the world which Poe makes possible in his stories. Once the great barrier between living and non-living matter is broken down, as it is for him, fantastic correspondences are discovered to exist. In "Berenice," for instance, Egaeus is a figure that only Poe could have created in that the distinction between reality and dream is quite without meaning for him. The realities of the world affected him as visions, "and as visions only, while the wild ideas of the land of dreams became, in turn, not the material of my every-day existence, but in very deed that existence utterly and solely in itself." [9] This is the nature of the inversion that took place in him. He had never loved Berenice in the days before her fatal sickness. Then, when she truly lived, "agile, graceful, and overflowing with energy," Egaeus was aware of her only as the Berenice of a dream. But after disease has wholly changed the mind, character, and the very person of the woman, when she has become no more than a walking corpse—at this moment Egaeus finds that he is consumed by a passion for her. When her transition from a living to a non-living state is nearly complete, she remains for him not the dream and abstraction she had been before, but becomes instead a real, embodied woman. And so in an act symbolic of physical possession, he violates her grave and tears the teeth from her head. This horrible deed has its own kind of logic. Poe does not make use of it in the story simply for the shock it provides as a scene of sadistic violence. For Egaeus, the teeth of Berenice symbolized ideas, and so *were* ideas, and as such he coveted them. "I felt that their possession could alone restore me to peace, in giving me back to reason." The significance of this becomes evident when we notice, as one of Baudelaire's notes suggests we do, the great fascination which the physical rather than the spiritual change in Berenice exercised over the sensibility of Egaeus.[10] He singles out a physical fact: the teeth; for him they become ideas. But ideas cannot be physically possessed; the teeth, however, can. When the real and actual world is supplanted, as it is for Egaeus, by the world of dreams, the entities proper to these two different realms exchange places. The actual becomes illusory, and illusion becomes actuality. The hero's appalling act is thus in keeping with the precise nature of his derangement.

The hard and fast lines by which we mark off one area of experience from another and, with the help of the barriers of definition, establish some order amid the flux of phenomena, meant very little to Poe. How little may be estimated from his procedure in "Berenice," in which a correspondence is established between the perfect white teeth of the woman and the clear and distinct ideas which Egaeus felt himself so desperately in need of. There is a similar if less striking illustration of the same thing in "The Island of the Fay." In describing the shadows of the trees falling on the water, Poe makes use of those words (*bury, impregnating, birth, entombed*) which will effect a metaphorical fusion of the phenomena of birth and death. The experience which this and many of his other stories provide is that of living in a world which manages somehow to preserve the recognizable features of the world we normally know, and which yet, and at the same time, is a world devoid of the postulates that underlie our notions of reality. For we assume that through differences in mode of being all that we perceive is divisible into disjunct, hierarchical categories. This was not Poe's axiom. Illusion and reality, dream and fact, death and life—these antithetical pairs do not exist as such in his vision but are instead continuous and often interchangeable. Forms and essences are deprived of their individuating principles; they merge with and take on the life of their contraries. For example, in one of his letters: "All things are material; yet the matter of God has all the qualities which we attribute to spirit. . . . There is a matter without particles. . . ." [11] It is a commonplace that Poe's stories are almost entirely without social relevance, and hence their lack of the kind of moral meaning that distinguishes such a writer as Hawthorne. Positively, it should be recognized that what Poe's stories *do* possess as their recurrent and perhaps ultimate source of interest is the author's preoccupation with ontology, the study of being. It is appropriate, in one way, that his career as a writer ended with *Eureka: An Essay on the Material and Spiritual Universe*. But in that treatise he took up the problem of being along an impossibly wide front; and although he called it a prose poem, a "Romance," and dedicated it "to those who put faith in dreams as in the only realities" —all this surely was by afterthought. There is nothing of poetry, romance, or dream in the disputatious tone of the book, and despite Valéry's essay on it, *Eureka* must be put aside as one of Poe's failures. He could not deal with his subject directly and by ordered demonstration. He needed imagery and dramatic action. Hence his success in fiction. The special quality of Poe results from his attempt to explore ontological problems through the medium of the imagination rather than the intellect.

We have seen thus far how a simple fact of physics becomes a biological mystery in "The Island of the Fay"; how the process of artistic creation in "The Oval Portrait" is an act of death; and how, in "The

Fall of the House of Usher," the water that reflected and so doubled the house becomes the agency of its complete obliteration. In each instance what is mirrored does not have its being duplicated, except in specious appearance. The mirroring water and the lifelike portrait are instruments of destruction. We might infer from this with what force the psychological phenomenon of the *Doppelgänger* would appeal to the imagination of Poe. In the preceding chapter an attempt was made to indicate its importance as one of his great subjects. Now, in the light of "The Island of the Fay," his interest in the *Doppelgänger* theme may be clarified in another way.

Otto Rank, in his study of the Double as a literary and psychological theme, calls our attention to the primitive belief that the shadow of a person is equivalent to his soul or spirit.[12] It was by means of his shadow that primitive man first saw his own body, and he equated it with his spiritual existence as the counterpart of the physical life that his somatic consciousness made him aware of. Hence the number of taboos —about breaking mirrors and walking on one's shadow—that were intended to preserve the "integrity" of the human shadow. Constantly emanating, however, it was as much a reminder of death as of life, and peril to the shadow was considered ominous of the fate in store for the body which cast it. Rank cites a case, recorded originally by the anthropologist Tylor, which has a very pertinent bearing on the nature of Poe's imagination. The belief was current in some primitive tribes that if a man were walking along a river bank in sunlight, a crocodile in the water could seize the man's shadow and swallow it. In "The Island of the Fay," it was the water itself which swallowed the shadows and thereby absorbed life from the objects which cast them. Poe's imagination, it seems, was of a sort which, in total ignorance of the findings of modern anthropology, could instinctively relive this ancient superstition. Breaking down the confines and compartments by which civilized man has brought some measure of order into the conditions of his mental existence, Poe asks us to experience the world in a way which humanity once knew but has long since forgotten. Through his ability to articulate these intuitions, he lays before us vestigial modes of feeling that lie buried in the depths of the human psyche. It may be that we should disapprove of this endeavor for literature, preferring to inspect such findings, codified and sterilized, and deprived of all their living human quality, in the casebooks of psychology and anthropology. If so, let us first make sure that we know what we are rejecting.

Is there not good reason, in any case, for taking the view that to dispose of Poe as merely a clever charlatan, to speak only of his melodramas, is to give evidence simply of misunderstanding? Poe was not exploiting a set of conjuring tricks, relying on the skill and versatility of his performance to keep the interest going and to distract attention from too close an inquiry into how each individual stunt is accomplished. He is an illusionist only in the sense that he wrote his stories in such a way that their surface and their latent meanings are not quite the same thing. When we read Poe with some sense of this fact, we are struck by the persistence in his work of a relatively small number of nearly obsessive concerns. Certainly his range was not a wide one. What serves as the dominant theme in one story will reappear in the form of variations in a num-

ber of others; or what may be found as a submotif in
one place will occur as the focus of interest in another.
This is why *Arthur Gordon Pym* makes such a good
starting place for a reading of Poe. The affinities that
exist between that book and stories apparently so diverse as "The Oval Portrait," "The Island of the Fay,"
"William Wilson," and "The Fall of the House of
Usher" indicate the homogeneity of what can easily
be mistaken as a nomadic and morbidly disordered
imagination. Story after story turns out to share some
measure of common ground.

Thus we may go on from the stories that have been
considered so far to a briefer mention of a number of
others in which the dominant idea is metempsychosis.
In "A Tale of the Ragged Mountains," a young man
in the Virginia hills relives an experience of action and
death in a battle fought long before in India. It develops that in him was reincarnated a British officer
who had fought and died in that battle a generation
earlier. In "Morella," a dead mother seems to enter
into and repossess the body of her daughter. So also in
"Ligeia," the soul of the narrator's first wife returns
from the grave to animate the corpse of another woman
and to alter her body into her own. In these three instances one notices how the theme of the Double exists
as a kind of lesser motif under the major one of metempsychosis; and how, in these and in all the other stories we have looked at, death provides the pervasive
context. Whereupon one recalls how often the experience of premature burial is dwelt on in Poe's writings. In every story in which metempsychosis is essential to the plot, this theme is necessarily present as well.
But it appears also in the stories of Madeline Usher,
and Berenice, and the victim of the pit and the pendu-

lum, whose rescue from the torture chamber was nothing else than a rebirth. To undergo the experience of death while still retaining the essential conditions of life—this is their plight; and it is likewise the one described in "The Facts in the Case of M. Valdemar." There, in what is possibly the most terrifying of all Poe's tales, a dying man voluntarily submits to hypnosis so that his soul may penetrate the wall of death though his corpse is meanwhile slowly decomposing on the bed. Finally, in "The Colloquy of Monos and Una," which is usually referred to only as an expression of Poe's contempt for the materialism of the nineteenth century, we find him recording another of his imaginative excursions beyond the bourne of mortality; and in this sense it belongs with his other tales of burial and resurrection. Throughout all these stories, as well as those in which the *Doppelgänger* theme and the pool and the portrait are the significant features, we discern the importance of Poe's obsession with death. Sometimes clearly visible, but usually present only implicitly, it is his conception of death as a transmutation of life—"the painful metamorphosis," he called it [13]—which, more than any other single factor, serves to give Poe's "dark" tales their odd and special character.

A partial explanation of the importance which this conception had for him may be derived from the fact that in his experience there existed an integral relationship between sleep and death. "By sleep and its world alone is *Death* imaged," he wrote in "Monos and Una." [14] It was through the experience of dreams —of daydreams and reveries as well as nightmares— that Poe attempted to investigate this mystery. "Eleonora" contains the capital text on this subject: "They who dream by day are cognizant of many things which escape those who dream only by night. In their grey visions they obtain glimpses of eternity, and thrill, in awaking, to find that they have been upon the verge of the great secret." [15]

To be sure, that secret is never disclosed, by Poe or any other writer. But if we are to account for the special effect which Poe's best stories have, we must grasp the purpose which underlies such themes as those of the Double, Premature Burial, and Metempsychosis. They are not used as ends in themselves, but as pretexts (as Mauclair termed them). Through them Poe found it possible to embark on an imaginative exploration beyond the frontiers of conscious knowledge. And Poe's unique ability as a writer consists in this: that when we read his stories with an awareness of what his ambitious intention was, we too may in some degree take part in this imaginative exploration. Through the spectrum of his stories the experience we have of the actual world, and the assumptions we make regarding it, come through in strange colors and fall into patterns that may have existed before for us, but only in those dreams that cannot be remembered. Poe well knew that the everyday world would call his visions fantastic, and so for most of his readers they seem to be. But so deep was Poe's apprehension of them that they took on for him the character of profound truths, grasped by the intuition rather than the intelligence, "upon the verge of the great secret." To read Poe properly we should realize that the experience which his stories uniquely offer us is that of participating in the life of a great ontological imagination. It is an experience of exploration and discovery that is offered us, a voyage of the mind. Invitation to this voyage was given its classic formulation by Baudelaire; and though Sainte-Beuve declined it, the record of the French response to Poe during the past hundred years is evidence that this invitation still stands.

NOTES & BIBLIOGRAPHY

NOTES

INTRODUCTION

1. Letter to Verlaine, dated 16 November 1885, in *Œuvres complètes de Stéphane Mallarmé*, ed. Pléiade (Paris, 1945), pp. 1509–10.

2. Jean Richepin, *L'Ame américaine à travers quelques-uns de ses interprètes* (Paris, 1920), p. 209.

3. Letter to Sara Sigourney Rice, dated 4 April 1876, quoted in Alex Pasquier, *Amérique, 1944* (Brussels, n.d.), p. 147.

4. Perry Miller, "Europe's Faith in American Fiction," *Atlantic*, CLXXXVIII (December, 1951), 52–53.

5. Eliot's essay on Poe appeared originally in a French translation by Henri Fluchère in *La Table ronde*, No. 12 (December, 1948), pp. 1973–92. The English text, curiously different in a few details from the French version, was published (not for sale) by Harcourt, Brace in New York in 1948, and was printed in *The Hudson Review*, II (Autumn, 1949), 327–42.

1

1. Baudelaire, *Correspondance*, I, 380. Unless otherwise indicated, all references to the writings of Baudelaire, his correspondence and his Poe translations, pertain to *Œuvres complètes de Charles Baudelaire*, ed. Jacques Crépet (Paris, 1923–1953), 19 vols.

2. D. R. Hutcherson, "Poe's Reputation in England and America, 1850–1909," *American Literature*, XIV (November, 1942), 223.

3. As reported by William Dean Howells in *Literary Friends and Acquaintances* (New York & London, 1901), pp. 60–64.

4. Whitman describes this occasion and sums up his impressions of Poe in *Specimen Days* (*Prose Works*, Camden edition, I, 284–87).

5. Eliot's essay has been cited. Those by Allen Tate may be found in *The Forlorn Demon* (Chicago, 1953.) In 1926, it was Edmund Wilson's opinion that "no recent American critic, with the exception of Mr. Waldo Frank in his article on the Poe-Allan letters, has written with any real appreciation of Poe's absolute artistic importance." The situation has not greatly improved, despite Wilson's own fine essay "Poe at Home and Abroad," from which this opinion is quoted. See *The Shores of Light* (New York, 1952), pp. 179–90.

6. See James's essay on Baudelaire in *French Poets and Novelists* (London, 1878), p. 76; P. E. More, "A Note on Poe's Method," *Studies in Philology*, XX (July, 1923), 309; Yvor Winters, "Edgar Allan Poe: A Crisis in the History of American Obscurantism," in *Maule's Curse* (Norfolk, 1938), p. 304.

7. *L'Art romantique*, p. 59.

8. *Journaux intimes*, ed. Crépet (Paris, 1938), p. 49.

9. Henri Mondor, *Vie de Mallarmé* (Paris, 1941), p. 104.

10. Letter to Gide in 1891, quoted in Berne-Joffroy, *Présence de Valéry* (Paris, 1944), p. 216.

11. See Valéry's preface to René Fernandat, *Autour de Paul Valéry* (Paris & Grenoble, 1944), p. ii.

12. Jules Lemaître, "Dialogue des morts," *Les Lettres et les arts* (1 January 1886), pp. 139–44.

13. *Le Symboliste* (7 October 1886), p. 1.

14. Albert Samain, *Carnets intimes* (Paris, 1939), p. 50.

15. *Correspondance*, IV, 277.

16. *Ibid.*, II, 212.

17. There is even greater irony in the fact, recently brought to light, that the first of these essays, "Edgar Poe, sa vie et ses ouvrages," was not original with Baudelaire! It has proved to be a translation of an article on Poe written by John W. Daniel and published in the *Southern Literary Messenger* in 1850. Baudelaire added some remarks of his own and some others which he found in an obituary notice on Poe written by John R. Thompson for the November, 1849, issue of the same magazine. See W. T. Bandy, "New Light on Baudelaire and Poe," *Yale French Studies*, No. 10, pp. 65–69. In a forthcoming edition of "Bau-

delaire's" first essay, Mr. Bandy will discuss the implications of this discovery. Meantime it may be said that this evidence does not help strengthen the assumption that the Poe revered in Europe may be dismissed as a figment of "the French imagination."

18. "Edgar Poe, sa vie et ses œuvres," in *Histoires extraordinaires par Edgar Poe*, p. xxviii.

19. "Notes nouvelles sur Edgar Poe," in *Nouvelles histoires extraordinaires par Edgar Poe*, p. xviii.

20. *Nouvelles littéraires* (23 September 1933), p. 3.

21. Similar assumptions underline *Edgar Allan Poe: A Study in Genius*, by Joseph Wood Krutch. This book antedates the work of Marie Bonaparte by seven years. It is still worth reading, but in wealth of explicative detail her *Edgar Poe* is on an altogether different plane.

22. *La Psychanalyse du feu* (Paris, 1938), p. 181.

2

1. *Correspondance*, IV, 48 (Baudelaire's italics).

2. *Ibid.*, IV, 6.

3. "The Facts in the Case of Monsieur Poe," in *Contemporaries and Snobs* (New York, 1928), p. 253.

4. *Ibid.*, p. 252.

5. *Ibid.*, p. 222.

6. *Ibid.*, p. 221.

7. Letter to Demeney in Arthur Rimbaud, *Œuvres complètes*, ed. Pléiade (Paris, 1946), p. 254.

8. Curtis Hidden Page, "Poe in France," *Nation*, LXXXVIII (14 January 1909), 32.

9. Régis Messac, *Influences françaises dans l'œuvre d'Edgar Poe* (Paris, 1929), p. 254.

10. *Ibid.*, pp. 74–78.

11. *Ibid.*, p. 129.

12. *Ibid.*

13. *Ibid.*, p. 98.

14. *Ibid.*, p. 59.

15. Rémy de Gourmont, "Marginalia sur Poe et Baudelaire," in *Promenades littéraires* (Paris, 1910), I, 351.

16. André Fontainas, *La Vie d'Edgar A. Poe* (Paris, 1919), p. 165.

17. Charles du Bos, "Poe and the French Mind," *Athenaeum* (7 January 1921), p. 26.

18. Marcel Françon, "Poe et Baudelaire," *PMLA*, LX (September, 1945), 841–59.

19. *Ibid.*, pp. 848–51.

20. Charles du Bos, "Poe and the French Mind," *Athenaeum* (14 January 1921), p. 54.

21. Charles Morice, *La*

Littérature de tout à l'heure (Paris, 1889), p. 202.

22. Guy Michaud, *Message poétique du symbolisme,* 4 vols. (Paris, 1947), I, 25.

23. Quoted in H. W. Hewett-Thayer, *Hoffmann: Author of the Tales* (Princeton, 1948), p. 382.

24. Quoted in Herbert Agar, *A Declaration of Faith* (Boston, 1952), p. 193.

25. See Albert Béguin, *L'Ame romantique et le rêve* (Paris, 1946), p. 365 (for Nerval), and p. 207 (for Novalis).

26. Hewett-Thayer, p. 384.

27. Fernand Vandérem, *Baudelaire et Sainte-Beuve* (Paris, 1914), p. 18.

28. *Histoires extraordinaires par Edgar Poe,* pp. 380–81.

29. *Correspondance,* II, 203.

30. *Les Aventures d'Arthur Gordon Pym,* pp. 262–63.

31. *Ibid.,* p. 264.

32. Léon Lemonnier, *Edgar Poe et la critique française de 1845 à 1875* (Paris, 1928), p. 296.

33. Cf. Claire-Eliane Engel, "L'Etat des travaux sur Edgar Allan Poe en France," *Modern Philology,* XXIX (May, 1932), 485.

34. Léon Lemonnier, *Edgar Poe et la critique fran-çaise de 1845 à 1875,* Part IV.

35. Jacques Vallette, "Chronique" [review of *The Centenary Poe,* ed. Slater (London, 1949)], *Mercure de France,* CCVIII (January, 1950), 162.

36. *Mesures,* VI (April, 1940), 89–127. A somewhat enlarged version of the article has been published as a book in 1952. In connection with Marion's monograph one should read Section IV, "Les Mystères de la rue Morgue," of Régis Messac's elaborate study *Le "Detective Novel" et l'influence de la pensée scientifique* (Paris, 1929). In this book, the first and most extended of all inquiries into an important phase of "popular culture," is to be found the fullest discussion ever published of Poe's ratiocinative tales and essays. Indeed Poe is the central figure and hero of the entire work, which comes to nearly 700 large pages. Concentrating on those writings of Poe in which logical analysis plays a dominant role, Messac argues that Poe should be seen as the descendant of the *Aufklärer* and the *Encyclopédistes,* "despite the great admiration the symbolists had for him" (p. 182). And yet Messac, like Marion, is aware that Poe's aggressive logic is,

after all, only logic "of a sort." See pp. 356–57, and p. 375.

37. Marion, p. 20.

38. André Faurès, "Edgar Poe," *Nouvelles littéraires*, XII (7 April 1934), 2; Suzanne D'Olivéra Jackowska, "La Réhabilitation d'Edgar Poe," *Nouvelle revue*, CXXIV (March, 1933), 106. Mme Jackowska was a singer of some distinction twenty years ago, and a very able translator of Poe's poetry. Her public readings of the poems seem to have been cultural events. "To celebrate the 124th anniversary of the birth of Edgar Poe, a ceremony took place on the 26th of February at the Sorbonne, in the Amphitheatre Richelieu, under the auspices of the 'Friends of the University of Paris.' Their excellencies the ambassadors of the United States, Poland, Belgium, Brazil, Sweden, Roumania, and almost the entire diplomatic corps, were represented."—*Ibid.*, p. 103. Mme Jackowska was the principal participant. But the occasion is remarkable for another reason: Poe's 124th anniversary! Is such a ceremony conceivable in this country?

39. Some of the evidence for this has been presented in the previous chapter. See also Téodor de Wyzewa, *Nos maîtres* (Paris, 1895), pp. 150 ff.; Charles Morice, *La Littérature de tout à l'heure* (Paris, 1889), p. 202; Jean Royère, *Clartés sur la poésie* (Paris, 1925), p. 87.

40. Jean Moréas, "Les Décadents," *Le XIXᵉ siècle* (11 August 1885), no pagination.

41. E. Noulet, *L'Œuvre poétique de Stéphane Mallarmé* (Paris, 1940), p. 150.

42. Gustave Kahn, "Les Poèmes de Poe traduits par Stéphane Mallarmé," *Revue indépendante* (September, 1888), 439–40.

43. *Ibid.*, p. 440.

44. Jean Dornis, *La Sensibilité dans la poésie française contemporaine (1885–1912)* (Paris, 1912), p. 40.

45. It seems that Laurière tried personally to fulfill the interminable demand that exists in France for books dealing with Poe. His 1904 volume was a doctoral *thèse* at the University of Paris. In 1911 he published a short study, *Edgar Poe*, and in 1934 appeared *L'Etrange vie et les étranges amours d'Edgar Poe*. It was followed the next year by *Le Génie morbide d'Edgar Poe*. Neither of these volumes is as intriguing as its title is meant to suggest.

46. Camille Mauclair, *Le Génie d'Edgar Poe* (Paris, 1928), p. xvi.

47. *Ibid.*, p. 214.

48. The fact that Baudelaire translated *Eureka* is enough to cast doubt on Mauclair's notion; and Baudelaire could speak of Poe as "a philosopher never refuted" (*Les Paradis artificiels*, p. 48), and as the author of "a seriously philosophical work" (*L'Art romantique*, p. 342). But Baudelaire's emphasis on Poe as a story-teller rather than as a thinker was all to the good, in my opinion. This emphasis has proved durable, whereas that proposed in Mauclair's book has not.

49. *Op. cit.*, p. xxiii.

50. *Ibid.*, p. 52.

51. *Ibid.*, p. 123.

52. *Ibid.*, p. 161.

53. *Ibid.*, p. 115.

54. *Ibid.*, p. 121.

55. Cyrille Arnavon, "Edgar Allan Poe, cent ans après," *Langues modernes*, XLIII (September–October, 1949), 292–303.

56. *Ibid.*, p. 299.

57. *Ibid.*, p. 298.

58. Albert Béguin, "Grandeur d'Edgar Poe," *Nouvelles littéraires* (27 October 1949), p. 5.

59. *Ibid.*

60. Arnavon, p. 295. The biography in question is that of Arthur Hobson Quinn.

61. Béguin, "Grandeur d'Edgar Poe," p. 5.

3

1. "Whenever a book is abused, people take it for granted that it is *I* who have been abusing it."—*The Complete Works of Edgar Allan Poe*, ed. Harrison (New York, 1902, 17 vols.), XVI, 155. After the appearance of "The Raven" in January, 1845, Poe's name became a household word in the United States. But, as Krutch observes, it was a transient notoriety rather than an enduring fame that Poe experienced in the four years before his death in 1849. See *Edgar Allan Poe: A Study in Genius*, pp. 152–64.

2. *The Letters of Edgar Allan Poe*, ed. Ostrom (Cambridge, 1948, 2 vols.), II, 336.

3. The details of the story of how Poe became known in France have been gone over by several investigators: by C. P. Cambiaire, in *The Influence of Edgar Allan Poe in France* (New York, 1927); by Léon Lemonnier, in *Edgar Poe et la critique française de 1845 à 1875*, and in *Les Traducteurs d'Edgar Poe en France* (Paris, 1928); and by Louis Seylaz, in *Edgar Poe et les premiers symbolistes français* (Lausanne, 1932). Lem-

onnier summarizes and corrects these accounts in the preface to his edition of the *Histoires extraordinaires* (Paris, 1946). For the most part, all three writers agree on the facts in the case, and in this section I make use of their findings. What promises to be a definitive history of the matter is in preparation by W. T. Bandy.

4. *Correspondance*, III, 41. See also the letter to his mother, dated 27 March 1852: "I have found an American author who has aroused in me an incredible sympathy, and I have written two articles on his life and work."—*Ibid.*, I, 160.

5. François Porché, *Baudelaire: Histoire d'une âme* (Paris, 1945), p. 163.

6. Charles Asselineau, *Charles Baudelaire* (Paris, 1869), p. 39.

7. *Ibid.*, p. 40.

8. *Journaux intimes* (Paris, 1938), p. 32.

9. Quoted in E.-J. Crépet, *Charles Baudelaire* (Paris, 1907), pp. 155–56.

10. *Op. cit.*, p. 8.

11. *Histoires extraordinaires par Edgar Poe*, p. 392.

12. Porché, p. 22.

13. *Œuvres posthumes*, p. 15.

14. *Correspondance*, I, 42.

15. *Ibid.*, IV, 277.

16. "Le Voyage" (*Fleurs du mal*, CXXXVII).

17. Porché, pp. 59–60.

18. *Correspondance*, I, 90.

19. [Jules Fleury] Champfleury, *Souvenirs et portraits de jeunesse* (Paris, 1872), pp. 132–33.

20. *Curiosités esthétiques*, p. 78.

21. *Journaux intimes*, p. 44.

22. Lemonnier, *Edgar Poe et la critique française de 1845 à 1875*, p. 12.

23. *Curiosités esthétiques*, p. 192.

24. *Op. cit.*, pp. 39–40.

25. *Ibid.*, pp. 45–48.

26. *Ibid.*, p. 41.

27. *Correspondance*, II, 212.

28. Esmé Stuart, "Charles Baudelaire and Edgar Poe: A Literary Affinity," *Nineteenth Century*, XXXIV (July, 1893), 66.

29. Jean Pommier, *La Mystique de Baudelaire* (Paris, 1932).

30. *Histoires extraordinaires par Edgar Poe*, p. 456.

31. *Ibid.*, p. 457.

32. *Ibid.*

33. P. Mansell Jones, "Poe, Baudelaire and Mallarmé: A Problem of Literary Judgement," *Modern Language Review*, XXXIX (July, 1944), 239.

34. *Works*, XVI, 71.

35. "Notes nouvelles sur Edgar Poe," in *Nouvelles histoires extraordinaires par Edgar Poe*, p. viii.

36. *Histoires extraordinaires par Edgar Poe*, p. 457.

37. *Journaux intimes*, p. 32; *Correspondance*, III, 278–89.

38. "Edgar Allan Poe, sa vie et ses ouvrages," in *Œuvres posthumes*, p. 286. Although this essay, as we noticed earlier, represents high-handed plagiarism on Baudelaire's part, the sentence quoted is his own.

39. *Histoires extraordinaires par Edgar Poe*, p. 458.

40. *Correspondance*, I, 161.

41. See Lemonnier's introduction to *Nouvelles histoires extraordinaires* (Paris, 1947), pp. xxiv–xxviii.

42. *Journaux intimes*, p. 65.

43. *Correspondance*, I, 191.

44. Jacques Crépet, in *Histoires extraordinaires par Edgar Poe*, p. 364. Unless other indications are given, my version of the history of Baudelaire's work as translator condenses the detailed account given by Crépet in notes to the five volumes of Poe translations.

45. Asselineau, p. 50.

46. *Journaux intimes*, p. 111.

47. Théodore de Banville, *Mes souvenirs* (Paris, 1883), p. 81.

48. Asselineau, p. 43.

49. Jacques Crépet, in *Les Aventures d'Arthur Gordon Pym*, p. 258.

50. *Correspondance*, IV, 207.

51. Jacques Crépet, in *Eureka par Edgar Poe*, pp. 214–17.

52. "Notes nouvelles sur Edgar Poe," in *NHE*, p. xxiii.

53. An important text, unpublished in Baudelaire's lifetime, is the translator's note which he intended to use as preface to a uniform edition of Poe's work. After reviewing the translations he had completed, Baudelaire wrote: "If my work could have been usefully continued in such a country as France, there would have remained for me the task of presenting Edgar Poe as poet and Edgar Poe as literary critic. . . . As for the second category of his talent, criticism, one can easily understand how what I might call the *Causeries de lundi* of Edgar Poe would have little prospect of interesting our frivolous Parisians. For they are not interested in the literary quarrels that divide what is still a young nation and that make North and South enemies, in literature as in politics." Quoted in *Eureka par Edgar Poe*, p. 233.

4

1. *Correspondance*, I, 381.

2. *Letters*, II, 309.

3. *Correspondance*, I, 327.

4. *Histoires grotesques et sérieuses par Edgar Poe*, p. 289.

5. See Lemonnier's introduction to his edition of the *Nouvelles histoires extraordinaires* for a discussion of the work of Hughes and the other translators contemporary with Baudelaire.

6. *Works*, III, 5; *Les Aventures d'Arthur Gordon Pym*, p. 1.

7. *Works*, VI, 138; *NHE*, p. 248.

8. *Works*, IV, 252–3; *NHE*, p. 166.

9. *Works*, V, 235; *HE*, p. 434 (Crépet's note).

10. Yves Le Dantec, "Baudelaire traducteur," *Le Correspondant* (10 January 1932), 98–112.

11. *Works*, II, 249; *HE*, p. 312.

12. *Works*, III, 290; *NHE*, p. 109.

13. *Works*, V, 89; *NHE*, p. 70.

14. *Works*, VI, 123; *NHE*, p. 233.

15. *Works*, IV, 251; *NHE*, p. 164.

16. *Works*, V, 75; *NHE*, p. 126.

17. *Works*, V, 72; *NHE*, p. 123.

18. *Works*, II, 250; *HE*, p. 313.

19. *Works*, II, 18; *NHE*, p. 80.

20. *Works*, II, 30; *HE*, p. 304.

21. Amiel, *Fragments d'un journal intime* (2 vols., Paris, 1927), I, 51.

22. *Op. cit.*, p. 111.

23. *Works*, IV, 254; *NHE*, p. 167.

24. *Works*, V, 70; *NHE*, p. 120.

25. *Works*, II, 19; *NHE*, p. 81.

26. *Works*, III, 273–74; *NHE*, pp. 91–93.

27. "Alas! even after all the progress we have for so long heard about, there will always remain enough evidence of Original Sin to prove its immemorial reality."—*L'Art romantique*, p. 392. See also *Journaux intimes*, pp. 80 and 92.

28. *Works*, V, 99; *HE*, p. 83.

29. *Works*, V, 102; *HE*, p. 86.

30. *Works*, V, 108–9; *HE*, pp. 93–94.

31. *Works*, V, 116; *HE*, p. 102.

32. *Works*, V, 123; *HE*, p. 108.

33. In Poe's "Marginalia" there occurs a passage, written well before the event, which serves admirably to

characterize the skill with which Poe was translated by Baudelaire: "Is it not clear that, by such dexterity, *a translation may be made to* *convey to a foreigner a juster conception of an original than could the original itself?* (Poe's italics).—*Works,* XVI, 106.

5

1. *Correspondance,* IV, 277.

2. "Edgar Poe, sa vie et ses œuvres," in *Histoires extraordinaires par Edgar Poe,* pp. xi–xiii.

3. *Ibid.,* p. ix.

4. Esmé Stuart, *op. cit.,* p. 167.

5. "Edgar Poe, sa vie et ses œuvres," p. xx.

6. *Letters,* II, 454.

7. *Correspondance,* I, 342.

8. *Ibid.,* p. 106.

9. *Letters,* I, 7 ff., 28 ff., 39 ff.

10. *Correspondance,* I, 233.

11. "Edgar Poe, sa vie et ses œuvres," p. xxi.

12. *Ibid.,* p. xvi.

13. E.-J. Crépet, *op. cit.,* p. 155.

14. *Correspondance,* IV, 312.

15. *Ibid.,* p. 313.

16. "Edgar Poe, sa vie et ses œuvres," p. ix.

17. *Ibid.,* p. xviii.

18. *Journaux intimes,* p. 88.

19. "Notes nouvelles sur Edgar Poe," in *Nouvelles histoires extraordinaires par Edgar Poe,* pp. vi–xiv.

20. See Ernest Marchand, "Poe as a Social Critic," *American Literature,* VI (March, 1934), 28–43.

21. "Notes nouvelles sur Edgar Poe," p. ix.

22. *Ibid.*

23. *Journaux intimes,* pp. 26–27.

24. *Works,* XIV, 207.

25. *Ibid.,* VI, 270; II, 122.

26. Poe quotes the aphorism in "Ligeia" (*Works,* II, 250) and in several other places.

27. *Curiosités esthétiques,* p. 224.

28. In his letter to Richard Wagner Baudelaire made a remark he might well have addressed to Poe: "It seemed to me at first that this music was familiar to me, and on later reflection I saw how the mirage came about; it was as if this music were *my own,* and I recognized it as any one will recognize the thing he is destined to love." *Correspondance,* III, 32–33.

29. *Curiosités esthétiques,* p. 119.

30. *Ibid.,* pp. 90–91.

31. *Ibid.*, p. 106.

32. *Ibid.*, pp. 14, 18, 107.

33. See E. Noulet, "L'Influence d'Edgar Poe sur la poésie française," in her *Etudes littéraires* (Mexico, 1945), pp. 100–109.

34. *Curiosités esthétiques*, p. 26.

35. *Ibid.*, p. 107.

36. And of plagiarism Poe was accused by one of the earliest students of the Poe-Baudelaire relationship. See Arthur S. Patterson, *L'Influence d'Edgar Allan Poe sur Charles Baudelaire* (Grenoble, 1903), Ch. XI.

37. "Notes nouvelles sur Edgar Poe," p. xx.

38. Jean Pommier, *La Mystique de Baudelaire* (Paris, 1932).

39. *Works*, VII, 31n.

40. Pommier, pp. 8, 72.

41. *Curiosités esthétiques*, pp. 249–50.

42. See "The Domain of Arnheim," *Works*, VI, 180–82.

43. *Ibid.*, XVI, 17–18.

44. *Curiosités esthétiques*, p. 274.

45. *Works*, XIV, 187.

46. *Curiosités esthétiques*, pp. 97–98.

47. "Notes nouvelles sur Edgar Poe," p. vii.

48. *Les Paradis artificiels*, pp. 16–17.

49. *Ibid.*

50. *Curiosités esthétiques*, p. 251.

51. *Les Paradis artificiels*, pp. 67–69; p. 233.

52. Georges Blin, *Baudelaire* (Paris, 1939); A. G. Lehmann, *The Symbolist Aesthetic in France, 1885–1895* (Oxford, 1951), pp. 85–87.

53. *Works*, XVI, 164.

54. *Ibid.*, XIV, 189–90; XVI, 164.

55. *Ibid.*, XVI, 88.

56. *Ibid.*, IV, 236 ("Eleonora").

57. *Ibid.*, VIII, 283.

58. *Ibid.*, XVI, 150.

59. Patterson, Seylaz, and, to lesser degree, Lemonnier, have emphasized the influence of Poe on Baudelaire; on the other side, Régis Michaud (in "Baudelaire et Edgar Poe: une mise au point," *Revue de littérature comparée*, XVIII [Oct.–Dec., 1938]), and P. Mansell Jones have belittled it.

60. *Journaux intimes*, p. 106.

61. See *Les Fleurs du mal*, ed. Jacques Crépet and Georges Blin (Paris, 1942), p. 213.

62. *Correspondance*, I, 266.

63. The text here is as quoted from the unpublished Journals of Kierkegaard by Walter Lowrie in his introduction to *The Concept of Dread* (Princeton, 1944), p. xii. W. H. Auden in *The Enchafèd Flood* (New York,

1950), p. 78, evidently uses the same quotation, but paraphrases it.

64. *Correspondance*, I, 195.

65. *Journaux intimes*, p. 88.

66. *Ibid.*, p. 43.

67. *Les Fleurs du mal*, ed. Crépet and Blin, p. 197.

68. *Ibid.*, p. 83.

69. *Ibid.*, p. 165.

70. *Ibid.*, pp. 86–87.

71. *Ibid.*, p. 133.

72. This was a recurrent idea with Baudelaire. See *Journaux intimes*, pp. 54, 63.

73. *Works*, II, 240.

74. *Ibid.*, V, 85.

75. *Ibid.*, II, 13.

76. See Mallarmé's letter to Cazalis, quoted in Henri Mondor, *Vie de Mallarmé*, p. 145.

77. *Works*, VI, 149–50. We might notice how "The Pit and the Pendulum" concludes: "An outstretched arm caught my own as I fell, fainting, into the abyss."

78. Quoted in *Les Fleurs du mal*, p. 270.

79. "Marginalia," *Works*, XVI, 167.

80. "Au lecteur," *Les Fleurs du mal*, p. 1.

6

1. Henry James, *The Golden Bowl* (New York, 1909, 2 vols.), I, 22.

2. Baudelaire's translation was the first to be made and has of course been the standard French version. But three other translations exist, and one of them, the work of Charles Simond, was published in 1887 and reprinted three times in the course of the next five years.

3. D. M. McKiethan, "Two Sources of Poe's *Narrative of Arthur Gordon Pym*," *University of Texas Studies in English*, XII (1933); Keith Huntress, "Another Source for Poe's 'The Narrative of Arthur Gordon Pym'," *American Literature*, XVI (March, 1944); J. O. Bailey, "Sources for Poe's *Arthur Gordon Pym*, 'Hans Phaall,' and Other Pieces," *PMLA*, LVII (June, 1942).

4. *Correspondance*, II, 212.

5. *Les Aventures d'Arthur Gordon Pym par Edgar Poe*, p. 265.

6. *Correspondance*, II, 76.

7. *Op. cit.*, p. 248.

8. Arthur Hobson Quinn, *Edgar Allan Poe* (New York, 1941), p. 264.

9. *Works*, III, 18.

10. *Ibid.*, p. 12.

11. *Ibid.*, p. 16.

12. *Ibid.*, p. 62.

13. *Ibid.*, p. 85.

14. *Ibid.*, p. 113.

15. *Ibid.*, p. 144.

16. *Ibid.*, p. 185.

17. *Ibid.*, p. 242.

18. Marie Bonaparte, *Edgar Poe* (Paris, 1933, 2 vols.), I, 374.

19. *Works*, III, 112–13.

20. Bonaparte, I, 406 ff.

21. *Works*, III, 17–18.

22. *Ibid.*, p. 17.

23. *Ibid.*, p. 33.

24. *Ibid.*, pp. 204–5.

25. Bonaparte, I, 389, 432.

26. *Ibid.*, I, 394.

27. Here I am following the preface which Bachelard wrote for a reprint of Baudelaire's translation, *Les Aventures d'Arthur Gordon Pym* (Paris, 1944). Another of his comments should be quoted: "When literature first began to interest me I found nothing but boredom in this book, and though I was an admirer of Poe from the time I was twenty I could never summon the fortitude needed to get through a reading of these interminable and monotonous adventures. When I came to understand the importance of the revolutions accomplished by modern psychology, I went back to my earlier readings and took up first of all those books that had proved tedious to me, a reader whose taste was warped along positivistic, realistic, scientific lines. In particular I resumed *Gordon Pym*, setting the drama this time where it really belongs, as all drama does, on the frontier between the conscious and the unconscious. I then became aware that this adventure, which in appearance hurtles across two oceans, is in reality an adventure of the unconscious, an adventure taking place in the nighttime of a soul. And this book, which to a reader of conventional literary tastes would seem weak and unfinished, was revealed instead as the full achievement of a remarkably unified dream. I thenceforth ranked *Pym* as among the great works of Edgar Poe." *L'Eau et les rêves* (Paris, 1942), pp. 80–81.

28. *Works*, III, 28.

29. Bachelard, Introduction, *op. cit.*, p. 15.

30. *Ibid.*, p. 12.

31. *Ibid.*, p. 21.

32. *Ibid.*, p. 23.

33. *Works*, III, 230.

34. *Ibid.*, VI, 147.

35. *Ibid.*, III, 44.

36. *Ibid.*, II, 14.

37. *Ibid.*, IV, 236.

38. Merton M. Sealts, "Melville's Reading," *Harvard Library Bulletin*, III (Autumn, 1949), 413.

39. *Moby-Dick* (London, 1922, 2 vols.), I, 258–59.

40. *Ibid.*, I, 7.

41. *Works*, III, 17.

42. *Moby-Dick*, II, 318.

43. *Ibid.*, II, 323.

44. *Ibid.*, I, 48.

45. *Ibid.*, II, 276. The discussion in this section is limited to making the point that the stature of *Arthur Gordon Pym* is by no means dwarfed when the book is set up against Melville's masterpiece. But this mention of the revolt theme brings to mind the fact that there are several other books by Melville which are relevant to Poe's story. *Benito Cereno* deals with the aftermath of a savage mutiny in a way strongly reminiscent of Poe: the conflict between white and black; the deceptive appearances which plague Captain Delano and make it almost impossible for him to differentiate between master and servant, friend and foe; Melville's reliance on documentary material covering the actual case so as to give a dry tone of authenticity to his version of the whole affair. In this last respect, Melville's reluctance to sound the symbolic depths of the story, the method of *Cereno* is especially close to that used by Poe. There is also the case of *Typee*. We might notice, among other things, the taboo on *whiteness*. But of special interest here is that the only really interesting episode in the novel, the perilous journey through deep crevasses and down tremendous cliffs, is an episode which reads very much like a reworking of Chapter XXIV in *Arthur Gordon Pym*. And the final page of Pym's narrative is like the sudden ending of *Mardi*.

46. *Ibid.*, II, 276.

47. *Ibid.*, I, 7.

48. *Ibid.*, I, 239.

49. Lemonnier, *Edgar Poe et les poètes français* (Paris, 1932), pp. 86 ff.; Seylaz, *op. cit.*, p. 158; Enid Starkie, *Rimbaud* (New York, 1939), p. 139.

7

1. Carl Jung, quoted in Brewster Ghiselin, ed., *The Creative Process*, Mentor Books (New York, 1955), pp. 212–13.

2. *Letters*, I, 130.

3. *Ibid.*, I, 57–58.

4. Napier Wilt, "Poe's Attitude Toward His Tales: A New Document," *Modern Philology*, XXV (August, 1927), 101–5; W. F. Taylor, "Israfel in Motley," *Sewanee Review*, XLII (July, 1934), 330–39.

5. J. W. Krutch, review of *The Letters of Edgar Allan Poe*, in *New York Herald*

Tribune Books (19 December 1948), p. 1.

6. T. O. Mabbott, "Introduction," *The Selected Poetry and Prose of Edgar Allan Poe*, Modern Library College Editions (New York, 1951), pp. v–vi.

7. Margaret Alterton and Hardin Craig, *Edgar Allan Poe, Representative Selections* (New York, 1935), Introduction, p. xxii.

8. Killis Campbell, *The Mind of Poe* (Cambridge, 1933), p. 22.

9. N. B. Fagin, *The Histrionic Mr. Poe* (Baltimore, 1949); Clark Griffith, "Poe's 'Ligeia' and the English Romantics," *U. of Toronto Quarterly*, XXIV (October, 1954), 8–25.

10. Edmond Jaloux, *Edgar Poe et les femmes* (Geneva, 1942), p. 97.

11. "Edgar Poe, sa vie et ses œuvres," in *Histoires extraordinaires par Edgar Poe*, p. xxx.

12. Thomas Mann, *The Short Novels of Dostoievski* (New York, 1945), Introduction, p. xvii.

13. As the epigraph to "William Wilson," Poe uses the lines: "What say of it? what say of CONSCIENCE grim/That spectre in my path?" He erroneously attributes the lines to "Chamberlayne's *Pharronida*."

14. *Works*, III, 300.

15. *Ibid.*, IV, 152.

16. *Ibid.*, p. 145.

17. *Ibid.*, pp. 134–5.

18. *Ibid.*, p. 140.

19. *Ibid.*, V, 94.

20. *Ibid.*, p. 88.

21. *Ibid.*, p. 90.

22. *Ibid.*, III, 325.

23. *Ibid.*, p. 297.

24. *Ibid.*, p. 276.

25. *Ibid.*, p. 282.

26. *Ibid.*, p. 291.

27. *Ibid.*, p. 281.

28. *Ibid.*, p. 289.

29. *Ibid.*, VII, xlii ("Letter to B——.")

8

1. *Works*, IV, 247.

2. *Ibid.*, p. 249.

3. *Ibid.*, p. 194.

4. *Ibid.*, p. 196.

5. *Ibid.*, p. 199.

6. *Ibid.*, p. 198.

7. *Ibid.*, p. 195.

8. *Letters*, I, 57–58.

9. *Works*, II, 17.

10. *Nouvelles histoires extraordinaires par Edgar Poe*, p. 384.

11. *Letters*, I, 260.

12. Otto Rank, *Don Juan: un étude sur le double* (Paris, 1932), pp. 88 ff.

13. *Letters*, I, 257.

14. *Works*, IV, 211.

15. *Ibid.*, p. 236.

SELECTIVE BIBLIOGRAPHY

Arnavon, Cyrille. "Edgar Allan Poe, cent ans après," *Langues modernes*, XLIII (September-October, 1949), 292–303.

———. *Histoire littéraire des États-Unis*. Paris, 1953.

Asselineau, Charles. *Charles Baudelaire*. Paris, 1869.

Bachelard, Gaston. *L'Air et les songes*. Paris, 1943.

———. *L'Eau et les rêves*. Paris, 1942.

———. Introduction, in *Les Aventures d'Arthur Gordon Pym*. Paris, 1944.

———. *La Psychanalyse du feu*. Paris, 1938.

Bandy, W. T. "New Light on Baudelaire and Poe," *Yale French Studies* No. 10, pp. 65–69.

Banville, Théodore de. *Mes souvenirs*. Paris, 1883.

Barine, Arvède. *Névrosés: Hoffmann, Quincey, Edgar Poe, G. de Nerval*. Paris, 1898.

Baudelaire, Charles. *Les Fleurs du mal*, ed. Jacques Crépet and Georges Blin. Paris, 1942.

———. *Journaux intimes*, ed. Jacques Crépet. Paris, 1938.

———. *Œuvres*. ed. Jacques Crépet. Paris, 1923–53. 19 vols.

Béguin, Albert. *L'Ame romantique et le rêve*. Paris, 1946.

———. "Grandeur d'Edgar Poe," *Les Nouvelles littéraires*, 27 October, 1949, p. 5.

Blin, Georges. *Baudelaire*. Paris, 1939.

Bolle, Jacques. *La Poésie du cauchemar*. Paris, 1946.

Bonaparte, Marie. *Edgar Poe*. Paris, 1933. 2 vols.

Boussoulas, Nicolas-Isidore. *La Peur et l'univers dans l'œuvre d'Edgar Poe*. Paris, 1952.

Cambiaire, C. P. *The Influence of Edgar Allan Poe in France*. New York, 1927.

Castelnau, Jacques. *Edgar Poe*. Paris, 1945.

Cestre, Charles. "Poe et Baudelaire," *Revue anglo-américaine*, XXI (April, 1934), 322–30.

Chassé, Charles. *Lueurs sur Mallarmé*. Paris, 1927.

Cowley, Malcolm. "Aidgarpo," *New Republic*, CXIII (5 November 1945), 607–10.

Dornis, Jean. *La Sensibilité dans la poésie française contemporaine (1885–1912)*. Paris, 1912.

Du Bos, Charles. "Poe and the French Mind," *Athenaeum*, 7 January 1921, pp. 26–27; and 14 January 1921, pp. 54–55.

Eliot, T. S. "Edgar Poe et la France," *La Table ronde*, December, 1948, pp. 1973–92.

———. "From Poe to Valéry," *The Hudson Review*, II (Autumn, 1949), 327–42.

———. "Note sur Mallarmé et Poe," *Nouvelle revue française*, XIV (November, 1926), 524–26.

Engel, C.-E. "L'Etat des travaux sur Edgar Allan Poe en France," *Modern Philology*, XXIX (May, 1932), 482–88.

Ferran, André. *L'Esthétique de Baudelaire*. Paris, 1933.

Fleury, Jules. *Souvenirs et portraits de jeunesse*. Paris, 1872.

Fontainas, André. "Ce qu'ont pensé de Poe ses contemporains," *Mercure de France*, CCXXV (15 January, 1931), 312–24.

———. *La Vie d'Edgar A. Poe*. Paris, 1919.

Françon, Marcel. "Poe et Baudelaire," *PMLA*, LX (September, 1945), 841–59.

Gourmont, Rémy de. "Marginalia sur Poe et Baudelaire," *Promenades littéraires*, Vol. I. Paris, 1904.

Hennequin, Émile. "Edgar Poe," *La Revue contemporaine*, I (25 January 1885), 24–56.

Huret, Jules. *Enquête sur l'évolution littéraire*. Paris, 1891.

Jaloux, Edmond. *Edgar Poe et les femmes*. Geneva, 1942.

———. "Rencontres avec Edgar Poe," *1935*, 27 March 1935. p. 9.

———. Review of Marie Bonaparte: *Edgar Poe*, in *Les Nouvelles littéraires*, 23 September 1933, p. 3.

Jones, P. Mansell. "Poe, Baudelaire, and Mallarmé: A Problem of Literary Judgement," *Modern Language Review*, XXXIX (July, 1944), 236–46.

———. "Poe and Baudelaire: The 'Affinity,'" *Modern Language Review*, XL (October, 1945), 279–83.

Jones, Rhys S. "The Influence of Edgar Allan Poe on Paul Valéry prior to 1900," *Comparative Literature Studies*, XXI–XXII (1946), 10–15.

Kahn, Gustave. "Les Poèmes de Poe traduits par Stéphane Mallarmé," *Revue indépendante*, September, 1888, pp. 435–43.

———. *Silhouettes littèraires*. Paris, 1925.

Lauvrière, Emile. *Edgar Poe, sa vie et son œuvre*. Paris, 1904.

———. *Edgar Poe*. Paris, 1911.

———. *L'Étrange vie et les étranges amours d'Edgar Poe*. Paris, 1934.

———. *Le Génie morbide d'Edgar Poe*. Paris, 1935.

Le Dantec, Y.-G. "Baudelaire traducteur," *Le Correspondant*, 25 December 1931, pp. 895–908; and 10 January 1932, pp. 98–112.

Lemaître, Jules. "Dialogue des morts," *Les Lettres et les arts*, 1 January 1886, pp. 139–44.

Lemonnier, Léon. *Edgar Poe et la critique française de 1845 à 1875*. Paris, 1928.

———. *Edgar Poe et les conteurs français*. Paris, 1947 .

———. *Edgar Poe et les poètes français*. Paris, 1932.

———. *Enquêtes sur Baudelaire*. Paris, 1929.

———. *Les Traducteurs d'Edgar Poe en France de 1845 à 1875*. Paris, 1928.

——— (ed.). Introduction, in *Histoires extraordinaires*. Paris, 1946.

———. Introduction, in *Nouvelles histoires extraordinaires*. Paris, 1947.

Mallarmé, Stéphane. *Œuvres complètes*, ed. Henri Mondor and G. Jean-Aubry. Paris, 1945.

Marion, Denis. *La Méthode intellectuelle d'Edgar Poe*. Paris, 1952.

Mauclair, Camille. *Le Génie d'Edgar Poe*. Paris, 1925.

Mendès, Catulle. Introduction to excerpts from Poe's *Margi-*

nalia in *La République des lettres*, 20 March 1876, pp. 131–32.

Messac, Régis. *Le "Detective Novel" et l'influence de la pensée scientifique.* Paris, 1929.

――――. *Influences françaises dans l'œuvre d'Edgar Poe.* Paris, 1929.

Michaud, Guy. *Message poétique du symbolisme.* Paris, 1947. 4 vols.

Michaud, Régis. "Baudelaire et Edgar Poe: une mise au point," *Revue de littérature comparée*, XVIII (October–December, 1938), 666–83.

Mondor, Henri. *Vie de Mallarmé.* Paris, 1946.

Moréas, Jean. "Chronique," *Le Symboliste*, 7 October 1886, p. 1.

――――. "Les Décadents," *Le XIXe siècle*, 11 August 1885. Unpaged.

Morice, Charles. *La Littérature de tout à l'heure.* Paris, 1889.

Morrisette, Bruce. *Les Aspects fondamentaux de l'esthétique symboliste.* Clermont-Ferrand, 1933.

Noulet, E. "L'Influence d'Edgar Poe sur la poésie française," *Etudes littéraires.* Mexico, 1945.

――――. *L'Œuvre poétique de Stéphane Mallarmé.* Paris, 1940.

Page, Curtis H. "Poe in France," *Nation*, LXXXVIII (14 January 1909), 32–34.

Patterson, Arthur S. *L'Influence d'Edgar Poe sur Charles Baudelaire.* Grenoble, 1903.

Poe, Edgar. *Letters*, ed. J. W. Ostrom. Cambridge, 1948. 2 vols.

――――. *Works*, ed J. A. Harrison. New York, 1902. 17 vols.

Pommier, Jean. *Dans les chemins de Baudelaire.* Paris, 1945.

――――. *La Mystique de Baudelaire.* Paris, 1932.

Porché, François. *Baudelaire: Histoire d'une âme.* Paris, 1944.

Poulet, Georges. "L'Univers circonscrit d'Edgar Poe," *Les Temps modernes*, CXIV–CXV (June–July, 1955), 2179–2204.

Praz, Mario. "Poe davanti alla psicanalisi," *Studi e Svaghi Inglesi.* Firenze, 1937.

Raymond, Marcel. *De Baudelaire au surréalisme*. Paris, 1947.

Régnier, Henri de. *Faces et profils*. Paris, 1931.

Rhodes, S. A. "The Influence of Poe on Baudelaire," *Romanic Review*, XVIII (October–December, 1927), 329–33.

Richepin, Jean. *L'Ame américaine à travers quelques-uns de ses interprètes*. Paris, 1920.

Riding, Laura. "The Facts in the Case of Monsieur Poe," *Contemporaries and Snobs*. New York, 1928.

Rosselot, Jeanne. "Poe in France," in *Poe in Foreign Lands and Tongues*, ed. J. C. French. Baltimore, 1941.

Rousselot, Jean. *Edgar Poe*. Paris, 1953.

Royère, Jean. "Edgar Poe et l'esthétique de poésie pure," *Clartés sur la poésie*. Paris. 1925.

Saisset, Léon, and Saisset, Frédéric. *Les Histoires extraordinaires d'Edgar Poe*. Paris, 1939.

Seylaz, Louis. *Edgar Poe et les premiers symbolistes français*. Lausanne, 1932.

Stuart, Esmé. "Charles Baudelaire and Edgar Poe: A Literary Affinity," *Nineteenth Century*, XXXIV (July, 1893), 65–80.

Saurès, André. *Portraits sans modèles*. Paris, 1935.

Tate, Allen. *The Forlorn Demon*. Chicago, 1953.

Valéry, Paul. "À Propos d'Eureka," *Variété I*. Paris, 1926.

———. "Situation de Baudelaire," *Variété II*. Paris, 1930.

Verhaeren, Emile. *Impressions*, Vol. III. Paris, 1928.

Wilson, Edmund. "Poe at Home and Abroad," *The Shores of Light*. New York, 1952.

Wyzewa, Téodor de. *Nos maîtres*. Paris, 1895.

Zimmermann, Eléonore M. "Mallarmé et Poe: précisions et aperçus," *Comparative Literature*, VI (Fall, 1954), 304–15.

INDEX

INDEX

ALLAN, John, 136, 139

Allan, Mrs. John, 137, 139

Allen, Hervey, 20, 56

American Imago, The, 20

Amiel, Henri-Frédéric, 128

Arnavon, Cyrille: on Poe's poetry, 62–63

Arnold, Elizabeth (mother of Edgar Poe), 137

L'Art Romantique, 12, 83

Asselineau, Charles, 71, 87, 88

Auden, W. H., 168, 289

Aupick, Jacques (stepfather of C. Baudelaire): effect of, on Baudelaire, 75–78 *passim*, 86

Aupick, Mme Jacques (mother of C. Baudelaire): effect of, on Baudelaire, 75–76, 97; parallel to Mrs. Allan, 138–39

BACHELARD, Gaston: psychoanalytical work on Poe by, 23–26, 55, 189–93, 201

Bacon, Francis, 145

Balzac, Honoré de: Poe reminiscent of, 34, 40; affected by Swedenborg, 90–91;

Baudelaire compared Poe to, 92

Bandy, W. T.: his work on Baudelaire, 280–81

Banville, Théodore de: on Baudelaire's exactness, 104

Baudelaire, Charles

—Opinions of Poe: stated, 9, 12, 17–19, 29, 55, 65, 84, 91–92, 107, 220; subscribed to by others, 12–13, 18–19, 26, 55, 59, 61, 63; questioned or denied, 29–30, 47–50, 173–74; evidenced in action, 87–89, 102, 104, 108

—Affinity with Poe; affirmed by Baudelaire, 15, 70, 135–36, 159; biographical, 73, 82, 135–41; aesthetic and intellectual, 141–66; doubted by admirers of Baudelaire, 157

—Impact of Poe on: described by Baudelaire, 15–16, 70, 135–36, 285; accounted for, 71–82

—Translations of Poe by: initial efforts, 89–98; his command of English, 96–98; *Histoires extraordi-*

naires: publishing history, 99–101; editorial plan, 111–14; *Nouvelles histoires extraordinaires:* publishing history, 99–101, editorial plan, 114–15, 262; *Les Aventures d'Arthur Gordon Pym,* 103, 118; *Eureka,* 104–5; *Histoires grotesques et sérieuses,* 106, 115–16; "Le Masque de la mort rouge," 119–20, 124–25, 128–29; "Petite discussions avec une momie," 118–19; "La Chute de la maison Usher," 122–23, 130–31; "Bérénice," 122; "Ligeia," 122–23, 125–26; "Le Coeur révélateur," 124; "L'Homme des foules," 124; "Le Puits et le pendule," 125, 129; "Morella," 126–28; "Le Démon de la perversité," 131; "Le Scarabée d'or," 131–34

—Works of: "L'Albatros," 78; *L'Art romantique,* 12, 83; "La Beauté," 167; "Correspondances," 150; *Curiosités esthétiques,* 83; "A une Dame Créole," 78; "Danse macabre," 59; "La Destruction," 153; "Le Flambeau vivant," 158; *Les Fleurs du mal,* 9–10, 46, 85, 102, 159, 165–67, 172; "Le Gouffre," 161–62; "Le Goût du néant," 162; "Harmonie du soir," 167; "Héautonimorouménos," 158; "L'Irrémédiable," 162–63; *Journaux intimes,* 12, 98, 142; "Au lecteur," 168; *Petits poèmes en prose,* 158; "A Sainte-Beuve," 76; *Le Salon de 1845,* 84; *Le Salon de 1846,* 84, 86, 147; "Le Voyage," 162

Baudelaire, Joseph-François (father of C. Baudelaire), 73

Beguin, Albert: quotation by Nerval and Novalis, 43; on Poe, 62, 63

Berman, Eugène, 254

Bertrand, Aloysius, 158

Blackwood's Magazine: style of articles in 1830's, 219–20

Boileau-Despréaux, N.: Poe's similarity to, 34, 40

Bonaparte, Marie: psycho-analytical study of Poe, 19–23, 37 and n, 55, 201; student of Freud, 20; discussion of *Arthur Gordon Pym* by, 183–88

Borghers, Alphonse: translator of Poe, 69, 98, 100

Bryant, William C., 11

CARLYLE, Thomas, 90

Charcot, Jean Martin, 36n

Charivari, Le, 67

Chase, Owen, 206

Chatterton, Thomas, 17

Chenier, Marie-Joseph; and convention of 1793, 42–43

Chute de la maison Usher, La (film): discussed, 257–59

Clemm, Mrs. Maria: in Poe's letter to Duyckinck, 67; Baudelaire's dedication to, 74, 101; parallel to Mme Aupick, 138

Coleridge, Samuel T.: and Poe's literary theory, 36, 38, 39; tone of, in Poe, 152; Poe critic of, 246–47

Commerce, Le, 68

Correspondences: concept of, 149–50, 153–55

Crépet, Jacques: definitive edition of Baudelaire, 9; on Baudelaire's translations, 104; on Baudelaire and Sainte-Beuve, 171–73

Curiosites esthétiques, Les, 83

DALI, Salvador, 254

Daniel, John M., 173

Daumier, H., 82

D'Aurevilly, Barbey: indifference to Poe, 13, 45; and *Le Pays,* 47–48, 100

Da Vinci, Leonardo, 12

Delacroix, Eugène: Baudelaire's art criticism of, 82, 83, 102; influenced Baudelaire, 46, 132

De la Motte, Houdart: on Schlegel and Poe, 36

Democratie pacifique, La: translations of Poe in, 69, 82, 85, 86

Descartes, René, 44, 90

Diderot, Denis, 91

Doppelgänger motif: in the tales, 115, 197, 198, 220–55 *passim,* 270–73; in detective stories, 198; in *Arthur Gordon Pym,* 196–97, 199

Dread, concept of: in Poe and Baudelaire, 160–67

Du Bos, Charles: ascribed French cast of mind to Poe, 35, 37–38

Duval, Jeanne, 80, 81, 99

Duyckinck, Evert: letter to, from Poe, 67

ELIOT, T. S.: on Poe, 8, 11; influenced by French Symbolist poets, 36n

Emerson, Ralph Waldo: held in higher esteem than Poe, 10, 35, 255; mentioned, 42, 90

Epstein, Jean: and filming of "Usher," 257–59

FAURÈS, André: praise for Poe, 53

Fleurs du mal, Les: lawsuit regarding, 46; appearance of, 102; themes in, 159; mentioned, 9, 85, 166, 167

Fontainas, André, 34

Forgues, Emile: translation of "Maelstrom," 68–69, 91, 98; translation of "Rue Morgue," 117

Fraisses, Armand: letter from Baudelaire to, 70

Françon, Marcel: criticism of Poe, 35–37 and n

Franklin, Benjamin, 49

Freud, Sigmund: Mme Bonaparte student of, 20; influenced by Charcot, 36n; mentioned, 94

Fuller, Margaret, 42, 166

GAUTIER, Théophile, 82

Gide, André, 13, 117

Goethe, J. W. von, 42, 91

Gourmont, Rémy de, 34

Griswold, Rufus, 136

HARDENBERG, Friedrich von. *See* Novalis

Hawthorne, Nathaniel: reputation compared with Poe's, 10, 63, 255, 269

Herder, J. G. von, 42

Hoffmann, E. T. A.: in France, 37, 42, 44, 88; is associated with Poe, 24, 63, 91

Hölderlin, Johann, 42

Holmes, Oliver Wendell, 11

Hughes, William: as translator of Poe, 98, 100, 117

Hugo, Victor: Morice on, 41, 45; mentioned, 44, 147

ILLUMINISM: spread of, in France, 93–95

Irving, Washington, 42

JACKOWSKA, Suzanne: praise of Poe, 53, 283

Jaloux, Edmond: praises Mme Bonaparte's study, 20; on *Blackwood's*, 219–20

James, Henry: on Poe, 11, 170; mentioned, 63

Jean Paul, 91

Jones, P. Mansell: belittled supposed significance of Poe on Baudelaire, 93, 289

Jung, Carl: on Poe, 216; on artistic creation, 218

KAHN, Gustave: criticism of "Usher," 54–55; criticism of "The Haunted Palace," 55, 249

Kant, Immanuel, 42

Keats, John, 38, 128

Kierkegaard, S.: concept of dread defined by, 160, 166

Kirkland, William, 66

Krutch, Joseph Wood, 217

LACLOS, C. de, 91

Lacordaire, Jean Baptiste, 28

Lauvrière, Emile: study of Poe by, 56–57

Lavater, J. K., 90

Le Dantec, Yves: on Baudelaire's translations, 122, 128

Lemaître, Jules, 13

Lemonnier, Léon: studies on Poe, 6, 48, 51, 72, 93

Lévy, Michel: publisher of Baudelaire's translations, 102, 105–6

Liberté de penser, La, 89, 91

Longfellow, Henry W., 11, 42

MADAME BOVARY, 83, 102

Maistre, Joseph de, 84

Mallarmé, Stéphane: high regard for Poe, 3, 4, 11, 12, 38–39, 48, 62; his translations of Poe's poems, 18, 51; mentioned, 6, 7, 165

Mann, Thomas, 221

Marion, Denis: criticism of Poe by, 51–52, 53

Massac, Régis: criticism of Poe, 32–34, 37, 282

Maturin, Charles, 91

Mauclair, Camille: study of Poe, 56–61 *passim*, 274

Melville, Herman: possible influence of *Arthur Gordon Pym* on, 205–15, 292; revival of interest in, 255–56; mentioned, 63

Metempsychosis: Poe's use of, 113–14, 272–73

Meunier, Isabelle: translations of Poe, 69, 71, 82, 91, 98

Michaud, Guy: study of Symbolist movement, 41–42

Michaud, Régis: belittled Poe's influence on Baudelaire, 289

Miller, Perry: at Poe celebration in Holland, 4

Moniteur universal, Le: Arthur Gordon Pym appeared in, 103, 116, 172

More, Paul Elmer, 11

Moréas, Jean, 13, 54

Morice, Charles: on Poe's success in France, 40–41

NERVAL, Gérard de: literary martyr, 17; compared hypothetically to Poe, 29; regard for Germany, 42, 43; as romantic, 44; Baudelaire on, 82

Newton, Sir Isaac, 90

Novalis (*pseud.*), 42, 43, 63

OSGOOD, Frances S., 66

Ossían, 37

PAGE, Curtis Hidden: criticism of Poe, 31

Pascal, Blaise: Poe compared to, 34; and Mauclair, 60

Pays, Le: Baudelaire's translations in, 47, 100–101

Petits poèmes en prose, Les, 158

Plagiarism: Forgues charged with, 69; on part of Baudelaire, 148, 280, 286

Plato, 3, 13

Poe, Edgar

—Great reputation in France: signs of its extent, 3–4, 11–14; contrasted with reputation in America, 10–11, 30, 217–20; sketched briefly, 14–26; surveyed, 28–65; theories to explain, 29–45; not unanimously endorsed, 47–52

—And the Symbolist aesthetic: 12–13, 53–56, 147, 165

—Motifs and themes: ratiocination, 51–52, 201–3, 252–53; metempsychosis, 113, 272; perverseness, 166, 193–94, 246; mystification, 175, 195, 204, 219–20; premature burial, 187–88, 190, 272–73; the *Doppelgänger,* 196–200, 220–47, 254, 270–71

—And Baudelaire: biographical parallels, 137–42; their views compared on: original sin, 131, 144–45; politics, 143; beauty, 144; inspiration, 147–48; originality, 147–48, 157; synaesthesia, 149–51; imagination, 151–52; dreams, 153–57; the concept of dread, 160–65; resemblance rather than influence, 157–59; differences between, 144, 149, 151, 155, 166–68

—Prose and verse compared: 247–55

—Imaginative quality defined: 259–74

—Works of: "Annabel Lee," 137; "The Assignation," 111; "The Balloon Hoax," 111, 113, 121–22; "The Bells," 137; "Berenice,"

97, 216–18, 224, 265, 267–68; "The Black Cat," 71–85, 95, 227; "The Business Man," 110; "The Cask of Amontillado," 116, 193; "The City in the Sea," 25; "The Colloquy of Monos and Una," 93, 273; "The Conversation of Eiros and Charmion," 93; "A Descent into the Maelstrom," 32, 59–60, 68, 164, 227–28; "The Devil in the Belfry," 13, 114; "The Domain of Arnheim," 111, 116; "Eleonora," 156, 273–74; *Eureka*, 21, 89, 94, 108; in relation to Poe's fiction, 266, 269; Baudelaire on, 18, 104–5; Marion on, 52; Mauclair on, 58; Samain on, 13; Valéry on, 18; "The Facts in the Case of M. Valdemar," 89, 113, 195, 273; "The Fall of the House of Usher," 25, 54–55, 130–31, 237–46, 264, 270; "Four Beasts in One," 59, 114; "The Gold Bug," 14, 52, 60, 68, 69, 131–34, 223, 225; "Hans Phaall," 101, 113, 195; "The Haunted Palace," 55, 158, 247–50; "How to Write a Blackwood Article," 220; "The Imp of the Perverse," 117, 131, 193; "The Island of the Fay," 262–65, 268; "The Journal of Julius Rodman," 111, 186; "King Pest," 82, 114; "Landor's Cottage," 111, 116; "The Landscape Garden," 111;

"Ligeia," 112–14, 122, 125–26, 198, 272; "Lionizing," 59, 110, 114; "The Literati," 66; "Loss of Breath," 22, 82; "Maelzel's Chess Player," 31, 107, 116; "The Man of the Crowd," 229–32; "The Man That Was Used Up," 22; "Marginalia," 151, 167; "The Masque of the Red Death," 119–21, 124, 129; "Mesmeric Revelation," 89, 93, 95, 96; "Metzengerstein," 113–14; "Morella," 113, 126–28, 198, 229, 272; "MS. Found in a Bottle," 32, 227–28; "The Mystery of Marie Roget," 116, 225; "The Murders in the Rue Morgue," 22, 67, 68, 226; "Mystification," 111; *The Narrative of Arthur Gordon Pym:* publishing history, 103–4, 169–70, 175; structure and themes, 176–83; its central importance, 193–205; its relation to the work of Melville, 206–15; Bachelard on, 25, 89–92; Baudelaire on, 171–74; Bonaparte on, 183–88; Mauclair on, 61; Messac on, 32–33; "The Oval Portrait," 259–62, 266, 269; "The Philosophy of Composition," 31, 107, 227; "The Philosophy of Furniture," 99, 107, 115–16; "The Pit and the Pendulum," 125, 129, 165, 193; "The Poetic Principle,"

107, 148; "The Power of Words," 115; "The Purloined Letter," 14, 22, 60, 225; "The Raven," 106, 189, 252; review of Hawthorne's *Twice Told Tales*, 201; "Some Words with a Mummy," 115, 118; "The System of Dr. Tarr and Prof. Fether," 116; "A Tale of the Ragged Mountains," 113, 198, 272; *Tales of the Grotesque and Arabesque*, 18; "The Tell-Tale Heart," 229, 233–36; "To Helen," 158; "Ulalume," 25, 252–53; "Why the Little Frenchman Wears his Hand in a Sling," 30; "William Wilson," 221–23

Porché, François, 71, 73
Presse, La, 69
Proust, Marcel, 117

QUOTIDIENNE, *La:* "Murders in the Rue Morgue" translated in, 68

RANK, Otto: study of double by, 270
Revue britannique, La: early Poe translations in, 68
Revue des deux mondes, La, 68, 71
Revue internationale, La: translation of *Eureka* appeared in, 105
Richepin, Jean, 3
Richter, Jean Paul, 91
Riding, Laura: criticism of Poe by, 29–30
Rimbaud, Arthur: pays respects to Poe, 13; cultivated "disordering of all the senses," 31; and Baudelaire, 78; possibly influenced by Poe, 214, 215

Romains, Jules, 170
Romanticism: lacked impetus in France, 41–43; Baudelaire on, 146–47

SAINTE-BEUVE, C. A.: indifference to Poe, 9, 13, 16, 26, 88; and Baudelaire, 45–47, 112; mentioned, 17
Saint-Martin, L. C., 90
Salon de 1845, Le: established Baudelaire as art critic, 84
Salon de 1846, Le: Baudelaire's art criticism in, 84, 86
Salut publique, Le, 86
Samain, Albert, 13
Schiller, J. C. F. von, 42
Schlegel, A. W. von: compared to Poe, 36
Scott, Sir Walter, 42
Seylaz, Louis: on Poe's influence in France, 6, 289
Shakespeare, W., 13, 206
Shelley, Percy Bysshe, 37, 38, 42
Southern Literary Messenger: Baudelaire collected copies of, 15; Daniel's article on Poe in, 173; first installments of *Arthur Gordon Pym* appeared in, 175; Poe's letter to White, editor of, 217
Spiritualism: in France, 93
Stevenson, Robert Louis, 202
Surrealism: Poe anticipated, 254

Swedenborg, E.: Baudelaire read, 83; vogue of, 90–93; designer of correspondence theory, 151

Symbolism. *See* Poe, Edgar; Symbolists

Symboliste, Le, 13

Symbolists: their attitudes to Poe, 34, 53–56, 62, 165; influence on T. S. Eliot and Wallace Stevens, 36n; study of, by Michaud, 41; as successors of Baudelaire, 147

TATE, Allen, 11

Taylor, W. F., 217

Tchelitchev, Pavel, 254

Ticknor, Elisha, 42

Tieck, Ludwig, 42

Tocqueville, Alexis de, 141

Tolstoy, Leo, 3

Transcendentalism: interest in, 35–36; Balzac not immune to, 90; Poe's antipathy to, 151

Tylor, Sir Edward Burnett, 270

VALÉRY, Paul: recognition of Poe, 6, 7, 12, 39, 61; essay on *Eureka*, 18, 269

Vallette, Jacques: as critic of Poe, 51, 53

Verlaine, Paul, 13, 38

Verne, Jules, 202

Virginia, University of: Poe affected by ideals of, 218

WAGNER, Richard, 83, 288

Wailly, Léon de, 98

Warren, Robert Penn, 117

White, Thomas W.: letter of Poe to, 217, 265

Whitman, Walt, 11, 266

Whittier, J. G., 11

Wilde, Oscar, 37

Willis, N. P., 66

Wilson, Edmund, 280

Wilt, Napier, 217

Winters, Yvor, 11